NAUMAN BRUCE

Hayward Gallery

sbc

This edition published by the Hayward Gallery
on the occasion of its presentation of the exhibition *Bruce Nauman*
at the Hayward Gallery, London, 16 July - 6 September 1998

The exhibition was initiated, conceived and realised by
the Centre national d'art et de culture Georges Pompidou,
Musée national d'art moderne-Centre de création industrielle

Exhibition conceived and curated by Christine van Assche
Co-ordinated by Cristina Ricupero

Centre national d'art et de culture Georges Pompidou

President: Jean-Jacques Aillagon
General Director: Guillaume Cerruti

Musée national d'art moderne - Centre de création industrielle
Director: Werner Spies

Production Director: Sophie Aurand
Exhibitions Department: Martine Silie, Valérie Millot
Art Handling: Annie Boucher, Naïma Kadri
Photographer: Philippe Migeat
Documentery Research: Andrea Lissoni, Misato Naïo

Hayward Gallery showing organised by Greg Hilty,
assisted by Marisa Culatto

Catalogue:

Conception and co-ordination: Christine van Assche
Research and realisation: Cristina Ricupero
Design: Neil Gurry
Translation from French: Charles Penwarden
Picture research: Elisabeth Harter
Documentary research: Elisabeth Harter, Andrea Lissoni
Editor-in-chief: Philippe Bidaine
Production co-ordination: Linda Schofield

Printed in Germany by Cantz Verlag, Ostfildern

Cover: *Rinde Spinning*, 1992
Photo: Katharina Faerber

French edition © Editions du Centre Pompidou, Paris 1997
English edition © The South Bank Centre 1998
Works by Bruce Nauman by permission of the artist

Hayward Gallery, National Touring Exhibitions and Arts Council Collection publications
are distributed by Cornerhouse Publications, 70 Oxford Street, Manchester M1 5NH
(tel. 0161 200 1503; fax. 0161 200 1504).

EXHIBITION TOUR

Kunstmuseum Wolfsburg
24 May - 28 September 1997

Centre Georges Pompidou, Mnam-Centre de création industrielle, Paris
16 December 1997 - 9 March 1998

Hayward Gallery, London
16 July - 6 September 1998

Nykytaiteen museo/The Museum of Contemporary Art Kiasma, Helsinki
17 October 1998 - 24 January 1999

Lenders

We would like to express our sincere and profound gratitude to the artist, museums, institutions and private collectors who agreed to contribute to the exhibition by lending their works:

Anthony d'Offay Gallery, London
Anthony d'Offay
Susanna Greeves
Lorcan O'Neal

Archives of American Art
Smithsonian Institution, Washington D.C.
Richard Wattenmaker
Elisabeth Joffrion
Joe Tallone

Benesse Corporation,
Naoshima Contemporary Art Museum, Kagawa
Soichiro Fukutake

Centre Georges Pompidou, Mnam-Cci, Paris
Werner Spies
Didier Schulman

Collection Sylvio Perlstein, Antwerp
Sylvio Perlstein
Esthel Rams

Katharina Faerber, Geneva

Froehlich Collection, Stuttgart
Josef W. Froehlich
Sylvia Froehlich
Anita Balogh

Galerie Konrad Fischer, Düsseldorf
Dorothee Fischer
Konrad Fischer †
Gundula Schulze

Pamela and Richard Kramlich, San Francisco

Kunstmuseum Wolfsburg
Gijs van Tuyl
Holger Broeker

Leo Castelli Gallery, New York
Leo Castelli
Susan Brundage
Patty Brundage
Amy Poll

Leo Castelli Graphics, New York
Maureen Mahony
Allan Dufy

Los Angeles County Museum of Art
Stephanie Barron
Christine Vigiletti

Nell and Jack Wendler, London

Jill and Jay Bernstein, New York

Art Institute of Chicago
Jeremy Strick
James Rondeau

Museum of Modern Art, New York
Glenn D. Lowry
Cora Rosevear

Rijksmuseum Kröller Müller, Otterlo
Evert J. van Straaten
Marianne Brouwer
Toos van Kooten

Selma and Jos Vandermolen, Ghent

Shoshana Wayne Gallery, Santa Monica
Shoshana Blank

Solomon R. Guggenheim Museum, New York
Thomas Krens
Lisa Dennison
Laura Latman

Sperone Westwater Gallery, New York
Angela Westwater
David Leiber
Karen Polack
Allison Plastridge

Staatsgalerie Moderner Kunst, Munich
Carla Schulz Hoffman
Ingrid Huber

Tate Gallery, London
Nicholas Serota
Catherine Clement

Vancouver Art Gallery, Vancouver
Alf Bogufski
Ian M. Thom
Andrew Hunter

Walker Art Center, Minneapolis
Kathy Halbreich
Peter Boswell
Gwen Bitz
Liz Glawe
Elisabeth Peck

Yasuda Fine Arts Inc., New York
Minoru Yasuda

Ydessa Hendeles Art Foundation, Toronto
Ydessa Hendeles

Electronic Arts Intermix, New York

Video Data Bank, Chicago.

CONTENTS

Susan Ferleger Brades   9 PREFACE

Jean-Jacques Aillagon   11 PREFACE TO THE FRENCH EDITION

Christine van Assche   12 PEOPLE DIE OF EXPOSURE

ESSAYS

Jean-Charles Masséra   20 DANCE WITH THE LAW

Vincent Labaume   34 BRUCE NAUMAN, ARE YOU *ROMAN* OR ITALIC?

François Albera   50 NAUMAN'S KINEMATIC CINEMA

Gijs van Tuyl   60 HUMAN CONDITION / HUMAN BODY
                            Bruce Nauman and Samuel Beckett

Christine van Assche   76 HEART BEAT AND SILENCE
                            An Interview with Meredith Monk

ANTHOLOGY

Marcia Tucker   82 PHENAUMANOLOGY

Willoughby Sharp   88 INTERVIEW WITH BRUCE NAUMAN

Chris Dercon   98 KEEP TAKING IT APART
                            A Conversation with Bruce Nauman

Joan Simon   106 BREAKING THE SILENCE
                            An Interview with Bruce Nauman

Tony Oursler   116 WAYS OF SEEING
                            The Warped Vision of Bruce Nauman

Michele De Angelus   120 INTERVIEW WITH BRUCE NAUMAN

APPENDICES

                       130 List of Works
                       135 Biography
                       136 Solo Exhibitions
                       139 Group Exhibitions
                       148 Bibliography
                       173 Credits

Beck's is pleased to sponsor the Bruce Nauman exhibition at the Hayward Gallery. The exhibition draws upon thirty years of work by this influential artist and we are proud to be associated with such an important event. The Hayward Gallery holds particular significance for Beck's, as the venue of one of our earliest large-scale sponsorships, *Gilbert & George 1982-1986*, in 1987. This was followed by Richard Long's *Walking in Circles* in 1991 and *Tatsuo Miyajima Big Time* in 1997. These three events occupy a special place in Beck's history as limited edition Beck's bottle labels were produced in collaboration with the artists to commemorate each exhibition.

We hope that a great many people enjoy this opportunity to see, at the Hayward Gallery, the first exhibition in Britain to span Bruce Nauman's remarkable career.

PREFACE

Bruce Nauman is without doubt one of the most significant artists working at the end of this century. For thirty years, his work has surprised and amazed for the breadth of its experimentation, the depth of its observation of the human condition, its abrasive engagement with the viewer and the wry humour with which it repeatedly questions - while continually asserting - the function of an artist in today's world.

In Britain, Nauman's considerable influence – especially among younger artists, many now themselves prominent in an international arena – has been built upon relatively few major showings: most notably at the Whitechapel Art Gallery in 1987, the Saatchi Gallery in 1989, several times at the Anthony d'Offay Gallery, and in 1996 as part of the Froelich Collection display at the Tate Gallery.

The present exhibition does not aim to cover the whole range of Nauman's career, a task admirably carried out by the retrospective organised by the Walker Art Center in Minneapolis, which travelled in the mid-1990s through the United States and to only one European city, Madrid. Instead, it offers a focused consideration of important themes arising from his earliest to his most recent works.

Over the past ten to fifteen years, Nauman has returned to the exploration of audio-visual technologies that characterised his early work, and has developed themes of existential self-scrutiny, of behaviour within determined parameters, of repetition, rhythm, and textual meaning, into a rich and varied body of work almost without parallel. This exhibition explores those themes, highlighting Nauman's major achievements in video, film and sound, but also encompassing drawing, neon, and sculpture.

The exhibition has been organised by the Musée national d'art moderne at the Centre Georges Pompidou, Paris, to whom we are profoundly appreciative for the opportunity to collaborate on such a compelling exhibition. In particular, I should like to thank the exhibition's curator, Christine van Assche, for her thoughtful and persuasive approach to Nauman's work. Together with her assistant Cristina Ricupero, she made the transfer of the project to London a pleasure. Thanks are also due to Martine Silie, and to many other staff in all departments of the Centre Georges Pompidou, who generously gave of their time and expertise.

The Hayward Gallery has benefited markedly from the experience of our colleagues who have also participated in the international tour of this exhibition. We thank most sincerely Gijs van Tuyl, Director of the Kunstmuseum, Wolfsburg, and members of his staff Veit Görner, Margarete Heck and Manfred Müller, for their considerable assistance; we have also appreciated the opportunity to work with Maaretta Jaukkuri in Helsinki.

A project of this kind depends crucially on the success of its technical realisation, and we are grateful for the expertise of many people: for the supply and maintenance of the audio-visual equipment, we thank MEKOM, in particular Axel Kirschbaum; for supervising the installation of all audio-visual equipment, we are grateful to Jem Legh, Tom Cullen and Heinrich Willecke; for installing the neon pieces we thank John Johnson and his team, who also lit the show at the Hayward. We have been privileged to work on the installation design with the architect Ian Ritchie, to whom I express my sincere thanks, as I do to his colleague Christophe Gérard.

PREFACE

We are grateful as well to the catalogue's designer Neil Gurry and to its translator
Charles Penwarden, and of course to all the authors, both of new and pre-existing material.
Cantz Verlag printed the publication with characteristic skill.

In our activities around the exhibition, through talks, workshops and related projects, we have
sought to inform our public about Bruce Nauman's work and to situate him both within an
inter-disciplinary context over the past thirty years, and within a continually evolving artistic
scene. I am grateful to all who have helped to achieve these ends.

We are delighted that the *Bruce Nauman* exhibition has presented an opportunity to collaborate
once again with Beck's, whose enlightened sponsorship has done so much to raise the profile
of contemporary visual arts in this country.

Like any exhibition, this one depends on the generosity and patience of lenders, and we are
enormously grateful to all those collectors, both public and private, who have permitted their
work to be included here.

The Hayward Gallery is above all deeply indebted to Bruce Nauman for his support of the
exhibition; sincere thanks are also due to the artist's assistant, Juliet Myers, and to his agents,
Angela Westwater in New York and Dorothée Fischer in Düsseldorf, for their wise and
practical advice.

Finally, but fulsomely, I thank all my colleagues in the Hayward Gallery and the wider SBC,
and very particularly Greg Hilty, the Hayward's Senior Curator, Exhibitions and Head of Public
Programmes, who has had responsibility for this project, for their characteristic dedication
in realising a most remarkable exhibition.

Susan Ferleger Brades
Director, Hayward Gallery

PREFACE TO THE FRENCH EDITION

By devoting a major monographic show to Bruce Nauman, in cooperation with the Wolfsburg Kuntsmuseum, the Hayward Gallery in London and the Nykytaiteen museo/The Museum of Contemporary Art Kiasma in Helsinki, the Centre Georges Pompidou hopes to give the French public a chance to become better acquainted with one of the major artists of our time, who is also one of the most complex: his work eludes classifications and divisions, drawing on a wide range of media in order to keep probing, questioning and experimenting.

This exhibition grew naturally out of the particular attention that the Centre has paid to Bruce Nauman over the last twenty years. This is reflected in the considerable space allotted to him in the collection of the Musée National d'Art Moderne-Centre de Création Industrielle, which has sixteen pieces, from the films and videos of 1967 to major installations such as *Going Around the Corner Piece*, 1970, or *Dream Passage with Four Corridors*, 1984. It is also reflected in the inclusion of Nauman's works in many of the Centre's major exhibitions. I am thinking in particular of *L'Informe* and *Fémininmasculin*, to name the most recent.

The Bruce Nauman exhibition is opening at what is a pivotal moment in the life of the Centre, which is entering into a key period in its evolution and development: the complete renewal of its spaces as a result of a major renovation programme which will enable it to approach the third millenium with the benefit of redefined, improved and readapted resources.

At the very moment, therefore, when the Centre is facing the experience of transformation and transition, and the concomitant questions concerning its own image and identity, as well as the questions concerning the space around it and its own constitutive space, the simultaneity of its existence inside and outside its physical setting, and, lastly, the need to develop a new kind of relationship with its users, it is more important than ever to make its voice heard and to assume its founding mission: to make contemporary culture and creation accessible to the widest possible audience.

Jean-Jacques Aillagon
President of the Centre Georges Pompidou

Christine van Assche

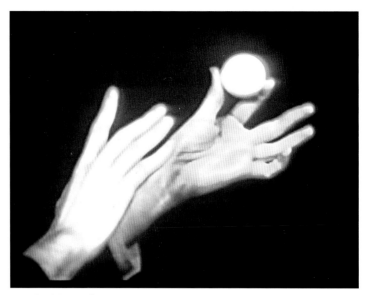

Falls, Pratfalls and Sleights of Hand. 1993

P E O P L E
D I E

O F   E X P O S U R E

Bruce Nauman is the creator of a prolific body of work
which eludes any possibility of categorisation
or enrolment into stylistic sections.
His works are rich and diverse in terms both of their processes
and of the modalities of perception they bring into play,
but also of their concepts, materials and genres.

Few artistic projects on the contemporary scene
are as complex or as multidisciplinary.
Few cover such a broad and incisive field of thought.

THE FRENCH CONTEXT

While it is true that the works of Bruce Nauman have been exhibited on numerous occasions, they have been seen mainly in the United States – his native land – in Germany and in Switzerland. A major retrospective organised by the Walker Art Center in Minneapolis, accompanied by a catalogue raisonné, presented Nauman's trajectory and his 'method'. This exhibition then toured to Madrid, Los Angeles, New York and Zurich in 1994 and 1995.

In France, though, we have had relatively few opportunities to see Nauman's oeuvre. An exhibition organised by the Whitechapel Art Gallery, London, was shown at the ARC in the Musée d'Art Moderne de la Ville de Paris in 1986. A number of exhibitions have also been held in Parisian galleries and a set of works held in the collections in the Musée National d'Art Moderne was exhibited in 1988.

Similarly, international thematic shows such as *L'Epoque, la mode, la morale, la passion. Aspects de l'art d'aujourd'hui, 1977-1987* at the Centre Georges Pompidou in 1987, and *L'Art conceptuel, une perspective*, at the ARC in 1989, featured a sizeable selection of works by Nauman.

The collections of the Musée National d'Art Moderne in fact possess a number of masterpieces: *Going Around the Corner Piece*, 1970, *Smoke Rings (Models for the Underground Tunnels)*, 1979, *Dream Passage with Four Corridors*, 1984, a set of prints from 1974-75, the *Merce Cunningham Portfolio*, and the complete set of videos and films from the 1960s and 1970s.

Coming up to the year 2000, the need to present a large selection of works by Bruce Nauman was becoming somewhat urgent.

However, there was no real justification for organising a new retrospective – the one in Minneapolis accomplished this task effectively and pertinently. It therefore seemed judicious to present Nauman's work from a more distinctively European point of view. Thus we have chosen a specific theme to articulate a generous survey of his production from 1966 to 1996.

This Bruce Nauman exhibition shares the same orientations as the other exhibitions organised by the New Media Department, which have included both established artists such as James Coleman and Chris Marker, and emerging figures such as Stan Douglas, Douglas Gordon, Johan Grimonprez, Mona Hatoum, Gary Hill and Thierry Kuntzel. One of the characteristics shared by these artists is that they extend the artistic possibilities of the body, of perception and of intelligence using current means of production: slides, neons, video projections, computers, sound tracks, etc.

These artists also manifest a real concern with the state of the world and concentrate their enquiries on the social, political, anthropological and even ontological aspects of the real. Direct experience is a key factor, and the involvement of the spectator is an essential element.

For most of these artists, written and oral texts as well as sound, music and images are necessary vectors for the acknowledgement of contemporary thought incorporating the ideas of, for example, Walter Benjamin, Marshall McLuhan, Ludwig Wittgenstein, Andy Warhol, Guy Debord, Gilles Deleuze and Jean-Luc Godard.

Manifestly, the work of Bruce Nauman goes much further than any concern with the specificity of any given media. It uses nearly all available materials, combines them with each other until their possibilities are exhausted, and renews them regularly in relation to developments in the economy, advertising and the media. However, Nauman is less interested in the object or material than in the experience itself, in the encounter with the Other.

NAUMAN UP TO NOW

Born in 1941 in Fort Wayne, Indiana, Nauman studied mathematics, physics, art, music and philosophy in Wisconsin then gained an MA in art at the University of California, Davis, where he subsequently taught, as he did at the San Francisco Art Institute.

In 1966 he settled in San Francisco, before moving to Mill Valley and then to Pasadena. He now lives in Galisteo, a small town in New Mexico.

Very early on, Nauman gave up painting for sculpture, performance, filmed performance, cinema and even holograms. When portable video equipment arrived on the market in the 1970s he made several taped performances exploring various parameters in his studio. He also designed video surveillance circuits for architectural installations. At the same time, the possibilities offered by the sound track led him to experiment with the orality, acoustic properties and rhythms of text. Subsequently, at a time when American buildings were covered with tubes of light, his uses of neon as a medium for texts and images allowed him to explore the complexity of their interrelations. More recently, a certain number of video installations deployed walls of video monitors like those to be seen in shop windows (*Violent Incident*),

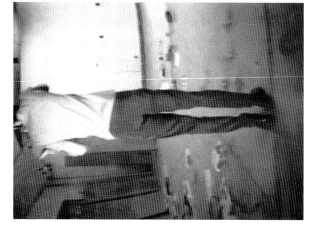

Violin Tuned D E A D. 1969

TV monitors in vitrines (*No, No, New Museum*) and large scale projection pieces (*ANTHRO/SOCIO (Rinde Facing Camera)*). In some cases, the precise, computer-assisted editing inevitably evokes the effects of the world of media and spectacle.

Parallel to his video work, Nauman continued to make sculptures, architectural environments and photographic compositions. This highly diversified practice – one of the most complex in the world of art today – also included a sizeable body of drawings, either working notes or autonomous pieces.

PROCESS

Although Nauman has been featured in surveys and retrospectives of Minimal and Conceptual art, as well as in Body Art shows, his work is independent of all movements. He has traversed the entire history of contemporary art without stopping at any given stage. It is true that, like the Minimalists, he was quick to take an interest in the relation of the work to its environment and to the involvement of the spectator, which he explored through installations pared down to the essential. He thus made several pieces in which he experimented with the constitutive elements of the artwork, including the role of the spectator. But this very singular artist has always been concerned with ontological, political, economic, anthropological and social issues as well as aesthetic ones.

Marcia Tucker made an attempt to define his method in her famous text 'PheNAUMANology': 'The structures of sound and movement as a basic function of human behavior and communication are the phenomena which

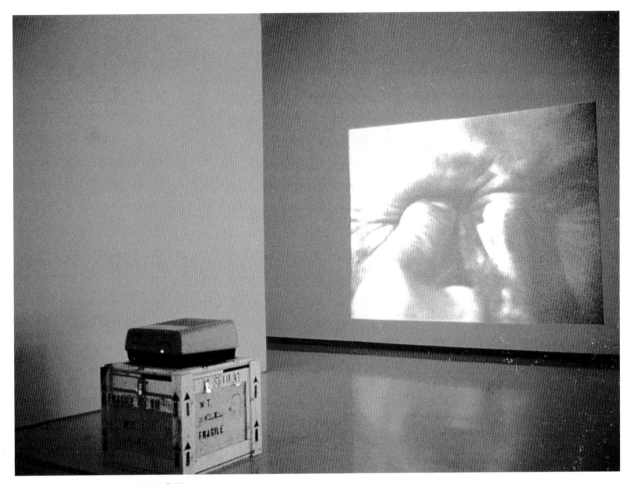

Poke in the Eye/Nose/Ear **3/8/94 Edit.** 1994

provide not only the artist, but the linguist, the anthropologist, the philosopher and the social scientist with the sources of our knowledge of man.'[1]

Each work is the result of an experiment in which the artist attempts to give a form to a question or an idea, while revealing its structure. In the 1970s, Nauman's heuristic method took the studio as its site and his own body as its medium. He explored all the permutations of a few simple actions taken from everyday life (Merce Cunningham). Subsequently, he transferred the site of his experience of the body to actors, mimes and clowns. But Nauman returns as the actor in the different versions of *Raw Material* and *Poke in the Eye/Nose/Ear 3/8/94 Edit.* He seems here to have come full circle.

The complexity of Nauman's questioning is never allowed to come between the work and its essential concerns. Living far from the art world and its fluctuations, Nauman has invented his own Blanchot-like working process, creating far away from any cultural context, proceeding alone in a far-away country. As he states in one of his rare interviews: 'So a lot of the work is about

that frustration and anger with the social situation, not so much of specific personal incidents but out of the world or mores.[2]

INFLUENCES

The influences that Nauman himself acknowledges having sought or undergone are highly diverse, including not only Marcel Duchamp, Man Ray, Jasper Johns, Samuel Beckett, Alain Robbe-Grillet and Vladimir Nabokov but also Steve Reich, Phil Glass and John Coltrane.

In an article entitled 'The Not So Holy Fool', Robert Storr argued that 'Nauman is the direct descendant of Marcel Duchamp and the cousin of Jasper Johns [...] If his ideas are not a simple extension of the Dadaist aesthetic and if his work enters a territory that his predecessors had only delimited, there are a certain number of affinities between Nauman, Johns and Duchamp; one of the most interesting is the diversity of his production.'[3]

It goes without saying that all these influences are of the utmost interest, all the more so since their conflation within a single body of work is the sign of remarkable originality.

DOUBLE STRUCTURE AND CONVOLUTION

The articulation of this exhibition is twofold, its elements both paradoxical and complementary. On the one hand, it explores the development of language, from mutism to a certain musicality, and, on the other, the different degrees of spectator involvement.

A. Language, sound, music, text

The exhibition affords an intent focus on Nauman's interest in language both written and oral, as music and as image: not only the enigmatic, metaphorical, playful and meta-conceptual language of Marcel Duchamp, but also the minimal, equivocal and incisive language of Samuel Beckett; the reversible, metonymic pictorial language of Jasper Johns; the fragmentary, experimental, disturbing language of Alain Robbe-Grillet. As for the writings of Ludwig Wittgenstein, in which Nauman took a considerable interest, they did not so much directly influence him as orient him towards a certain area of thought.

'Language games', writes Jean-Christophe Amman in 'Wittgenstein et Nauman', 'replace the old theory of symbols – the proposition is, by virtue of its logical form, an image of facts, and language is therefore an image of the world – insofar as language is part of an activity or a form of life.'[4]

Nauman's interest in mathematics and logic is certainly not without its effect on the structure of his texts, a structure also evident in the composition of his neon pieces and drawings, and in the editing of the sound tracks.

Already, the first films and videos made patiently in the artist's studio in the 1960s and 1970s used a repetitive structure articulated in accordance with an ascending or descending rhythm. Speaking of an early video entitled *Violin Tuned D E A D*, Nauman declared: 'I thought it would just be a lot of noise but it turned out to be musically very interesting. It is a very tense piece. The other idea I had was to play two notes very close together so that you could hear the beats in the harmonics'.[5]

What is developed in the sound pieces (and texts) that follow is a diachronic, binary structure made up of alternating full passages and blanks, positives and negatives, affirmations and gaps. The music of Steve Reich and Phil Glass and, astonishingly, John Coltrane, have clearly made an impression here.

The 'Cage-like' silence of the surveillance installations (the *Corridors*, the *Double Steel Cage Piece*, etc.) and of certain sculptures (the *Tunnels* and *Carousels*) represents the other side of this approach. The spectator is often physically and psychologically included in an intermediary space where he or she is subjected to constant surveillance, condemned to silence and almost imprisoned.

The binary structure becomes more complex at the end of the 1970s and in the 1980s. By the late 1980s and 1990s it has become a polyphony based on permutations, gaps, inversions, shifts and repetitions.

B. The place of the spectator

The second orientation of the exhibition can be perceived as its structural backbone. This is the awareness and development of the different levels of spectator participation. There are three processes at work here:

1. References to space and time through the presence of Bruce Nauman as actor and author carrying out his various experiments on and with his body as medium (*Art Make-Up*, *Lip-Sync*, *Poke in the Eye/Nose/Ear 3/8/94 Edit*, etc.). Increasingly, the artist withdraws from the work, transferring his role to others – a mime, a clown, the actor, the spectator – and thus enacting a transition from a kind of subjectivity to alterity.
2. Opposing forces deployed in a rhythmic pattern that suggests narrativity while confronting the spectator with an aspect of the human condition (*Violent Incident*, *Chambres d'Amis (Krefeld Piece)*). *Consummate Mask of Rock* prefigures the adoption of a more complex structure.
3. A spectacularisation of the parameters in the work draws the spectator into a network of dislocating political, social and anthropological energies. There is no longer a gradual development of complicity with the author and the work, but a radical implication in the 'society of spectacle' (*Shadow Puppets and Instructed Mime*, *ANTHRO/SOCIO (Rinde Facing Camera)*).

Initially, the emphasis is on subjectivity, the field of personal experience, the silence of the subject – the artist making himself up in several colours (*Art Make-Up*), the subject speaking and repeating a few more or less identical gestures (the *Raw Material* series), then putting

Shadow Puppets and Instructed Mime. 1990

his finger in his eye (*Poke in the Eye/Nose/Ear 3/8/94 Edit*) as if to remind us of his first works, and the distance between then and now.

Gradually this relational mode is replaced by an onus on the Other, who is progressively integrated in the work, at first by narrative *mises-en-scène*, and later through the interstices and artifices of the montage, assemblage and collage of images and sounds.

The sequence of the exhibition highlights the increasingly complex and subtle forms of spectator involvement, rather than following the strict chronological order of the works.

Nor are the works acoustically isolated from one another. The idea of this exhibition is to set up correspondences between the works, in order to create synergies between the different compositions and rhythms.

Between the first and last section in this progress is placed the complex, intricate *Consummate Mask of Rock*. This work institutes a strange mathematical logic, in the form of stones laid out on the floor, while the complementary text expresses a playful poetics. This work is

an allegorical illustration of the artist's dilemma, his ambiguous position as a soothsayer who tries to remain hidden behind a mask. *People Die of Exposure* is his conclusion to the text.

This piece also expresses the distinction between two opposing attitudes: to consume; to burn, wear away, wear out, spend time, be passive, and to consummate; to perfect, complete, accomplish, be active.

Two works made in 1996 constitute precise reiterations of this tension: *World Peace (Projected)* and *World Peace (Received)*. In the first, five large-format video projections feature actors who seem to be trying to communicate with each other (some play deaf and dumb people) and with the spectator. Simple, highly 'Beckettian' sentences are exchanged. A fast-moving edit switches the image and voice from one screen to another. The spectator is encouraged to move around in this installation in which he or she can grasp only fragments of text. However, the spectacular in this installation disorients him more than it encourages him to take an interest in the characters.

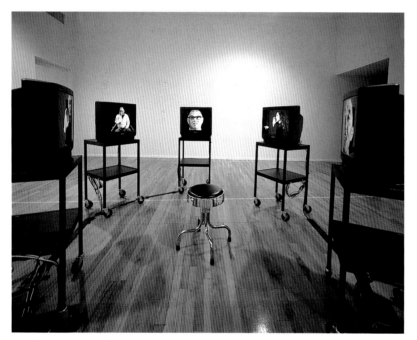

World Peace (Received). 1996

In *World Peace (Received)* on the other hand, the spectator is encouraged to take a seat amid five monitors in a rather more intimate space. Although the spectator is surrounded by the same actors and their attempts to communicate, the work evokes the relationship established between television and its viewers. The gestures and phrases are the same as before; only the montage is different, with an extremely fast rhythm leaving the viewer very little mental space.

These two installations, whose titles evoke obvious political questions, present two modes of reception and two modes of media communication. These two modes are also evident to varying degrees throughout the other works chosen for this exhibition.

THE CATALOGUE

Most of the texts written about Nauman hitherto have focused on his work in general, on the role of the artist, his vision of the world and his relation to history. For this catalogue we have chosen to analyse specific aspects of his work: the choreographer Meredith Monk, who produced a performance with Nauman in the late 1960s, considers the musicality of his work; François Albera looks at the cinematic dimension of Nauman's art; Jean-Charles Masséra studies the process of the instrumentalistion of the body and negation of the subject in the recent installations; Vincent Labaume examines Nauman's textual complexities and Gijs van Tuyl traces his work's correspondences with that of Samuel Beckett.

The catalogue also includes reprints of interviews and articles published in reviews, such as Marcia Tucker's seminal 'PheNAUMANology', plus a previously unpubished interview by Michele de Angelus.

At a time of great change, this presentation of aspects of the complexity of Bruce Nauman's work is very much in keeping with the mission of a contemporary arts programme that seeks to address the essential questions of our century.

World Peace (Projected). 1996

NOTES

1. Marcia Tucker, 'PheNAUMANology', *Artforum*, no. 4, New York, December 1970, p. 38.
2. Michele de Angelus, 'Interview with Bruce Nauman', *Archives of American Art*, Smithsonian Institution, Washington, May 1980, pp. 120-128.
3. Robert Storr, 'Bruce Nauman. Le Fou-pas-si-saint', *Art Press*, no. 89, Paris, May-June 1973, p. 10.
4. Jean-Christophe Amman, 'Wittgenstein et Nauman', *Bruce Nauman*, ARC, Musée d'Art Moderne de la Ville de Paris, Paris, 1986, p. 29.
5. Willoughby Sharp, 'Interview with Bruce Nauman', *Avalanche*, no. 2, New York, winter 1971, p. 29.

Jean-Charles Masséra

DANCE

WITH
THE LAW

Shit in Your Hat–Head on a Chair. 1990

In the late 1960s and early 1970s, Bruce Nauman's work seemed to be marked
by one of the last modern utopias: that of constructing a subject
cut free from all psychological, social, and historical determinisms.
Conceiving a subject outside the sound and fury, in the abstract space
of the studio or the white cube; exhibiting a neutral, transhistorical body.
The symbolic space and the historical dimension of experience were repressed.
Since the early 1980s, Nauman's installations have incorporated
a historical dimension of experience, particularly through their insistence on
certain processes of the body's instrumentalisation and the subject's negation.

'LAW-OFF' AND THE REDUCTION OF THINKING TIME

1990. *Shit in Your Hat–Head on a Chair.* An off-screen voice, settled, steady, and neutral: 'Put your hat on the table. Put your head on your hat. Put your hand on your head with your head on your hat.' On a hanging screen, an androgynous mime docilely executes the orders. 'Sit on your hat, your hands on your head. Shit in your hat. Show me your hat. Put your hat on your head.' No sign of suffering or humiliation on his face as he must successively shit in his hat, show it, then put it back on. Contrast between the nature of the orders and their assiduous execution. The will to submit is even more stupefying than the nature of the abasement. Make one's body a gift to power. 1975. *Salò or The 120 days of Sodom:* the abasement of the victims staged by Pasolini is comparable in nature, but here the torturer (the power) has a name and a face: a duke, a bishop, the president of a tribunal, a banker. 'The face or body of the despot or god has something like a counterbody: the body of the tortured, or better, of the excluded', remarked Gilles Deleuze and Félix Guattari. [1] *Shit in Your Hat–Head on a Chair:* the body of the tortured is no longer a counterbody because the despot and God were stripped of their power long ago. The orders now come from elsewhere. The site of enunciation is off-screen. A voice-off.

And if the body of the tortured is still a current theme, the exercise of power has become more cerebral, no longer marking bodies. The body reduced to slavery (to nudity) by political, religious, legislative, or economic power, exposed in *Salò or The 120 days of Sodom,* has been replaced by the body employed for the execution of highly precise tasks, in specific working garments (the mime's clothing). The face has lost the marks of torture. Emancipation has erased its very traits with cosmetic powders. A white face, ready for use. Power (the voice-off) can write on it, impose its desires, without leaving its mime the least possibility of representing what he desires. The mime is no longer the master of his gestures. He gives form to speech which is not his own. His androgynous body carries out a statement (a desire) of which he is not the subject, but the instrument. A body dispossessed of its sex and its desires.

1935. *Modern Times* [Chaplin]. The division of labour deactivates the full range of possible bodily functions, using only one for each body. The chain-structure of the assembly line dispossesses Charlie of his body, specialises it for the tightening of bolts. The body takes the form of its function and lives to the rhythm of that function's execution. But the reduction of a body to a function is only possible by stepping up the pace imposed by the factory director, whose face appears on the section leader's control screen: 'Workshop 21: Maximum speed.' The pace of task execution takes possession of the bodies. The reduction of break time transforms the subject into a tool of economic rationality. Longer breaks between bolt-tightening sessions would have allowed Chaplin to become conscious of what growth in productivity really means (the labour-organising phase). Slower and more varied movements would have allowed him to regain awareness and possession of his body (access to leisure activities). The speed of command sequences and the lack of breaks prohibit any rise in the mime's consciousness. After a certain speed of enunciation (of task execution) the absurdity and abjection of the commands are no longer legible. Pacing as a mode of the subject's execution.

For Chaplin, the rationality of self-dispossession has a face: the face of the boss who appears on the screen of the section leader. If 'the face is a veritable megaphone', if 'a language is always embedded in the faces that announce its statements and ballast them in relation to the signifiers in progress and subjects concerned', [2] what then shall we make of these commanding words broadcast from nowhere? For the mime, the rationality of self-dispossession has no face. The master's law has been replaced by a law-off. [3]

SERVILE, SERVICES, SEVERITY: NORMAL DESIRES

When the body is no longer a counterbody (martyr or slave), when it is no longer the mechanical arm of an assembly line (blue-collar worker), then it takes back its senses in order to enjoy the products which were formerly forbidden (consumer). 1985. *Porno Chain:* seven neon silhouettes form a horizontal chain carrying out all the possible varieties (product lines) of sexual intercourse. Whoever does not feed the chain with offers and demands – whoever does not feed off it – is invisible. Produce pleasure and reproduce it, or blink out. Consumer logic. Pasolini saw *Salò* as 'a visionary representation which, via sexual relations, becomes a metaphor between power and subject. The sadistic relation is nothing other than the commodification of the body, its reduction to a thing.' [4]

Today the abstract economic *machine* has beheaded the Prince (the single subject of enunciation). Power can no longer be located (off-camera) because it is fragmented,

P.P. Pasolini, **Salò or The 120 Days of Sodom**. 1975

diluted in an interweave of networks and interests.
1982. *Sauve qui peut (la vie)* [Godard]. Seated at his
desk, a boss organises a pornography chain whose
departure and arrival point is himself. The system's functioning rests entirely with him. Each body must carry out
a task (lick, suck, penetrate) at the moment when the
preceding body in the chain gives the sign (a foot on the
breast, fellatio, and so forth). [5] The bodies are employed
to produce the supply (the pleasure) to which they enchain
themselves. *Porno Chain:* the commodified bodies are
dissociated from the command sequence that sets them
into place and determines their function. Godard's
pornographic system reconstructs the meaning and the
symbolic chain that links economic agents to their direc-
tives. The economic machine has beheaded the Prince,
but its agents still need to represent, indeed, to embody,
the power that is exerted upon them (to put a face on
the command). Thus the last link of the chain receives
the command to 'put some rouge' on the pale, dispirited
face of the boss (the service director), as though the
boss had to produce an image of his power ('Okay, the
image'll do', he blurts out while putting it all together).
As in *Shit in Your Hat–Head on a Chair,* the absurdity of
the orders reveals the naked exertion of power on the
bodies and their reduction to things. Bodies employed
in the service of a law-off, and dispossessed of their
free will.

Speech and the forms it produces all flow along a
one-way traffic route through the bodies of the mime, the
employees and the neon silhouettes. They blink and flow

in us until we are nothing more than the desire for the
product: *Hanged Man*, 1985. The life and death of a man
hanging from norms. Three phases: waiting for the
message (only the gibbet is lit), reading the message
(the man lights up), consumption-consummation (erection
and orgasmic possession of the product). The totality of
this man's body is occupied by the message. The mass
destination of the supply entails standardisation of those
who demand. The neon silhouettes refer less to individuals
than to types. Consumption disfigures (they're all platinum
blondes) and the consumers take on the forms of the
things they consume. The reign of statistics denies
interiority and individuation. Successful distribution
calls for nothing but reflexes or programmed behaviour.
The mechanicality of desires replace the mechanicality
of production (*Modern Times*). The neon man has no
individual features because the economic machine only
produces the habits and reflexes of consumption,
which deny any possible individualisation of experience.
The machine offers combinatory possibilities, arrange-
ments of goods and services. Just let yourself be shown
around. *Normal Desires.* If you're not turned on, you're
invisible.

All this places the demander in a posture of immediate consumption: the flashy, attractive colour pages
of our advertising, the rhythm of our fashion parades,
the absence of causes and reasons in favour of sheer
effects (porn star Tracy Lord always moans when she
meets someone). *Masturbating Man, Masturbating Woman.*
The distributed model and the model economic agent
fuse together in neon. The effect that the message
provokes in the man becomes the message to switch
on another neon man. To be turned on by a product,
to be hot for it – or not to be. Light up for a product or
just blink out – without feeling the pleasure.

Only actions come to light (the active population):
marching, getting a hard-on, in *Five Marching Men...*
Greet, suck, kill and commit suicide in *Sex and Death
by Murder and Suicide.* The neons are a chain of states,
positions, reactions and effects without pauses or connections, reflecting nothing but demand (the movement
of growth). The blinking signals and the hypnotic repetition of the postures are like promises of an event that
never comes (a TV viewer in suspense until the next
episode). The speed of the blinking and the assembly
of the phases are the events. Never leaving one's seat,
satisfaction with the pure clash of images (channel
hopping). Don't be the subject of your desires, just
satisfy them, right now. You can be sure to pick up
your programme wherever you left off.

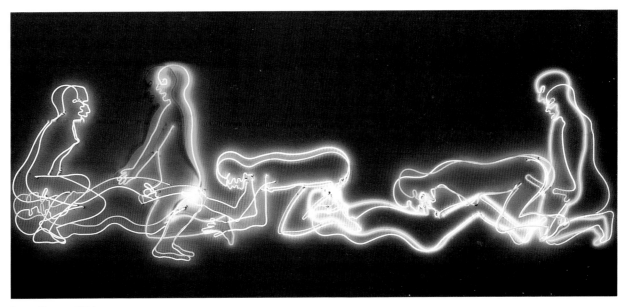

Seven Figures. 1984

DANCE WITH THE LAW

A word or a message becomes effective when it circulates through bodies. Whatever the future ways of instrumentalising bodies, the movements of the future mime or the future hanged man will necessarily melt into the motion of their chains or networks (keeping up with the times). The law is a cadence, a rhythm that circulates through bodies. The more your drives are synchronised to the rhythm of the law, the easier the execution of the task. Let feeling make a word effective. Help us feel pleasure at the effectuation of a message. 1968.

J.-L. Godard, **Sauve qui peut (la vie)**. 1979

Two loudspeakers set in the walls of an empty room, addressing any visitor who happens by: *Get Out of My Mind, Get Out of This Room.* A few footfalls, then those two injunctions repeated ceaselessly in tones that make you want to run when they are throaty or even mucous, but also to linger when the rhythm shifts: a ritornello, a bouncy little jig that makes you want to dance. The spectator is led to acquiesce to a discourse, to dance to words he no longer hears and that reject him (get out of my mind, get out of this room...). Slip into the cadence of your own eviction. The inscription of the law is a matter of feeling. Like a room left free so that a subject – the spectator in this case – might come to actualise a text. *Dancing in your head...*

The chain of behaviours and reactions that the boss tries to put into motion is slow to produce the desired image, because the employees have to learn as they go along. But the mime's execution is immediate, the image of the hanged man is composed in a flash, because the first has been trained and the second has been programmed. Michel Foucault speaks of school-children's training: 'All the activity of the disciplined individual must be punctuated and sustained by injunctions whose efficacy rests on brevity and clarity; the order does not need to be explained or formulated; it must trigger off the required behaviour and that is enough. From the master of discipline to him who is subjected to it the relation is one of signalling: it is a question not of understanding the injunction but of perceiving the signal and reacting to it immediately, according to a more or less artificial, prearranged code.' [6] Four columns of affirmative, imperative phrases written in neon on the wall: *One Hundred Live and Die.* Some fifty attributes and action verbs combined with the words 'live' and 'die', blinking on and off in binary patterns: 'SHIT AND DIE… SING AND LIVE… SMILE AND LIVE… SMILE AND DIE…'. An empty room big enough for a group of people (learning process): the same proposals are chanted in a welter of childish voices. An invitation to turn in circles. Once learned, these obsessive combinations will turn us into the mimes and hanged men of tomorrow. Tables or chants designed to 'place the bodies in a little world of signals to each of which is attached a single, obligatory response: it is a technique of training, of *dressage,* that despotically excludes in everything the least representation, the smallest murmur'. [7] The mime and the hanged man are non-representations. The mime is just the representation of the spoken word; the hanged man's erection is a reaction triggered off at the proper time.

The content of the command can be read immediately. The structure of *One Hundred Live and Die* is generative. It proposes formations of possible phrases (actions) – formations into which one could insert other verbs, other qualities. Once the jig has been assimilated, once the melody is on your mind, not only does it become difficult to shake it off (to think of anything else), but more importantly, the most absurd, indeed, the most dangerous contents can be absorbed and broadcast by this obsessive little jig, without the subject even batting an eye: 'YELLOW AND DIE… KILL AND LIVE'. The pause in which consciousness – critical thinking – could react is reduced to zero; no time to say 'no' or not follow orders (refuse to join the dance). How many listeners or TV viewers have the time (the consciousness) to realise the incoherence of certain pieces of information strung together in a single phrase? 1991. 'According to Pentagon sources, the tonnage of bombs dropped in the past few hours is one and a half times greater than that of the bomb dropped on Hiroshima; according to Pentagon sources, twenty-three civilians have died.' This montage of two pieces of contradictory information broadcast by the media during the Gulf War forces our assent (just say 'yes'). Media metrics skip all transitions (no ordering of the factors at the origin of the event). It beats time without analysing, hollows a void around the salient facts of the day. The event is an inflection (numbers without the matching story). The chain of selected facts is pulled by too quickly, and the over-explanatory, over-lengthy articulations – the ones that could imperil the transformation of the public into true believers – have been edited out. Media metrics call for dancers who can be made

amenable to the pursuit of operations. The image hits hard but ricochets away. The commentaries of our special reporters as modes of structuring our collective behaviour. The break in the beat, the halt of the cadence means critique (opposition journalism).

Whether command ('HEAR AND LIVE'), commercial ('YOUNG AND LIVE'), warning ('FUCK AND DIE'), or educational diatribe (*Good Boy, Bad Boy*), the messages gain in effectiveness when they merge into a simple binary rhythm, easy to grasp and hang on to: 'We are segmented in a *binary* fashion, following the great major dualist oppositions: social classes, but also men-women, adults-children, and so on… . It is a particularity of modern societies, or rather State societies, to bring into their own duality machines that function as such, and proceed simultaneously by biunivocal relationships and successively by binarized choices.' [8] As though all the possibilities that punctuate existence had their contrary (good and evil, integration and exclusion, right and left, etc.). As though they fit together in a logical chain necessarily linking cause and effect ('FUCK AND DIE'). As though each situation implied a choice between two contradictory possibilities (refusal or acceptance, success or failure). Our reflexes and decisions respond to a binary logic: yes or no – drink or drive. But each choice has its consequence (the right choice, the wrong choice) and its sanction ('KILL AND DIE'). Punish or reward.

In Foucault's description of the society that emerged after the collapse of the *ancien régime*, the art of punishment had to be 'as unarbitrary as possible'. It rested on 'a whole technology of representation': 'an art of conflicting energies, an art of images linked by association, the forging of stable connections…. it is a matter of establishing the representation of pairs of opposing values, of establishing quantitative differences between the opposing forces, of setting up a complex of obstacle-signs that may subject the movement of forces to a power relation'. [9] This society is now being replaced by one which eliminates quantitative differences in favour of a game based on the arbitrary. 'When I take the game, I take it out of context and apply it to moral or political situations.' [10] *Musical Chairs:* the slowest one is left standing (learning to compete). A kid's game becomes an adult pastime. *Hanged Man:* whoever gets it wrong wins an erection. The game as structure of our imaginary. The cruelty of an imaginary structured by the taste for business ventures, the taste for risk, the pleasure of exclusion. But in this adults' game 'the parts of the figure are put into place without you'. [11] The hanging doesn't follow from your difficulty at spelling a word – it's just in the programming.

Hanged Man. 1985

The very restricted freedom afforded the spectator in Nauman's most recent works corresponds to the restricted freedom that power gives the subject. 1996. *World Peace (Received):* five monitors, each playing back the words of a sincere-looking speaker. They're set in a circle around a chair (do sit down), they address you with an aggressive drone – 'I'll talk, you'll listen to me' – while assuring you they're listening: 'You'll talk, I'll listen to you. They'll talk, we'll listen to them.' Just try to slip a word in edgewise. The TV talks to you (talks for you). Stymied promises of dialogue.

It remains to decide if one can be satisfied with this demonstration of the processes whereby the subject is negated and reduced to a machine. If you agree that Bruce Nauman's works have something to say, then no doubt – at that very point, you have to admit that they say nothing else. Yet each exhibition confronts you with a choice: accept or refuse the way the works work on you ('STAY AND DIE/LEAVE AND LIVE').

NO

1987. *Clown Torture, Clown Taking a Shit.* Must we accept the cacophony of what the clowns tell us ('Pete and Repeat were sitting on a fence. Pete fell off. Who was left? Repeat. Pete and Repeat...') and the cacophony of what they don't want to tell us ('No!... No!... No!... No!...')? Why remain caught in the vice-like grip of a low-ceilinged room amidst a profusion of monitors and wall projections showing us one clown having a jar of water poured over his head, another stamping 'no no no' with his feet, a third taking a shit? Their torture becomes ours. Looking and listening become impossible and unbearable, just as they were on the chair surrounded by the five droning monitors. Unable to say anything to us, these installations attack us. The neat little jig (*Get Out of My Mind, Get Out of This Room*) has disintegrated into a cacophony, but the effect is only magnified. As soon as you get in you have to get out.

1991. For the exhibition *DISLOCATIONS*, a gallery at MoMA is plunged into semi-darkness. *ANTHRO/SOCIO (Rinde Facing Camera):* close-up on a shaven-headed face projected on three walls and six monitors, screaming with deafening intensity: 'Feed Me/Eat Me/Anthropology... Help Me/Hurt Me/Sociology... Feed Me, Help Me, Eat Me, Hurt Me'. The installation turns into a demonstration of strength. The gallery acts like a sounding box that amplifies the scansion of the cries. Sensurround. A process that surprises us 'like getting hit in the back of the neck.... The kind of intensity that doesn't give you any trace of whether you're going to like it or not.' [12] Creation of a three-dimensional acoustic ambience bringing a sensation of depth to the chanted phrases. The repetition of the imperative inflections and the simplicity of the injunctions obsess us. The alterity of the piece forces contact upon us. Reach out or reject. The neon silhouettes can suck each other, kill each other, but they don't concern us directly. Rinde's face becomes inescapable, compelling us to recognise his demand. Feed him and feed off him, help him and do him harm. Confused feelings of attraction and repulsion. *Get Out of My Mind, Get Out of This Room:* the tone and rhythm make us enter the dance that rejects us. 'Feed Me, Help Me', calls the chant. 'Eat Me, Hurt Me': it circulates inside us, to the point where our hearts beat to the pulse of the other's destruction. Embody the output of the chant (beat to the rhythm of the text). Let yourself be swept away by speech that reduces you to silence. The amplification system and the dimensions of Rinde's shaven head refer to other faces, other commanding words. Linkages of hammered commands that call for an impulsive response. Unlike *Clown Torture, Clown Taking a Shit* or *World Peace (Received),* the installation no longer appears to be addressed to a single person or to a small group of persons, but to a crowd – to the social body. Stadium logic. Bass-note logic, dispossessing us of the desire for any other thing except this chant. Let yourself be fascinated by the spectacularisation of power, or leave. *RUN FROM FEAR.*

The mix between the fascination of power and the aggressive force of the decibels raises a question that Bruce Nauman formulates with respect to certain earlier works: '[…] how does normal anger – or even hating someone – evolve into cultural hatred? At what point does one decide it's OK to wipe out an entire race? How do you become Hitler? Where does it stop being something personal and turn into the abstract hatred that leads to war?'[13] No doubt the moment when this obsessive chant (this rhythmic beat) is imprinted in us – the moment when we enter the dance – is the moment when we pass over to the stage of adherence (alienation). A discourse becomes effective when it penetrates bodies. Michel de Certeau: 'The *credibility* of a discourse is what first makes believers act in accord with it. It produces practitioners. To make people believe is to make them act.… Because the law is already applied with and on bodies, "embodied" in physical practices, it can accredit itself and make people believe that it speaks in the name of the "real".'[14] Rhythm as a means of structuring an opinion. Nauman's installations never name the nature of power. The only things shown are the forms of its application to bodies and the conditions in which the subject becomes a *believer.* At what point are we dispossessed of our own free will? At what moment do we become the objects of power?

CONFISCATED BODIES

1988. *Learned Helplessness in Rats (Rock and Roll Drummer).* An improvised installation, almost ridiculous. On the ground, an empty perspex labyrinth scanned by a video camera. Against the wall: video images of a terrorised rat seeking to escape from the same labyrinth (document), images of a drummer launching into a wild solo (clip), images of the labyrinth scanned by the camera (live). In the early 1970s, the combination of constraining spaces for the body and the use of closed-circuit video surveillance was inscribed in the field of pure aesthetic experience. Enter a first corridor to follow your own progress on a control screen; go out, then enter a second corridor to observe the comings and goings of those who are still in the first one. The relative control of the spectator is replaced by the total control of the laboratory animal. Ambiguity of the title: who is put in a situation of helplessness? The rat because it has no chance to get out of the labyrinth, or the spectator because he can do nothing but look?

Bruce Nauman: 'My work is basically an outgrowth of the anger I feel about the human condition. The aspects of it that make me angry are our capacity for cruelty and the ability people have to ignore situations they don't like.'[15] Let yourself be seduced by the rock rhythm or become conscious of the violence done to the lab animal. Although the title of the piece can imply that the rat is terrified by the drummer, nothing in the installation proves that anybody was drumming while the rodent's movements were filmed. The alternating playback of the three image sources seems to deny the possibility of simultaneity. What's more, the speed of the rat's movements does not necessarily mean it has been placed in a situation of distress… . The association of these two images (the editing) would then be no more than the projection of a fantasy: watching the rodent's movements in the labyrinth exhibited at our feet. The installation exposes and blends voyeurism (the empty labyrinth), pleasure (the solo) and compassion (the rat). The guinea pig is not where you think it is. The installation's object shifts. The second version of the piece – *Rats and Bats (Learned Helplessness in Rats II)* – renders the hypothesis of the suffering rat still more unlikely: a baseball player has replaced the drummer, while the labyrinth, now spread over four stories, has taken on grotesque proportions. The aggressivity inherent in numerous other installations fades into derisiveness here. The images lose their force. The sound takes hold of the body and separates it from judgement. Headless body.

After having sacrificed it to power (the slave and the conscript), then to industrialisation (the blue-collar worker), the subject is now separated from his body (the consumer). Giorgio Agamben: '. . . the process of technologization, instead of materially investing the body, was aimed at the construction of a separate sphere that had practically no point of contact with it:

The multiplication and repetition of the images and sounds prohibit any linear reading (or comprehension) of this domestic drama. A trivial story which leaves only a few peaks of intensity in the mind. The narrative and reasons for the dispute disappear beneath the insults, screams, toppling chairs and sounds of fighting bodies. We rediscover the media logic that links violent actions

Masturbating Women. 1985

what was technologized was not the body, but its image. Thus the glorious body of advertising has become the mask behind which the fragile, slight human body continues its precarious existence'. [16] *Porno Chain, Five Marching Men, Sex and Death by Murder and Suicide:* conductive body for commodified behaviour simplified to extremes (greatest common denominator). The behaviour can be outdated (marching in time), reprehensible (murder), emancipated (sex) or social (greeting each other). The sexualisation and spectacularisation of an organless body. The programmed linkage of sequences and the repetition of certain bodily postures deny the event, the gap, the existence of desire. Technologisation and commodification as processes for the devitalisation of bodies.

1986. *Violent Incident:* twelve monitors forming a video wall, four video decks. Twelve key moments in a candlelight dinner which begins with someone pulling away the chair as the other sits down (practical joke) and ends with two knife thrusts. All in eighteen seconds.

in a chain, eliminating the transitions and the order of causal factors. The televised event is an inflection, a flow. But here, the splintering of the scenario leaves us at a respectable distance: the blasé TV viewer. This distance confirms the constitution of an exclusively spectacular body and the development of a sphere and a temporality which have been entirely separated from the subject (exclusion).

Shit in Your Hat—Head on a Chair: hanging in front of the screen on which the mime's body loses all dignity (all will), is the green cast of a head with its eyes closed, laying on a chair. A head severed from its body and its activity. An activity that unfolds on the screens or in the neons. An activity severed from the subject. Where certain activities of the early 1970s 'force you to be aware of your body' [17] the later installations seem to deprive the subject of his body of experience. The shrinking corridors acted to heighten the awareness of the senses and the sentiment of self. The acoustic and visual juxtaposition exposed by the simultaneous functioning of the monitors and mural projection in *Clown Torture, Clown Taking a Shit* puts our bodies in a situation of hyperaesthesia. It's the paradox of a hearing test that denies the spectator even the slightest room for reflection. Hyperaesthesia turns into sensory deprivation.

Touch and Sound Walls (1969): two walls twelve metres apart. By touching the first, the spectator produces a sound which the second wall echoes after a slight delay.

Clear yourself a path through couples and communities of heads. Monochrome casts of wrinkles, expressive mouths and eyelids. Frozen interiorities. Subjects without a body of experience. Subjects disembodied of their individual history. The hanging of these heads at eye height reveals the ground and the empty space at the base of the necks. A space that the installation invites us to occupy,

Self-consciousness depends on the experience of delay (hearing oneself think). The *retrospective* awareness of one's own bodily activity. *ANTHRO/SOCIO (Rinde Facing Camera)… World Peace (Received):* a room with a chair that invites us to have a seat, faces that address us and let us know that we are considered the actors of a process, that we have access to speech… But these spaces of free being and speech prove limited. These faces (sounding boxes) give us an illusory consciousness of ourselves. By eliminating the delay (the step back) that is necessary for comprehension, the intensification of speech flow imposes an immediate reception that bars any possible access to consciousness. The time of the subject (the time of understanding) is interstitial and silent. The time of media speech is continuous. Severed temporalities.

1989-91. Return to silence. Other heads, hanging from threads at eye height: *Hanging Heads… Ten Heads Circle/In and Out… Ten Heads Circle/Up and Down… Four Pairs of Heads…* Confiscation of a body.

underscoring the frail and fragile presence of our own body, its precarious existence. The wax, the monochromy and the hanging as a fragilisation of our own field of experience. The closure of faces (private experiences) imposed by continuous, deafening speech. *One Hundred Live and Die:* the verbs and attributes do not articulate in any particular experience (generative grammar). 1985. *Good Boy, Bad Boy:* two actors – a man and a woman, each on one monitor – link together a few commonplaces of existence in various intonations, from persuasive inflections to aggressivity: 'I'm bored. You're bored. We're bored. Life is boring/I like to drink. You like to drink. We like to drink. This is drinking.' Playback of an 'I' which is not a particular case, of a 'you' which is hypothetical, of a 'we' which denies any possible singularity. The media don't tell us anything; they base their generalities on the sum total of the subjects of generic experiences (listening/viewing public). Subjects and verbs without complements (specific experiences). Faces without histories.

Ten Heads Circle/Up and Down, 1990

In the late 1960s and early 1970s, a number of Minimal sculptures and performances worked toward the construction of a subject of experience and enunciation. In the years that followed, the installations of some of Bruce Nauman's contemporaries integrated the psychological, social, anthropological, cultural, or even political conditions of subject-formation which had been repressed until then by Modernism. In Nauman's recent works, the subject is neither neutral, nor embodied in a specific figure; instead, the subject is exposed to processes of instrumentalisation and negation of exactly that which constitutes it as a subject. Since the mid-1980s, the relations we maintain with certain installations are power relations. With the spectacularisation of media forms, the activation of imperative language, the recourse to certain allegorical figures and constrictive systems, we are confronted – or thrust violently up against – the experience of a threshold, a turning point: at what moment does the pressure exerted on us become unbearable? At what moment do we move from the state of subject to that of a *target* for certain types of speech? And when the pressure eases off, when the installation offers us breathing spaces, room to move, then the critical attitude (distance) becomes an alternative to rejection (dissidence) or acceptance (the docile body). Make the links between the symbolic tenor of the dislocated objects (a chair, a head, etc.) and the language played out. Imagine the latter's context of enunciation and field of effectuation, and inductively reconstitute (retrace) the chain of assigned roles. Work back from the facts to the law-off.

NOTES

1. Gilles Deleuze and Félix Guattari, *A Thousand Plateaus: Capitalism and Schizophrenia*, tr. Brian Massumi, The Athlone Press, London, 1988, p. 115.

2. *Ibid.*, p. 179.

3. In French I play on words: 'law-off' (or 'command-off'), a translation of 'loi off', is a made-up expression which comes from 'voix off' ('voice-off' or 'off-screen voice'). I mean that it's impossible to know where the command comes from. You can hear the command but you don't know where it's coming from. In Bruce Nauman's piece *Shit in Your Hat—Head on a Chair*, the mime hears an off-screen voice (an 'off-screen command') and the viewer doesn't know who gives the commands. On the contrary, Chaplin knows where the command comes from. The command has a face (the one of the director, which appears on the control screen). The command of Nauman's mime is faceless – it is separate from the hanging screen on which the mime executes the commands.

4. Pier Paolo Pasolini, *Une vie future*, Associazione 'Fondo P.P. Pasolini'/Ente Autonomo Gestione Cinema, Rome, 1987, p. 306.

5. 'The boss – You Nicole, lay on your back, there… Thierry, put your thing in her mouth. Isabelle, come on over here… Bend over.
The assistant – I lick her ass?
The boss – I haven't said a thing yet…
The assistant – Excuse me boss.
The boss to Isabelle – Okay, you're going to put make-up on me but only when he licks your ass. And you Thierry, you lick the crack of her ass only when she blows you… . And you, you start the blow job each time I touch your tits with my feet. So let's try it… Okay, the image'll do, now we're going to work on the sound. When I touch your tits with my shoe you say "Ahh!" and you blow him. Go ahead: "Ahh!" You, Thierry, when she sucks you, you say "Ohh!" and you lick her crack. Let's do it: "Ahh!"… "Ohh!"… And you, when he eats your ass, you go "Ayy!" And don't respond if he's not on target. Go for it Thierry: "Ayyyy!" And then you put a little make-up on him, just once. And if I ever smile at you, you kiss me. So let's do it: "Ahh!"… "Ohh!"… "Ayy!"…'

6. Michel Foucault, *Discipline and Punish: The Birth of the Prison*, tr. Alan Sheridan, Vintage, New York, 1995, p. 166.

7. *Ibid.*

8. *A Thousand Plateaus, op. cit.*, pp. 208-10.

9. *Discipline and Punish, op. cit.*, p. 104.

10. Interview with Joan Simon, 'Breaking the Silence', *Art in America* 75, no. 9, New York, September 1988, pp. 140-49, 203.

11. *Ibid.*

12. *Ibid.*

13. Quotes excerpted from a text by Kristine McKenna, 'Bruce Nauman: Dan Weinberg Gallery', *The Los Angeles Times*, Los Angeles, 27/01/91, pp. 4, 84, reprinted in *Art Press* 184, Paris, October 1993, pp. 21-23.

14. Michel de Certeau, *The Practice of Everyday Life*, tr. Steven Randall, University of California Press, Berkeley, 1984, p. 148.

15. *Cf.* note 12.

16. Giorgio Agamben, *The Coming Community*, tr. Michael Hardt, University of Minnesota Press, Minneapolis/London, 1993, p. 51.

17. Interview with Willoughby Sharp, 'Body Works', *Avalanche* 1, New York, autumn 1970, pp. 14-17.

I would like to thank Vincent Labaume and Pierre Leguillon for their precious help.

To all the words from mother's tongue.

And his finger-tips touched the two secret openings to her body,
time after time, with a soft little brush of fire.

D.H. Lawrence

It's not a matter of articulating messages.

Piero Manzoni

Vincent Labaume

A Rose Has No Teeth (Lead Tree Plaque). 1966

BRUCE
NAUMAN

ARE YOU
ROMAN

OR ITALIC
?

An artist who invents always disorients the art lover. But while the latter ultimately learns to enjoy, the chances are that the former will gain acceptance only for his invention as a big paradox, a product of knowledge unaffected by the total ignorance of its necessity: as cultural added value. He may soon find himself supporting a pure convention, an invention gone stale, with novelty as a mere sales pitch and zero philosophical content. If he wants to last, the artist who invents is bound to keep repeating this inaugural gesture whereby he became an artist, and which endlessly distances him from himself, plunging him into 'new tricks, new scams' (to borrow the arriviste motto of the Pieds-Nickelés and Marcel Broodthaers); he must keep repeating himself in the role of agent of novelty, but without ever being able to invent himself, as a revelation. The artist who invents does not invent himself. 'Invent something to say', as Ignatius de Loyola urged, then invent something to be. But how is it possible to invent oneself without repeating oneself?

As with most artists whose oeuvre is more than the result of a specific activity, but stems from a risk-taking and innovative historical understanding of art – Andy Warhol, say, or Piero Manzoni, Marcel Broodthaers, Joseph Beuys, Michel Journiac and Art & Language – Bruce Nauman is indebted to the work of Marcel Duchamp. But if the other artists mentioned here took from Duchamp the obscure, fragmentary and sometimes anecdotal elements that set their own approach in motion, Nauman could stand as the heir to every facet of this oeuvre. For he made no attempt to isolate some 'bachelor' action from within this challengingly anachronic body of work that he might then develop for his own purposes in order to derive a new creative process from it – which, to varying degrees, is what did Manzoni with the *Standard Stoppages*, Journiac with the *tonsure*, Broodthaers with the *Rembrandt for Ironing*, Art & Language with 'It is the spectators who make the picture' and Warhol with the *Chocolate Grinder*. Rather, Nauman set out to repeat and develop each singular gap opened by Duchamp's oeuvre, instituting in his own work a kind of academy of exceptions as rich and diverse as the one that used to prepare students for the Beaux-Arts.

Thus, just as Duchamp recapitulated the whole of modern art at the beginning of the century, so, since the mid-1960s, Bruce Nauman has explored and conquered each of the major formal problems of his time. Steeped in the work on specific form that crystallised around the American Minimalists, Nauman's oeuvre would now occupy an eminent position in most of the categories of contemporary artistic activity: from Body Art to drawing, from spatial sculpture to photography, from the object to video, from figuration to language games. Likewise, he is familiar with every kind of material; he has made casts with anything that can be cast, from lead to plastic via high-definition police wax; he has used neon and polyurethane foam, marble and concrete, and even flour; he has made works out of sound and music. Nauman comes across as a protean artist capable of mastering any modern form of visual expression. And yet his oeuvre is far from seeming governed by a methodical determination to work through all the registers of art that have developed since the historic explosion of the twentieth century shattered the traditional formal limits of its reception, painting and sculpture. For this oeuvre is not just multiple in terms of its registers: within each of these it also carries out series of variations in an exponential proliferation of pieces that generates a new multiplicity: an internal multiplicity that is more than the accumulation of a simple motif, gesture or manner that could be identified with a unique authorial subject. For each piece in this body of work is a *bachelor* (i.e. singular) that puts a specific question to the modality it has adopted, and the answer to this question cannot be found in the cumulative continuity of a strategy. Each piece by Nauman is, in the end, a *solitary problem*, posed in a given formal register and needing to be solved using only the elements that it brings together. Finally, Nauman's body of work could also be considered multiple in the details of its crafting: the artist regularly varies his 'handmade' effects – recently, he even called on a professional to re-execute of one his pieces – so that this facture is never fixed as pure proficiency. Nauman is polymorphous right down to the details of each piece.

Within the teeming corpus of this diversified oeuvre, those pieces based on the plasticity of language, using words or expressions as either scores for performance or material presences, constitute a distinct and highly developed, indeed bacciform, ensemble in which the general profusion of the oeuvre is, in a sense, regularly replenished and recast (rewound). The artist first used language in his sculpture in *A Rose Has No Teeth (Lead Tree Plaque)*, 1966. Taken from Wittgenstein's *Philosophical Investigations* (1953),[1] the words are engraved in relief on the convex side of a lead plaque curved in order to be fixed to a tree trunk. Nauman had originally intended the plaque to be attached to a young trunk so that, as it grew, the tree would obscure and

Consummate Mask of Rock. 1975

ultimately destroy it. 'I thought that outdoor sculpture was usually big and durable, but that seemed very dumb, because it's already very nice outside, with trees and fields, and I didn't want to put something there and change it all. So I thought I'd make something which fell apart after a while – which would return to nature. Like dirt or paper. Then I made this piece… . After a few years, the tree would grow over it, and finally cover it up, and it would be gone.' [2] Note in passing the very 'natural' laconicism of Nauman's remark, which brings in the idea of 'dirt' when evoking the destiny of an artwork that deals with a philo-sophical meditation containing a statement about roses.

Anticipating by a short interval some of the most original propositions of the exponents of Land Art – an aesthetic movement which set out to appropriate and transform an untouched natural space by means of artistic activity, and whose leading figure, Robert Smithson, produced outdoor constructions that were themselves destined to disappear by virtue of the entropic principle of destruction on which they were based – this piece by Nauman short-circuits registers and genres in a surpris-ing way: by addressing a 'language sculpture' to the 'outdoor sculptor', Nauman ironically confronts 'outdoor' sculpture (Land Art) with nature itself, considered here

as a fine, very 'nice' sculptor in its own domain. Moreover, by engraving a 'dirt sentence', a conceptual aberration that is fated to disappear, Nauman takes an explicit swipe at those who, like that other reader of Wittgenstein, Joseph Kosuth, confuse the immateriality of words with the intemporal concept of art and are convinced that roses really do have no teeth. 'For where should a rose's teeth have been?' they ask, echoing the question of the Viennese philosopher.

In a sense, and although *Philosohical Investigations* was Nauman's bedside book during his formative years, *A Rose Has No Teeth* seems just as much a skit on the very Wittgensteinian idea of the 'bi-polarity' linking words and objects as a homage to the philosopher. By showing that an absurd proposition – although, to quote Wittgenstein again, 'It is even surer than that a goose has none' – can be concretely and conclusively 'objected to' by the natural order in which it is considered incapable of intervening, Nauman is ridding himself of Wittgenstein more than he is seconding him (but still 'saying it with flowers'). *A Rose Has No Teeth*: to English ears, the words have a figurative meaning which is shared by expressions such as 'the law has no teeth'. Surely, Nauman, who is so attentive to word-play, to palindromes and double

Consummate Mask of Rock. 1975

37

Love Me Tender, Move Te Lender. 1966

meanings, must have picked up on this idea of impotence. A rose is powerless. Is this an ecologist's cry of protest to those who trample flower beds? Only if we forget that this plaque, with its teeth-like block capitals in relief, which also resembles a dental plaque (plaque on the teeth) will, its own teeth notwithstanding, gradually but inexorably be bitten by the powerful jaws of the earth and that soon this 'whole cloud of philosophy condensed into a drop of grammar' (as Wittgenstein says in his next paragraph) will also lose all its teeth. Even if the natural and linguistic (or cultural) orders have only one polarity, nature always has the last word: *an idea has no teeth. An idea is powerless.*

It is interesting that Nauman should have chosen to cast Wittgenstein's words in lead, a material not exactly synonymous with the lightness or immateriality of the conceptual domain. Here, however, the material is used primarily on account of the fusibility which enables it to be cast and recast, just as the printer's lettering can be combined to write and print anything, both truths and falsehoods – or, in Nauman's case, a truth contradicted by the way it is placed, a truth countered: a counterfeit truth. In fact, the artist's stroke of genius here consisted in casting a kind of immobile rotary press, to be bolted to a tree – in other words, to the main source of paper – one which, rather than printing itself on the tree, making its mark on it, takes on the conventional presence of a forest sign, like a plaque saying 'private land' that is itself destined to be one day expelled from the estate. Resonating at a distance with some of the 'textual' paintings of Magritte, in which the real is booby-trapped by its redundant designation as image and language, this piece condenses and generates the same disruptive effects as some of Piero Manzoni's pieces, particularly his *Socle du monde* (Base of the World), a steel cube with its title engraved inside out, made in 1961 and installed in a park in Herning in 1962.

Not long afterwards Nauman produced a sequel to this work, using the mould that had shaped the original lead plaque to produce casts in tinted polyester resin. These were sent around the world to all the people Nauman knew. The original plaque destined to be destroyed by vegetation is now carefully kept by Thomas Ammann in Zurich. If, in the end, Nauman did manage to get rid of it, to 'break it up', he did so by multiplying and scattering it to the four corners of the earth. Engraved in workaday plastic, this worldwide mailshot would provide Wittgenstein's purely negative utterance with the universality it previously

Make Me Think Me. 1994

lacked. There is a sense in which, for Nauman, it is not the viewer who makes the work but the addressee who destroys it. Like many others by Nauman, this piece, about which one could write a thick tome without exhausting its reserves, is above all a lesson, and as it happens a good lesson, a lesson in *bons mots* and truths – but then, is it possible to give a bad lesson? A lesson from a dullard barely able to read or look?

The True Artist Helps the World by Revealing Mystic Truths (Window or Wall Sign), 1967, is perhaps not Nauman's best known work, but certainly one of the most frequently reproduced and mentioned. Nauman has it set up at the entrance to all his retrospective shows, and acknowledges its position as a manifesto or emblem of his activity. Made of coloured neon tubes, like a street sign, it consists of an outward-tending pink spiral containing the eponymous words in blue neon. The sentence follows the same spiral pattern as the pink neon, starting at the centre. Now, are we supposed to read the sentence (The true artist helps the world by revealing mystic truths), or to look at it? Do we read it as a figure, in a genuinely spiralling movement and direction? In this case, to read would mean following the infinite outward movement. Generally speaking, when people describe something as mystic, there is every reason to believe that they're not going to reveal a thing. And, as we see it here, rolled around the centre of the sign, the 'true artist' can always hide behind the revelations inspired by a mechanical and purely self-absorbed drawing. This drawing is not, as we see when we follow it, the simple ornament of a profound truth: on the contrary, it constitutes the sole meaning of a statement that is in fact rather flat, or is made flat by the accumulation of layers of profundities ('true artist', 'revealing mystic truths', 'help the world'), the accumulation of words that make signs seem deep. And if this clichéd statement has a special place among the 'mystic truths' that 'help' us, this is not unrelated to the little twist that turns it and rolls the true artist away from his navel-gazing ego, towards the other, the world, the exterior, through the window, into the street. The movement of this open spiral constitutes a kind of figural mould for many other pieces by Nauman which make the viewer or passer-by turn in space, go back on their tracks, and then pushes them out towards the exit: 'one little turn and off we go'. Sometimes the expulsion is more direct, as in the sound installation *Get Out of My Mind, Get Out of This Room*, 1968, in which speakers sunk in the wall of the empty space take turns to drum out the order of the title in a whole range of tones of voice.

The visual sign of a cliché (in both the semiotic and commercial sense of the word) written in light and colour, this work is unlike the tree plaque in that it does not pit language against an external force that would counter or break it down. Rather, it points to its own signifying power, by the arbitrary sequence of sign-words, of interchangeable signifiers which order, or rather, adumbrate, a meaning. A 'real' understanding of this totally esoteric sentence has more to do with a 'mystic' belief in the cult of the 'true artist' than with a rational analysis of its contents. Here, the form of the work gives the words an antagonistic or exoteric meaning worthy of a banal piece of public information on a sign on a wall or in a window. One of the most troubling constants of Nauman's pieces lies in this particular form of vulgarisation which they bring into play with deep utterances from some arduous branch of knowledge, and which, as we have seen, are made accessible to all in a naive illustrative reduction. This form of vulgarisation is also applied to pure clichés, commonplaces or coarse statements taken from the narrowest of lexicons, going all the way to pornography (this vulgarisation of pornography is not the least of Nauman's strengths). Like Racine, Nauman uses a limited number of words. He also eats them a lot.

Of the eleven colour photographs in the portfolio from 1967-70 (including the famous *Self-Portrait as a Fountain*, a chest-high shot of the naked artist in a joyous posture spouting from his mouth a jet of water whose fall is at a tangent with the image plane), several theatricalise the popular idiomatic expression contained in their title. They are sometimes visually accompanied by a concrete representation of words. *Eating My Words*, for example, shows the artist sitting at a table in a very basic kitchen decor spreading jam on big pastry letters that we see in his plate. Together they spell 'words'. The vulgarisation of the expression is here effected by a literalisation of the suggested organic content of this figure of speech. Moreover, the literalisation is even flatter if we consider that what we see really is, without any wordplay, someone eating cakes in the form of a word which he has himself made. The word 'words' really does belong to the person eating it: 'These are my words and I am eating them myself.' Surely this is the burden of this photograph whose professional studio execution further underlines the stripped-down solemnity of the artist's autophagous meal. If, in this image, Nauman has reduced a linguistic utterance to a visual image, in its most common form as a gag-cum-Freudian slip, he is also reducing the

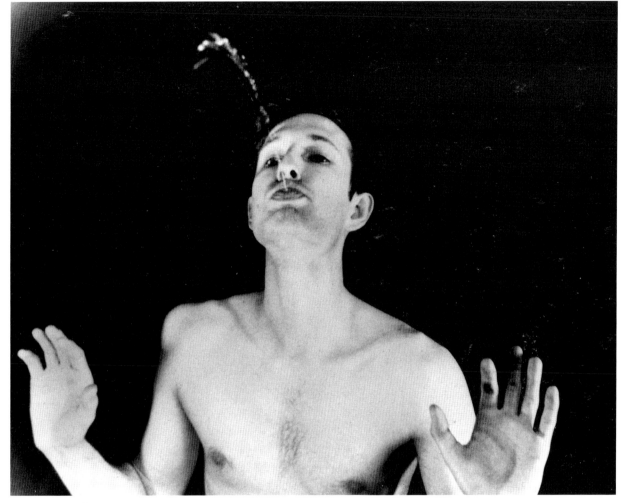

Self-Portrait as a Fountain. 1966

image to its minimal figurative content, to the flattest and most 'objective' part of the expression. In a way, Nauman is opening up a channel for a verbal use of photography, but this he only hints at. [3]

The slick, 'advertising standards' aestheticisation of Nauman's portfolio contrasts with the artist's usual stylistic indifference to 'finish'. With his neon corridors, for example, as Benjamin Buchloh puts it: 'Bruce Nauman has reversed the formalist aestheticism of Flavin's fluorescent lights. By reinstalling them simply and functionally in his corridors, he allows an immediate and authentic experience of the elements of the work: architectural space, light, colour and the observer's reactions to them.' [4] With these photographic images, it is as if Nauman had first tried to neutralise the reactions of the observer by submitting a pure sampling of photogenic renditions (bleed backgrounds and screens with textural effects, out of focus and mirror, gloss and matt finishes)

whose visual content is of interest only because of the light and shade that plays across it. No doubt these images could be seen as shots of shots (clichés of clichés), doubly emptied of their content, literally sacrificed, reduced to (eaten up by) the neo-retinal approach of professional standards. And yet... they do express something. In what language, though? English or half-baked English?

What is the language spoken by the many neon signs made by Nauman since 1967? From the absurd but true (the plaque) to the true proposition that is void of meaning (sign no. 1), then to the visual incarnation of a figure of speech (the photo), Nauman had kept to secondary linguistic entities that are complex and rich in figurative processes: phrases. These phrases, which unroll a carpet of empty meaning, nonetheless contain a residual sense which means that they are perceived as the genuine statements of the artist delivering his 'ideas

Live and Die. 1983

about the world.' In the later neon pieces, Nauman gets rid of phrases and focuses on limited syntagmata, on groups of words or ordinary expressions, messages whose articulation is graphic and rhythmic, acoustic and visual. A number of his signs function in the mode of a binary rhythm, of the signal-response type, linking together two anagrammatical messages of which the second suspends, deflates or renders absurd the impact of the first when it lights up. *None Sing Neon Sign*, 1970 presents the words 'none sing' in ruby-red neon above the words 'neon sign' in white neon. The two messages are in script and light up alternatively. The bright red of 'none sing' is of the kind generally used in theatres or TV studios to enjoin silence or prohibit smoking. This unusual statement, which would seem to apply to an audience of birds or of children humming incessant and imbecilic jingles more than it does to art lovers, is followed by the milky white 'neon sign' message. The second, which reflexively designates its own material reality as object, reacts against the first signal by deflating its somewhat authoritarian pretensions. 'Sing! Look! it's only a simple sign, just a neon sign!' Moreover, the second 'neon sign' message provides a retroactive explanation of the first: it is an anagram of the one that follows. The utterance 'none sing' is in fact

secondary to 'neon sign', even if it is the first to light up. It is as if Nauman begins by provoking a kind of *faux pas*, or Freudian slip, and then tries to correct it, to make up for and erase it as best he can. But here the artist has included a third, unexpected twist which restores the claims of the first utterance. For how can a purely visual neon sign cancel a purely aural statement? We thus have a rather ill-defined juxtaposition of two utterances, which oscillate between an 'objective' and descriptive form concerned with the visual scheme of things (indeed, neither of the neon signs sing), and a performative form concerned with the aural regime. Each of these utterances is confirmed in its own regime and contradicted in the other. It is a war waged in private, in which each of the spheres misses the other, in a chase that is like those children's stories that go round and round in circles by virtue of the articulation between two words: 'Pete and Repeat'... .

Another sign from 1970, *Raw War*, suspends or diverts the visual message by superimposing a hidden message which is actuated only by the diachronic order in which the letters light up. The sign is the simple word 'War' in roman capitals consisting of a double line of coloured neon. In this piece, the sequence in which the word lights up breaks down into three phases: 1) the letter 'R' lights up on its own; 2) the letter 'A' lights up on its own; 3) the three letters of the word 'WAR' light up all together. The word 'RAW', which is like the mirror inversion of 'WAR', cannot be read in the same space. For a continuous right-to-left reading is made impossible by the spatial orientation of the letter 'R' which, unlike 'A' and 'W', cannot be read in a mirror. Only the sequence in which the letters light up, from right to left, can end this sort of 'figural censorship' of the letter which means that 'RAW' can only be read in one direction. This is the word which lights up the word 'WAR' and is dissolved in it in the luminous saturation of the sign where its trace is consumed, except in the retinal memory of the spectator. 'Raw' is the anamnestic reminder which lights up all wars. In this piece, Nauman stirs up two antagonistic conceptions: a vulgar and reactive one; 'war is raw' and an intellectual, positive and evidently Heraclitean one; 'raw (materials) mean war'. But neither is really fully accomplished and independent. Spatially (in the vulgar version, you might say), the 'R' blocks the reversal (WAR = RAW); and temporally, the complete sequence of illumination gives us 'RAWAR', which means nothing. Nothing but a war sign, a bloody standard that has only a word to its name: 'WAR'. [5]

LIVE AND DIE	LIVE AND LIVE	SING AND DIE	SING AND LIVE
DIE AND DIE	DIE AND LIVE	SCREAM AND DIE	SCREAM AND LIVE
SHIT AND DIE	SHIT AND LIVE	YOUNG AND DIE	YOUNG AND LIVE
PISS AND DIE	PISS AND LIVE	OLD AND DIE	OLD AND LIVE
EAT AND DIE	EAT AND LIVE	CUT AND DIE	CUT AND LIVE
SLEEP AND DIE	SLEEP AND LIVE	RUN AND DIE	RUN AND LIVE
LOVE AND DIE	LOVE AND LIVE	STAY AND DIE	STAY AND LIVE
HATE AND DIE	HATE AND LIVE	PLAY AND DIE	PLAY AND LIVE
FUCK AND DIE	FUCK AND LIVE	KILL AND DIE	KILL AND LIVE
SPEAK AND DIE	SPEAK AND LIVE	SUCK AND DIE	SUCK AND LIVE
LIE AND DIE	LIE AND LIVE	COME AND DIE	COME AND LIVE
HEAR AND DIE	HEAR AND LIVE	GO AND DIE	GO AND LIVE
CRY AND DIE	CRY AND LIVE	KNOW AND DIE	KNOW AND LIVE
KISS AND DIE	KISS AND LIVE	TELL AND DIE	TELL AND LIVE
RAGE AND DIE	RAGE AND LIVE	SMELL AND DIE	SMELL AND LIVE
LAUGH AND DIE	LAUGH AND LIVE	FALL AND DIE	FALL AND LIVE
TOUCH AND DIE	TOUCH AND LIVE	RISE AND DIE	RISE AND LIVE
FEEL AND DIE	FEEL AND LIVE	STAND AND DIE	STAND AND LIVE
FEAR AND DIE	FEAR AND LIVE	SIT AND DIE	SIT AND LIVE
SICK AND DIE	SICK AND LIVE	SPIT AND DIE	SPIT AND LIVE
WELL AND DIE	WELL AND LIVE	TRY AND DIE	TRY AND LIVE
BLACK AND DIE	BLACK AND LIVE	FAIL AND DIE	FAIL AND LIVE
WHITE AND DIE	WHITE AND LIVE	SMILE AND DIE	SMILE AND LIVE
RED AND DIE	RED AND LIVE	THINK AND DIE	THINK AND LIVE
YELLOW AND DIE	YELLOW AND LIVE	PAY AND DIE	PAY AND LIVE

None Sing Neon Sign. 1970

which now seems highly paradoxical in the light of the tremendous creativity of the 1960s and 1970s, which constituted the second great aesthetic revolution of the twentieth century, one just as rich and profound as that of modern art itself – the statement made by Nauman with neon was more radical and ambitious at the time than any other. By his desire to really 'play the game' with an advertising form identified with and inseparable from the modern urban landscape, particularly the American one, Nauman was one of the first artists to take up a form from outside the world of art without bringing it back to art or the idea or specific definition of art, using it instead in a practice that was itself resolutely based on advertising and makes its form and its message public. Inaugurating the slow relegation of specifically aesthetic forms, Nauman later confirmed with his corridors and surveillance videos what Buchloh called the new, 'simple and functional' relation he wanted to get from public forms of expression.

While neon proved its aesthetic and formal qualities in the work of Lucio Fontana and, above all, Dan Flavin, and demonstrated seductive conceptual possibilities in that of Joseph Kosuth who, in 1965, made the sentence 'Five Words in Blue Neon' in blue neon, it was not until Nauman that it really become a tool for exploring the figural and linguistic sign. This is because, beyond the specific properties of neon which made it possible to draw in coloured light – one of the great modern utopias of painting, uniting Cézanne's stroke of colour with electric light – Nauman was not trying to introduce a ready-made industrial technique into art, but really did want first and foremost to make a sign that could mix with the concert of real signs in the street. Speaking of the first *Wall Sign*, 1967, he said: 'I had an idea, that I could make art that would kind of disappear – an art that was supposed to not quite look like art. In that case, you wouldn't really notice it until you paid attention. Then, when you read it, you would have to think about it.'[6] If the neo-Hegelian idea of the disappearance or 'death of art' was fairly common at the time – a fact

In December 1969, in the first major American interview about his work, Joseph Beuys declared that, of all the work done by the American artists he had met, that of Bruce Nauman seemed to him the closest to his own. But he attached to this statement of proximity a serious reservation: it all depended on the 'inner intentions' underlying Nauman's work for, as he said, 'I attach the utmost importance to inner intentions.'[7] Today, thirty years after this declaration, and with Beuys' work under vengeful attack from those who would never have dared confront him when he was alive,[8] this proximity with Nauman's work has remained uncontested – indeed it is no doubt one of the most intriguing and thought-provoking proximities in recent art history: a blind proximity. A comparative and systematic study of their respective oeuvres, with regard both to their internal processes of development and their sensory impact, would no doubt constitute a decisive critical contribution to understanding the conceptually competitive and economically tense bi-polarity of the dominant versions of contemporary art, the American and the European. I would like to take a modest example touching on the

Run from Fear, Fun from Rear. 1972

question considered here, written language, to try to approach and compare the inner intentions of the two men, as revealed in their work.

A Beuys drawing of 1963 in oil and watercolour on a piece of 'Bristol Light' card from a pad and entitled *Lightbox* presents two occurrences of the word 'lightbox' traced one over the other in black on a black ground. If the unlikely light given out by this *Lightbox* does not bring a shine to its own name, which is written even darker than the ground, then what exactly is this lightbox lighting up? By tracing a vertical strip in the left corner of the cardboard that allows segments of the white paper to show through, is not Beuys paying a discreet homage to the support, Bristol Light, whose second word obviously

refers to luminosity as well as weight? In that case Beuys would have covered the white paper in black in order to highlight its fundamental iconic property: to make visible, by contrast, in drawing or in words. This negative and dialectical lighting-up could be compared to a piece by Bruce Nauman entitled *Dark*, 1968. This is a square plaque of steel, in standard industrial format (about 120 x 120 cm and 10 cm thick), laid out on the ground with, as the artist remembered it twenty years later, the word 'dark' painted in yellow in indelible ink on its lower – and therefore invisible – side. It could be said that in this piece Nauman adopts an approach that is symmetrically opposed to that of Beuys: by turning over the inscription and hiding it, it is not the scriptural or iconic properties of the steel plaque that are highlighted, by an operation

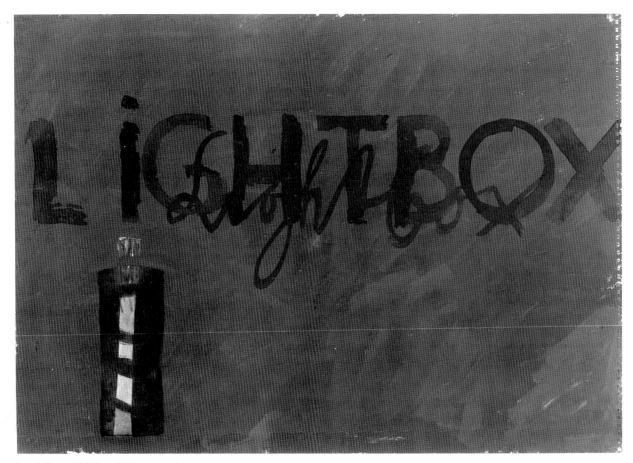

Joseph Beuys, **Lightbox.** 1963

of covering-over combined with writing and colour. It is simply the objective material qualities of the steel that are being reaffirmed: cut, dimensions, weight, thickness and surface. As for the word 'dark', although it is traced in a luminous, indelible colour, the lack of light due its position against the ground does make it effectively dark: and its darkness in no way clarifies the manifest form of the material. But – and this is the great irony of Nauman – this does not raise the standard sheet steel to the particular dignity of a work of art, as it might in the work of certain American Minimalists such as Carl Andre or John McCracken from the same period. Nauman's plaque is still fundamentally an inscription, and even an inscription that is currently in conformity with its meaning and will remain so up to the moment when someone decides to turn the plaque over.

If, in a certain sense, light for Beuys is always the result of a revelatory transition through darkness, the shade or death, with Nauman, light is always light and darkness. Their alternation in the winking of the neons, for example, contradicts and cancels the order or the message originally perceived: but the conflict of interpretations is not resolved for all that, and with the next blink the initial message starts all over again. Like the persistent retinal illusion of a stick that looks as if it is broken when it is put in water, even though we know very well that it is straight and whole, Nauman's alternating messages seem to keep breaking each other, but are also continually righted against each other, restored to their wholeness as colour and light. Here it is the spectator who is called upon to choose, to select from among the utterances without being able to take control of or consummate their synthesis, except in the purely retinal apprehension of fluorescent colour effects. When everything lights up, the retinal pleasure reaches a peak: each of the messages strikes up its own solo score amidst the saturated concert. But, to conclude, let us come back to this very strange double inscription of the word 'lightbox' in Beuys's drawing. The first is in regularly spaced roman capitals and takes up the whole length of the card. The second, in script, written over the first word, forms a kind of knot that is tangled at the centre. This double writing, in which the subjectivity of the handwritten words are added on top of the erect, official and anonymous letter-ing of the law, like a countersignature authenticating its own name by crossing it out, encloses what in a way is the key theme of Beuys' work: the creative 'flux' of meaning bridging the separation of death in order to achieve a reconciled, organic and plastic communication with life. As for Nauman, he has developed an impressive physical grammar of crossings-out and deletions which is the natural result of the spatio-temporal imbroglios studied in pieces like *Raw War*. *Seven Virtues and Seven Vices*, 1984 presents the names of the seven classical virtues engraved in roman capitals, and those of the corresponding vices in italics, superimposed on each other on blocks of granite (Nauman also produced a neon version of this piece a year before). Each virtue, each vice, is thus crossed out by the addition of its antonym. However, the slant of the italics is not the manifestation of a subjectivity present in the work of the signature or ligature of the law, it is a modality that rivals with roman capitals, one invented by the great Venetian printer Alde Manuce, the first publisher of the great Greek and Latin texts. In this murky business of Virtue triumphing over Vice, and vice versa, Nauman is in fact reviving a printers' war that goes all the way back to the Renaissance: is not the sloping letter vice-ridden? By setting it violently against roman characters, Nauman sets the two together in the granite of the endless con-flict that makes them appear now as Virtue against Vice, now the contrary, eternally confronted with their other and incomprehensible for all.

In contrast to Beuys, whose oeuvre rests on a metaphysics of expression which assigns to the linguistic sign a 'message of light for the darkness', drawing creativity from the dialectical union of contraries, Nauman's work with language is based on a 'physics of expression' which limits itself to the competing interfaces of signs that engage a reflex reading that is simultaneously provoked and repelled, leaving the reader-spectator the essentially tragic alternative of having to choose anew every time the lights blink. Nauman's works are not so much com-positions as appearances (before a judge). What Beuys saw as the proximity between his and Nauman's work was indeed predicated on a certain ignorance of Nauman's 'inner intentions'. It was, for the German, a *blind* proximity: not for a moment did he consider that the intentions of the American could be, in a Biblical sense, very shallow intentions, intentions at work in surfaces and interfaces, full of sound and fury, a tale told by an idiot entranced by a flashing sign.

One Hundred Live and Die, 1984 is an imposingly large wall of signs (about 3 x 3.3 m and 50 cm deep) containing a hundred three-word injunctions, all ending, alternately, in 'DIE' or 'LIVE', divided up into four columns of double multicoloured neons. These imperatives light up according to a random distribution pattern. Each message faces its own antithesis in the neighbouring column. Thus, working downwards from the tops of the two left columns we see 'LIVE AND DIE – LIVE AND LIVE/DIE AND DIE – DIE AND LIVE/SHIT AND DIE – SHIT AND LIVE'. Among these crude, brutal and seem-ingly disjointed, disorganised orders (further on, we see 'SUCK AND DIE – SUCK AND LIVE'), one is struck by the grammatical oddity of some of the messages, rather as if their clarity of elocution had become blurred, just as when, carried away by the rhythm, one sometimes rattles off instantaneous phrases or last-minute school exercises with bits missing: 'GOOD AND DIE – GOOD AND LIVE' or 'YOUNG AND DIE – YOUNG AND LIVE' followed by 'OLD AND DIE – OLD AND LIVE'. In fact, some of these anomalous messages seem to be no more than padding, as if the artist had suddenly run out of verbs ('BLACK AND DIE – BLACK AND LIVE/WHITE AND DIE – WHITE AND LIVE' and 'YELLOW AND DIE – YELLOW AND LIVE'). Except that this is no pupil who has forgotten his verbs, it is a giant wall sign, a monument in light dispensing a terrifying lesson in what the artist calls 'the attributes and actions of man', these being systematically co-ordinated with life or death. The anomalous substitution of colours for verbs thus seems justified, here, as pure padding: when you are at a loss for an action to put with death or life, there's always a colour. Rose pink, as Duchamp nearly said, is life. To be copied out a hundred times.

NOTES

1. Ludwig Wittgenstein, *Philosophical Investigations*, 1953, Basil Blackwell, Oxford, 1983, pp. 221-222.

2. Coosje van Bruggen, *Bruce Nauman*, Rizzoli, New York, 1988, p. 113.

3. The photographic images of Michel Journiac's *24 Heures de la vie d'une femme ordinaire*, 1974, formulate a similar viewpoint to these photographs by Nauman. By acting out, as an 'ordinary transvestite', the twenty-four most important moments and twelve major fantasises in the life of a woman, as gathered by a survey of the women's press, Journiac also enacted a double incarnation of a cliché – here that of the feminine ideal – as it is reified and standardised in a series of postures: 'making up', 'the meal', 'washing', using the form of the photo-story as the reflection of a 'travestied' action. Here, the relation of language to representation contains, as in Nauman, a trap, one based on the rules not of idiom but of the political and ideological score of the sexes. Journiac said that each of his pieces was like 'a trap for which we have to invent the way out'. Could we not say the same of Nauman's works?

4. Benjamin H. D. Buchloh, *Formalism and Historicity, Authoritarianism and Regression. Two Essays on the Artistic Production of Contemporary Europe*, trad. fr. Claude Gintz, Territoires, Paris, 1982, p. 39.

5. A drawing by Nauman (1968) describing how the piece works includes the following commentary: 'Sign to hang when there is a war on.'

6. Interview with Brenda Richardson, *Bruce Nauman: Neons*, exhib. cat., Baltimore Museum of Art, Baltimore, 1982, p. 20.

7. Willoughby Sharp, 'An Interview with Joseph Beuys', *Artforum*, New York, December 1969, pp. 40-47. In this interview, when Sharp asked Beuys what he thought of the work of Heizer, Oppenheim, Smithson and Sonnier, Beuys replied that Bruce Nauman was the only artist he felt close to, and revealed that he had spoken with him in Bern, no doubt at the famous exhibition organised by Harald Szeemann, *When Attitudes Become Form*, one of the major manifesto shows of the 1960s.

8. For fear, perhaps, of 'being turned into a work of art', if we are to judge by the 'very official' justification given by the SDP Prime Minister of Rhineland Palatiante, Johannes Rau, in 1968, for his refusal to dialogue with Beuys. Nowadays, when artists are generally considered as suppliers of services to the cultural and political powers that be, it is hard to imagine an artist being able to *frighten* his contemporaries so badly, and stir a fantasied terror worthy of a super-powerful comic-book hero.

I would like to thank Sandra Cattini and Jean-Charles Masséra for their precious help, their support and their infinite patience. I know that I am indebted to many others.

Knows Doesn't Know. 1983

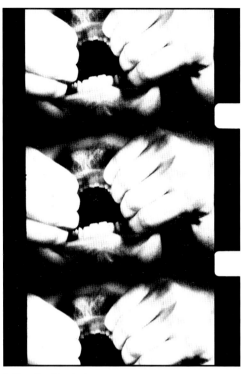

Pulling Mouth. 1969

François Albera

NAUMAN'S
KINEMATIC CINEMA

Is it paradoxical to link Bruce Nauman's work to the cinema,

or to point up its 'kinematic' dimension?

Already, this distinction shows that there are two 'ways in' to this question,

and that the answer depends on how we define our terms.

Kinematics, the French *cinématique*, is, the dictionaries tell us, the science of motion 'considered without reference to the matter or objects moved'. We come across the term in Etienne-Jules Marey, where it is used to describe the motoricity of movement in human or animal gestures. The term widens with Canudo and others, serving as an adjective for the cinema but also more than that. Something *cinématique* relates to the cinema without necessarily belonging to it. It designates the domain, you might say, of 'expanded cinema'. This was the meaning taken up by Eisenstein when he used the French term to designate any set of 'cinematographic' techniques or figures, whose characteristics he also saw prefigured in other symbolic spheres (poetry, dance, the art of knots, painting, music, etc.), and even in forms of thought: the Bororo language is cinematic, El Greco is cinematic, as are Pushkin, Prokofiev, and so on.

Eisenstein's *cinématisme* ultimately became identified with the general principle of montage. However, while it reflects an attitude that is manifestly reacting to the artistic revolution brought about by the cinema (the problematic expounded by Benjamin), the word above all offers the practical advantage of not restricting us to the closed field of the specificity of the medium. Whatever we think of it in itself, it has a heuristic value, it is a tool: for reading and for producing.

Although this word can be considered exclusively in relation to the word 'cinema' – the English 'cinematic' is synonymous with cinematographic – we cannot overlook its origin in *mechanics*. For it does retain something of the idea of cinema as a 'mechanical' art or technique which can thus 'mechanise' filmed movements by the process of breaking down and recomposing to which it subjects them. This is what Eisenstein called the *Urphänomen des Films*, i.e. the production of the illusion of movement by the superposition of two immobilities following each other in time. Superposition and not succession or juxtaposition. This material law of film, this '(optical) technical foundation', from which he set out to 'deduce the essence, the stylistic principle and the opinion of a film' [1] was observed by Walter Benjamin to be spreading, affecting even the actors: 'The gestures of Charlie Chaplin, the fragmentation of his movements, his jerkiness', he wrote, 'are the result of an extension of the law governing the sequence of images in a film to the law of human motricity'. [2] This argument – which Benjamin removed from the definitive version of his article – is of a piece with the utopia of the body-machine or 'human motor' dreamed up in the late nineteenth and early twentieth century in the search for total human efficiency, out of which grew a certain form of functionalism and the Taylorian organisation of work. [3]

NAUMAN AS CINEMATOGRAPHER

But let us begin by acknowledging that Nauman made a dozen or so 16mm films between 1966 and 1969 (notably *Fishing for Asian Carp* and *Revolving Landscape*), and then moved on to video (1968-1973: *Wall-Floor Positions*, *Manipulating a Fluorescent Tube*, etc.) before coming back to the cinema in 1976. Then there are all the installations which use filmed sequences, particularly *Good Boy Bad Boy*, *Violent Incident*, *Clown Torture* and, above all, *Falls, Pratfalls and Sleights of Hand*, which uses projection, in a sense reactivating the structures of cinema.

However, it must be repeated that Bruce Nauman's *cinema* cannot be reduced to Bruce Nauman's *films*, or even to his films and videos.

As attested by the reference to Duchamp's *Anemic Cinema* made by the neon spiral of *The True Artist Helps the World by Revealing Mystic Truths*, and the frequent allusions to Man Ray as a film-maker (*Emak Bakia* [4]), his relation to cinema is much wider than that; it can be actuated on other supports than film.

This relation to cinema in fact implies that we first get rid of the restrictive definition of the cinematic and consider it above all as, in a sense, *outside film* – as a model whose structural techniques have been adopted in another field: cinema outside film, which is to say, apprehended in terms of its techniques, figures and constructive principles, its effect, its concept.

In 1985-86 (notably with the three neon works *Human Sexual Experience*, *Hanged Man* and *Mean Clown Welcome*, and *Crime and Punishment*, which was done on paper), Bruce Nauman worked on the very foundation of the 'cinema effect', the *Urphänomenon*.

Given that in the 1960s Nauman shot several films (notably *Art Make-Up, Nos. 1-4, Playing a Note on the Violin While I Walk Around the Studio, Black Balls*), as well as numerous videos recording the duration of a performance (*Slow Angle Walk (Beckett Walk), Manipulating a Fluorescent Tube*, etc.), we cannot but note this attention to the minimal relation between two phases of a movement, two stases as the inscription of time issuing from a discontinuity, for we can suppose that it *grew out of* these same experiences which, in contrast, played on the continuity of the sequence (a single shot) and undivided temporal unfolding. One could consider, in fact, that by questioning this 'given' of recording by means of the discontinuities that he presents in terms of framing, angle and the movements of the filmed subject, Nauman has managed to produce the opposite effect and go back to the '(optical-)technical foundation' of cinema.

Already, the photograph *Failing to Levitate in the Studio*, 1966 recorded two successive moments by means of a double exposure on the film which showed the body in two different positions in the same image (lying horizontally between a chair and a step and half-seated on the floor).

We know that the Italian Futurists rejected photography because it fixed and contracted life, that Bragaglia tried to capture the trace of movement (light trails, double

permutational structure that removes all possibility of linear classification: each part could be before or after the other, depending on its position within the panel of twelve monitors offering a constantly renewed series of vertical and horizontal associations.

So, we can see that the temporalisation of the artwork is disengaged from vectors of forward movement; it comes and goes and transfers the problem of vectorship to the perception of the spectator.

Tony Sinking into the Floor, Face Up and Face Down. 1973

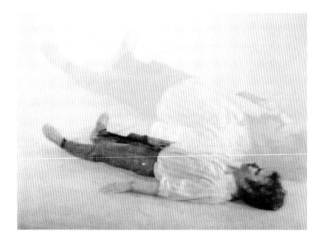

exposures), and that their position, which argued for 'photodynamism', was opposed to that of Marey's chrono-photography, and to Duchamp's *Nude Descending a Staircase*. They were just as hostile to the cinema which, in Bergsonian terms, they accused of subdividing movement, of imposing on it arbitrary mechanics just as the 'needle of the chronometer divides time when in fact it flies in a continuous and constant flux'.

By marking two states (lying/sitting), Nauman's photograph immediately creates an ambivalence, which is reiterated in several later pieces, regarding the chronological order of the two phases shown. True, the title does impart an order to the two states by stating that an action, levitating, and its failure, have occurred in keeping with a before/after time vector which coincides with the parameters high/low (*levitate/fall*[*fail/fall*]), but, at the moment of perception, their visual simultaneity contradicts this narrative orientation (he levitates, he has fallen or he falls, he has levitated; one of the states represents the spectral aspect of the other as either its memory or its anticipation). This orientation, which is reprised in *Hanged Man* (erect/soft, hanged/not hanged, each state could precede the other), is taken further in the installation *Violent Incident*, in which the narrative phases, the action sequences, are ordered within a

BODIES FALLING

The second point to be noted regarding *Failing to Levitate in the Studio* and several other propositions mentioned above (*Hanged Man*, etc.) is that the change of state is the result of applying a law, that of gravity, the fall of bodies.

Here, dance, the second source of this work, combines with cinema to explore another question linked to the origins of the cinema, which was taken up and reworked by Modern Dance (see Yvonne Rainer as spectator of *A bout de souffle*), who handed it down to artists such as Morris, Serra, Acconci and Nauman: that of the body, its orientation, gravitational attraction and balance.

This cinematic recreation of movement in film brings to the fore walking, running, jumping, wrestling – see the exercises Marey imposed on his models – and therefore falling, a repressed modality of choreography.

From optical toys (standing/lying, etc.) to the burlesque.

In *Inside In*, Steve Dwoskin goes through variations on the fall of a body which, because it is invalid, cannot remain erect, even though the whole of society enjoins it to do so.

The correlative of this observation is the negation of this law of gravity. Méliès and Zecca make their characters walk on walls as if they were flies. Fred Astaire dances on one, as does Trisha Brown in *Walking on the Wall*, or the astronaut in *2001: A Space Odyssey* and Nauman himself in *Slow Angle Walk (Beckett Walk)*.

Now for the third aspect of the question: this observation of the discontinuous states of bodily movement, this reflection on the given categories of representation

used by Merce Cunningham (and many others) suddenly becomes aerial, detached… (it is used in a great many of Nauman's sculptures, paintings and videos).

This brings us back to Moholy-Nagy, El Lissitzky and their floating spaces full of contradictory and suddenly changing perspectives.

Falls, Pratfalls and Sleights of Hand brings together all these different parameters which were previously dispersed or explored individually.

of the human figure – verticality, equilibrium, continuity of movement – implies a reflection on point of view.

The fixity of the frame, of the camera, means that the *performer* of *Slow Angle Walk (Beckett Walk)* leaves the field of view then partially returns to it, is decapitated, etc., as a result of the controlled but contradictory movements. When the camera is turned over we see the filmed subject walking on the ceiling or at right angles; it 'lightens' this body compelled to go through a wearisome physical exercise, perturbs our perception of it. Unlikely shots (from below) allow the characters to float, at last.

The continuous duration recorded on video in *Slow Angle Walk (Beckett Walk)* is diffracted by the fact that the fixed frame in which the performance takes place starts to *exist* as the place of separation: the body loses its permanence, its integrity, when it leaves the field of view, transgresses the limits of the screen and therefore postulates an extension of the out-of-frame, when it overturns the relations of scale within the frame. The movement and the gesture enacted – standing on one leg, moving forward, pivoting, switching position – are no longer legible because they are fragmented by the proximity of the spectator's position.

The variations on the *chair*, an object whose very definition denotes the equilibrium of its four legs placed on the ground, are emblematic in this respect. This accessory

THE CINEMATOGRAPHIC MECHANISM

First, though, we must come back to the minimal form of this questioning which is clearly articulated by the neons: the erect/soft hanged man (hanged man/hard-on, we might say, à la Nauman), and Serra's open or closed hand (*Hand Catching Lead*, 1969) – for, by acknowledging discontinuity, it introduces the reversibility of time: of the before and after. The hanged man has an erection when the noose tightens around his neck, but the contrary state could just as well as precede or follow the hanging. Two photograms follow each other but could easily do so in the opposite direction. In silent films, the camera could film backwards (the diver leaping backwards out of the water and returning to his position on the diving board) and not only to project backwards (which the Lumière Brothers started doing very early on in their film shows).[5]

The Bergsonian repulsion for the 'cinematographic mechanism' – in other words, for discontinuity (as opposed to flux) and the instant (as opposed to duration), was at the centre of the controversies of the years 1910 and the 1920s (Benda, Bragaglia, Vuillermoz, L'Herbier), for one of the distinctive questions touching on approaches to film was (and remains) whether the image it presented

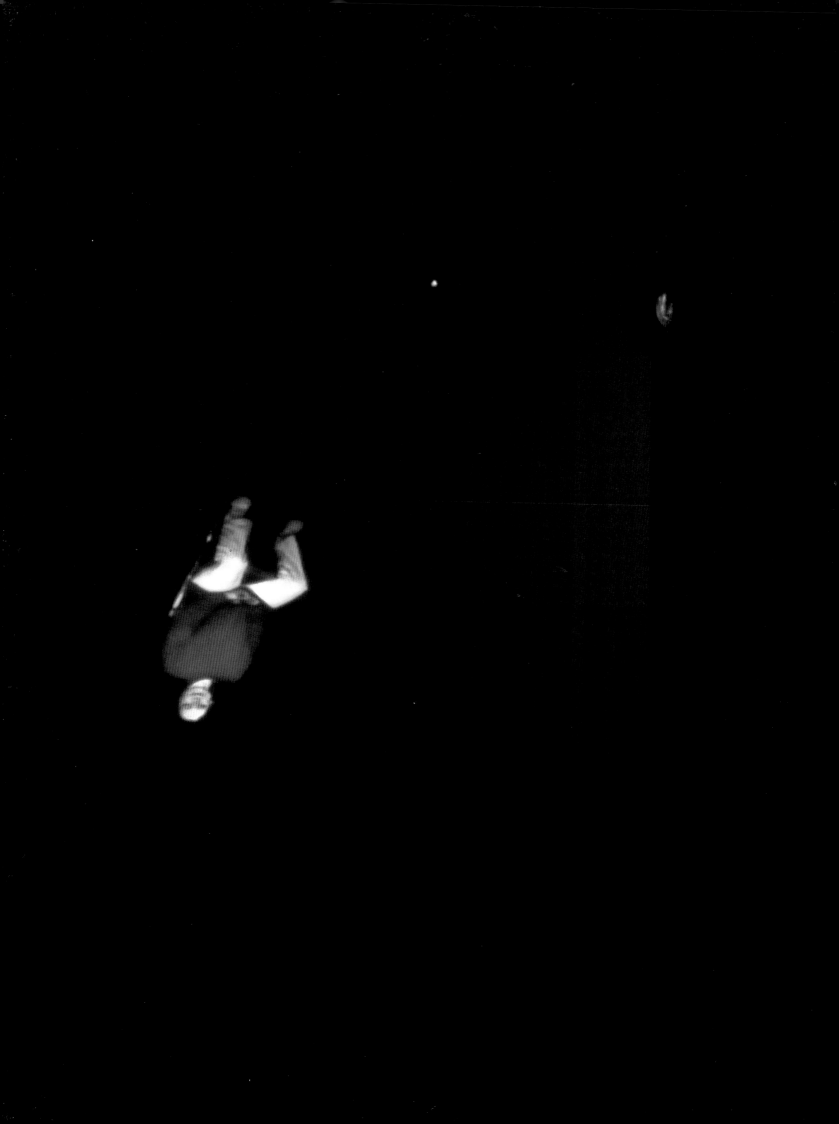

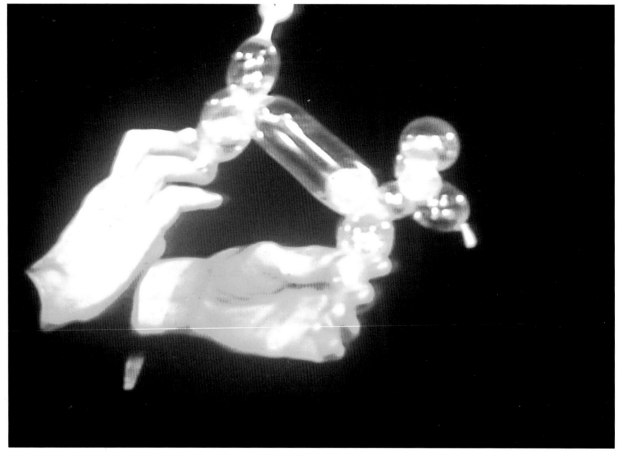

Falls, Pratfalls and Sleights of Hand. 1993

was, *from the outset,* a mobile image, a moving image that develops a duration, if only a minimal one, or whether it was an impression of movement in a given stretch of time which is that of the accomplishment of the phenomenon.[6]

The recognition of discontinuity implies an idea of montage which, for Eisenstein and Vertov, or Kubelka and Nekes, resides in the relation of one frame to another: the *kineme,* or the question of the interval.

Nauman adopts this affirmation, but makes it conditional because of the reversibility of time.

If we go back to the comparison with optical toys and the experiments of Marey as opposed to the films of the Lumière Brothers, we come back to the circularity and repetition of phenomena which incorporate a temporality within themselves.

SLEIGHTS OF HAND

*Falls, Pratfalls and Sleights of Hand,*1993, the group of five large video projection screens, constitutes a provisional totalisation of the concerns we have considered so far.

Two screens show medium (full-length) shots of figures, and the three others offer close-ups of active hands. On one of the screens – in a loop – a man walks and slips on a banana skin in slow motion, in the manner of a comic character, a foot rises ridiculously high in the air, the body twists as if devoid of internal structure then falls into a heap. In another, a woman sitting on a chair, filmed from below through a transparent floor, suddenly falls from her seat, which moves or folds beneath her, and comes to rest on the floor and yet hovering. The close-ups of hands show, on the third screen, vanishing tricks played with an egg or small ball; on the fourth (dominated by the colour pink), hands playing around with an animal-shaped ball; on the fifth (where green dominates) card tricks.

These walls of images form three sides. Standing facing them, the spectator becomes aware of relations between the different screens, relations which play on the

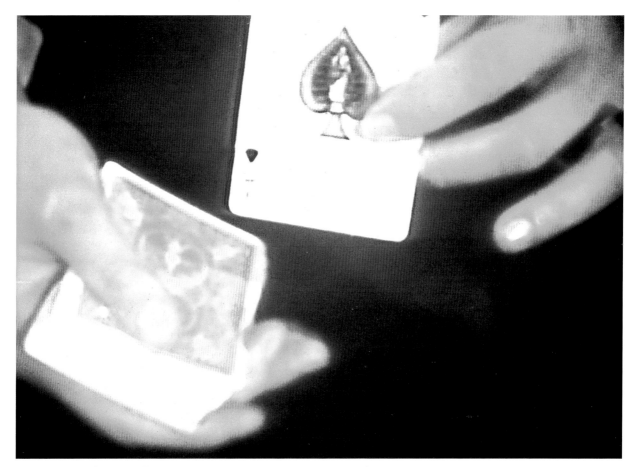

Falls, Pratfalls and Sleights of Hand. 1993

repetitions in these looped sequences and the multiple links, responses, repulsions and differences that arise from their simultaneous presence in space. However, we also note a greater complexity than in *Violent Incident,* whose narrative element, although circular and in tatters, elicits a very different kind of activity on the part of the spectator.

In *Falls, Pratfalls and Sleights of Hand*, we come back to the primary character of simple, basic actions, that are filmed and looped in such a way that they are put on the level of the circular subjects of the zoetrope (walking, running, jumping, etc.), which are wrested from their onward sequence by slow motion and from graphic proficiency by the 'poor' definition of the enlarged, distended electronic image. The temporal slow motion corresponds to the distension of the components (lines, pixels).

Contrary to the sequences of the zoetrope or optical toys, contrary to the burlesque sequences, here the human mechanism is slowed, broken down, the human motor is made to experience fatigue, deflation – in complete contrast to the 'healthy' and 'joyous' mechanisation saluted by Sigfried Giedion.[7]

DISSOLUTION

The last piece in the Zurich exhibition, *Poke in the Eye/Nose/Ear 3/8/94 Edit*, 1994 accentuates this insistence on the materiality of the medium, with slow motion and enlargement causing the raster lines to become the suffering, tortured 'flesh' of the subject. If these images evoke the close-ups of Jean Epstein, or those of Blaise Cendrars in his *ABC du Cinéma*,[8] what is proposed to the spectator has nothing to with this inquisition into the substance of things by the cine-eye, the super-eye of the camera that unveils the invisible to imperfect human vision. Before the infinite slowness, the inexorable violence of the finger penetrating a nostril, an ear, or rubbing against the eye, the spectacle we are called on to witness is of another type: there is none of the splendour of the never seen, but a disaster, a disintegration, an 'end of the world'. Corporeal integrity undergoes a 'telluric' upheaval that leads the spectator not to the side of the fragmented body (as in fragment-ation by means of close-up: see *The Battleship Potemkin*, *Un chien andalou*, etc., and their use of metonymy),

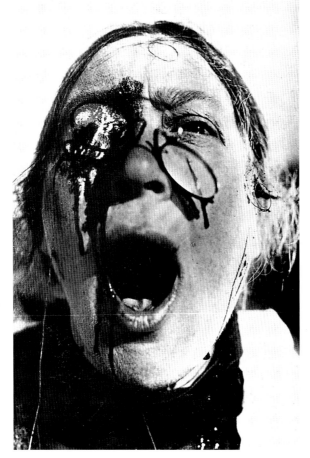

S. Eisenstein, **The Battleship Potemkin.** 1925

to our own faculties of representation and also imitates to a certain extent its changeability'.[9]

Nauman's highly individual practice of *temporality* (which cannot be reduced to the inevitable looping of the exhibition video which it usually includes) far from relies on this ductility, this speed of succession which led many to believe in the isomorphism of cinema and the unconscious, or cinema and the psyche (from Hans Sacks to Dr Allendy).[10] This situates his kinematics a long way from Benjamin and Valéry's 'aesthetics of clashes', and even from the practice of montage, of intervals, etc.: all these presuppose a discursive articulation, if not narration, even if they spare the spectators from active participation in their *blanks*. In contrast, even when he organises a structure of aggression as in *Clown Torture* (cries, brutal zooms, jump cuts, etc.) Nauman builds a trajectory of dispersion, of dissolution. This trajectory is perhaps too explicitly stated in *Learned Helplessness in Rats* (the set-up including video which is probably the closest to the carousels of hanging animals in his sculpture), whose literal reference to rats and all their Freudian connotations shows clearly where this trajectory leads – but it is more subtly implied in most of the pieces involving images on screens or TV monitors.

We can now understand better the reasons for the recurring falling, disappearing, floating and sliding: these are all figures of destabilisation in the perceiving subject, all dismemberings that the spectator shares as part of his own tropisms: he knows the role of the law of gravity, of equilibrium, and his presence in a Nauman installation, because it is usually slowed down, repetitive and reversible, solicits both his readiness to indulge foetal regression and his capacity to break free from it! (The paradoxical video corridors where we move further from our image the closer we get to the monitor are part of the same approach.)

If we now come back to one of the references made above, to the floating space of Vertov, Moholy-Nagy or Lissitzky, we cannot but recognise another function of Nauman's practice: whereas the Constructivists pluralise the perceiving subject (ultimately making it into a collective subject), Nauman programmes its dissolution. The experiment is obviously very different, and radically anti-utopian.

but to that of the dissolution of the body, of rejection, of abjection.

It would thus be interesting to compare Buñuel and Dali's eye cut by a razor, or even the smashed eye in Eisenstein, with this banal gesture of rubbing against the eyelid, in order to measure the gap between them. For while we can turn away from the horror of the former (shock, trauma, transgression), we are pulled into the latter. It is an entirely different form of experience.

Lou Andréas Salome expressed surprise that 'cinema plays absolutely no role' for psychoanalysts when its 'technique… is the only one that permits a rapidity in the sequence of images which just about corresponds

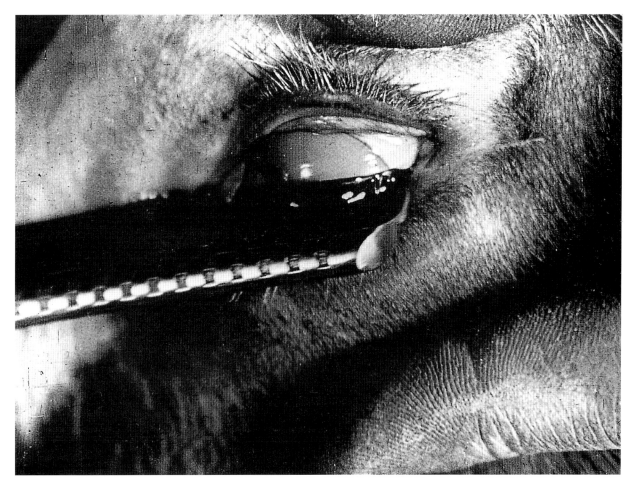

S. Dali and L. Buñuel, **Un chien andalou.** 1929

NOTES

1. Talk for the Stuttgart FIFO (*Film und Foto*), 1929: 'Dramaturgie der Filmform'.
2. Walter Benjamin, 'Paralipomenes'. 'The Work of Art in the Age of Mechanical Reproduction', in *Écrits français*, Gallimard, Paris, 1993, pp. 175-176.
3. Anson Rabinbach, *The Human Motor. Energy, Fatigue and the Origins of Modernity*, Basic Books, USA, 1990. It is striking that Chaplin, the 'hero' and embodiment of this new idea (Léger, Stepanova and many other artists saw him as the prototype of 'assembled' man), chose to change direction in *Modern Times*. where he attacks 'the extension of the law' of mechanics to 'the law of human motricity' while keeping the actual film on the side of the machine (in the sequence where he is swallowed up by the assembly line, the reverse movement whereby he is rescued from its cogs uses the 'reverse movement' of the film, or backwards filming).
4. The preparatory drawings for this short film used Marey's graphics and 'kinematic' body movements.
5. In the days of the manual camera, thanks to a rather *ad hoc* system, the film recorded the event in the order of its occurrence, but laid it out in the reverse order on its band (a process that remained current in amateur 8 mm and Super 8 films through to the 1960s).
6. Thierry Kuntzel gives this problem the name of 'running' (défilement) and has pursued his reflections on this in his video work.
7. Sigfried Giedion, *Mechanization Takes Command: A Contribution to Anonymous History*, Oxford University Press, New York, 1948. Giedion warns against the process whereby technology would take the place of social organisation, but his criticism of its 'excesses' is presented in the name of a rather abstract humanism.
8. Blaise Cendrars, *ABC du Cinéma* (1917-1921), Ecrivains Réunis, Paris, 1926: '... Train the lens on the hand, the corner of the mouth, the ear, and drama takes shape, grows against a background of luminous mystery'. Fernand Léger was fascinated by the disproportionately enlarged close-up of a nail.
9. *Journal*, 19 February, 1913.
10. We can observe a related quality of attention in the work of Douglas Gordon: the slowness of *24 Hour Psycho* leads the spectator to unfold the virtualities of the image that are invisible at twenty-four images a second. The film/psyche relationship is located in the temporal density of the image, rather than in the running.

Gijs van Tuyl

HUMAN CONDITION
/ HUMAN BODY

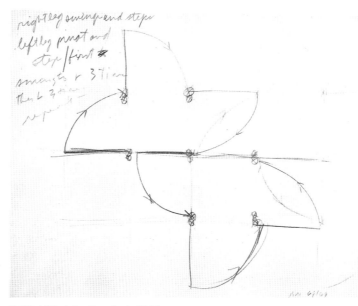

Untitled (Study for Slow Angle Walk),
also known as **Beckett Walk Diagram II.** 1968-1969

BRUCE NAUMAN AND SAMUEL BECKETT

Bruce Nauman and Samuel Beckett. Samuel Beckett and Bruce Nauman.
What do they have in common besides the century,
world renown and the English language?
Nauman is familiar with Beckett's work.

I. FIVE VARIATIONS FOR AN INTRODUCTION TO A FIVE-PART POLYPHONY, INCLUDING THESE FIVE VARIANTS.

Begin the beginning. One, two, three, four five; a, b, c, d, e. Five numbers. Five letters. Five words. Five sounds. Five rhythms. Five beginnings to this essay. Bruce Nauman plays through variant after variant in his work in a kind of Wittgensteinian linguistic game, unconcerned with the truthfulness of the result. His exhibition in Konrad Fischer's Düsseldorf gallery in 1968 was presented like an arithmetical exercise: *Six Sound Problems for Konrad Fischer*. Nauman gave a systematic series of performances which were recorded on reel-to-reel audio tapes first played at the opening and subsequently for the duration of the exhibition:

1. Monday – Walking in the gallery. / 2. Tuesday – Bouncing two balls in the gallery. / 3. Wednesday – Violin sounds in the gallery. / 4. Thursday – Walking and bouncing balls. / Friday – Walking and violin sounds. / Saturday – Violin sounds and bouncing balls. A different programme every day, for six days, like arithmetical variations on a musical theme. There were also methodical trials with linguistic variants. In the *First Poem Piece* of 1968 the sentence 'You May Not Want to Be Here' was variously transformed into 'You May Want to Be Here', 'You Want to Be', 'You May Not Want to Be', and so forth.

Five opening moves, thought out and noted down on paper, like chess openings. Chess was Samuel Beckett's great passion. He often played, usually against painter-friends. He was an assiduous reader of Marcel Duchamp's chess column in *Ce Soir* and a great admirer of the French artist's book, analysing as co-author the endgame. [1] The two men often played each other, although Beckett hardly ever won. But he was good at variants, witness *Molloy*: 'I had four ways of wearing my shirt. Front to front right side out, front to front inside out, back to front right side out, back to front inside out.' [2]

Beckett envisaged a fascinating chess variant: not to move the pieces at all, but leave them in their initial positions. It was a strategy designed to avoid the final, fatal phase of the endgame, for pawns inevitably advance towards their doom. Do nothing, was his motto. Take the beginning and end of *Waiting for Godot*. The first sentence is 'Nothing to be done'. And just before the curtain falls Vladimir says: 'Well? Shall we go?' and Estragon: 'Yes, let's go'. (They do not move). [3]

An interpretation of immobility which in my case would have resulted in blank pages.

Bruce Nauman and Samuel Beckett. Samuel Beckett and Bruce Nauman. What do they have in common besides the century, world renown and the English language? Nauman is familiar with Beckett's work. Beckett liked Caspar David Friedrich's *Two Men Looking at the Moon,* 1819, his source of inspiration for *Waiting for Godot,* [4] and he acknowledged a bond with the Dutch painter Bram van Velde, who lived in Paris. Nauman makes language three-dimensional, shaping words into neon letters and presenting them as images, like a billboard written on the moon. Beckett, on the other hand, evokes images by means of language. Beckett's fame came slowly, Nauman's fast. Nauman likes Beethoven's late string quartets. Beckett preferred the interventions and silences of the Seventh Symphony.

And this is start number four. Writing this text is like making one's way through a labyrinth. Physical and psychological disorientation resemble the experience of being in an architectural installation by Nauman. Or Molloy searching for his mother, Moran searching for Molloy or the Unnamable in search of himself, of his I. It is one thing to set forth, but getting there is another matter.

Establishing a connection between a hand in Nauman's work and a mouth in a Beckett novel is not a proper starting point, nor is explaining an ear in the work of one by comparing it with an eye in the work of the other. Could Beckett have been spawned by Nauman? You never can tell. Wasn't Shakespeare Hamlet's son, as James Joyce suggests in *Ulysses*? The philosopher Theodor W. Adorno, though, thought that Hamm, the principal character in Beckett's *Endgame*, was descended from Hamlet. [5] Names prompt people to make all sorts of associations, as was continually happening to Beckett, to his chagrin. That is not the right way of going about things, then.

This is the end of the beginning. Images in space which possess many aspects, and which can be seen from many viewpoints, disrupt the strict temporal order of language. To commence, seize, begin, open, leave. Arriving where? Beckett sometimes even links a story's end and beginning. He does so in *Molloy*, repeating the two opening sentences at the end of the second and final chapter, rather like a film loop: 'It is midnight. The rain is beating on the windows.' With the paradoxical modification: 'It was not midnight. It was not raining.' [6] We are left guessing. Nauman's films of performances can be shown as loops, as motions and actions repeated *ad infinitum*. An eternal *Wiederkehr*. One of the clowns

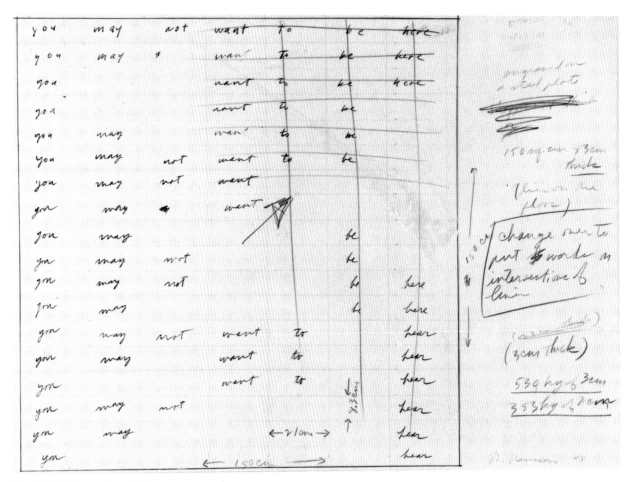

Study for First Poem Piece. 1968

in the video work *Clown Torture* of 1987 keeps on repeating the nonsensical text 'Pete and Repeat were sitting on a fence. Pete fell off. Who was left? Repeat. Pete and Repeat were sitting on a fence...' .

Beginning and end are handcuffed together, departing from the straight path of linear time. The reader or viewer gets the impression of a space-time continuum. The same kind of thing happens in Beckett's plays: 'Instead of a linear development they present their author's intuition of the human condition by a method that is essentially polyphonic; (...)' [7]

II. BECKETT, NAUMAN AND THE HUMAN CONDITION

Nauman and Beckett share an obsessive interest in the human condition. Both artists evince a profound sympathy with the lot of man in their work. They register and portray the human condition in the modern and post-modern world.

It would be hard to imagine a more penetrating portrayal of modern man's situation than in *Waiting for Godot*, in which life is characterised as an endless waiting, with an endlessly repetitive story, with actions which do not take place, and with the threat of power and violence lurking in the background. Beckett's credo is best expressed in his observation about two of his closest friends in Paris, the Dutch painters Bram and Geer van Velde: 'Basically, they are not interested in painting at all. What interests them is the human condition.' [8]

The leitmotif of the human condition is quite explicit in Nauman's suspended geometric metal sculptures of the 1980s with centred chairs, expressing his reaction to political violence in South America. His deep concern about world affairs, and his feelings of responsibility or frustration, affect his work: 'My work comes out of being frustrated about the human condition. And about how people refuse to understand other people. And about how people can be cruel to each other. It's not that I think I can change that, but it's just such a frustrating part of human history.' [9]

Clown Torture. 1987

The essence of human existence, with all its attributes and activities, is magnificently captured in the monumental neon relief *One Hundred Live and Die* of 1984. It is a multicoloured neon display with words flashing on and off, issuing the dramatic commands: LOVE AND DIE – LOVE AND LIVE; HATE AND DIE – HATE AND LIVE; FUCK AND DIE – FUCK AND LIVE – a hundred in all. The human condition is intimately linked with human nature: the contradictory experiences of pain and pleasure, of hate and love, of indifference and concern, of ignorance and knowledge and ultimately of death and life, as proclaimed a year previously in the round neon sign: *Human Nature/Life Death/Knows Doesn't Know*, 1983.

By the selfsame token he expresses notions of guilt and sin in his work. Take *French Piece*, 1968, in which the word *Guilt* is hidden away underneath a gilded steel plate, signifying guilt and gilt. And *Seven Virtues, Seven Vices*, 1983, brings mediaeval morality to the public's attention, executed in neon or engraved in stone. The seven vices

are taken to the extreme consequence in Dante's *Inferno*. The appearance of Dante's name in the anagrams of Nauman's *Steel Channel Piece* of 1968 is not fortuitous. The letters describing the object as 'lighted steel channel' are shuffled in such a way that the word 'Dante' is coupled with 'delight' and 'light' – not without moral irony. Beckett regarded the *Divine Comedy* as the most profound exploration of the human soul and is said to have never gone anywhere without a copy. Indeed, his entire oeuvre can be read as a modern paraphrase and transformation of the *Divine Comedy*.

Some of Nauman's architectural installations have an infernal character. The unsuspecting visitor is assailed with screams, wails, groans and shrieks issuing from glaringly illuminated or murky, oppressive, swirling, clamorous or deathly silent rooms. Sometimes the impressions are too overwhelming even for him, as in *Yellow Room (Triangular)*, 1973: 'The room is very hard to stay inside of – I can't stay very long myself.'[10] Rooms like that recall the description of the colossal breathing cylinder in

Beckett's *Le Dépeupleur (The Lost Ones)*, peopled with figures moving around or standing still or climbing up ladders towards niches. The lurid light reinforces the hopelessness of the situation. It has been suggested that the cylinder represents a gigantic lens, an allusion to Beckett's eye affliction.[11] The association with a closed cell in the underworld or hell is more plausible.[12] Nauman's

Seven Virtues and Seven Vices. 1983

Room with My Soul Left Out, Room That Does Not Care, 1984 – corridors leading to a square room, with yellow light – is pervaded with the same dismal mood.

The play on words in the title *Cones/Cojones*, a project realised in the Leo Castelli Gallery in 1975, conceals worlds, perhaps even hell itself. 'Concentric rings of masking tape at the floor were meant to represent cross sections of gigantic cones that begin at the center of the earth and project into the universe and in which the viewer was to imagine himself or herself centered.'[13] 'Cojones' means balls, in the vulgar sense as well. Nauman's subterranean rooms and tunnels of the second half of the 1970s embroider on the theme. It doesn't take much imagination to associate these environments with the mediaeval vision of hell.

Dante's *Inferno* is a yawning, conical void reaching into the depths of the earth. The damned, depending on their sins, are banished to different circles around the rim of the crater. Confronted with similar installations by Nauman, with images like those in *Le Dépeupleur*, with the deep abyss of the human condition, the beholder is aghast, filled with terror, as if on the very brink of hell:

I found myself – I know not how it was –
Upon the brink of the abyss of woe,
That thunders with the sound of endless wails.

It was so dark and deep and full of mist,
That, though I peered intently in the depths,
I could not make out any object there.[14]
(Dante, *Inferno IV*, 7-12)

Truth is paramount in both Nauman's and Beckett's work; more important than beauty or goodness. The figure caught up in a treadmill in Nauman's film *Pursuit* of 1975 was originally meant to keep its eye fixed on the significant word TRUTH. The schematic, cognitive-theoretical representation is fraught with irony, keeping truth permanently out of reach.

Nauman's work does not afford the pleasure of Matisse's sensual decoration or the nirvana of Mondrian's eternal beauty, but the torment of *De Profundis*. The spectator's senses are given a severe drubbing; he is disoriented, exposed to aggressive noise, glaring light and above all to the dire earnestness of human activity, notwithstanding the occasional touch of gallows humour. This is existence, not entertainment.

In their attempt to probe the darkest corners and most hidden areas of the human condition, both Nauman and Beckett operate in the borderlands of art – where those borders are not clearly defined, where the outcome of their explorations is not preordained. Such a mission transcends the choice of artistic medium. Neither Nauman nor Beckett feels bound by a particular medium, and accordingly their work is untrammelled by a uniform style with specific characteristics. Nauman is not interested in producing objects of art, in making paintings. His fundamental preoccupation is with art's potential as an instrument for investigating human existence.[15]

Beckett renounced external form and other adornments of language back in 1937: 'And more and more my own language appears to me like a veil that must be torn apart in order to get at the things (or Nothingness) behind. Grammar and Style. To me they seem to have become as irrelevant as a Victorian bathing suit or the imperturbability of a true gentleman. A Mask.'[16] He even turned to writing in French, 'without style', as a means of avoiding the temptations of automatic associations and obvious allusions. Using French also enabled him to 'cut away the excess, to strip away the colour' and to concentrate more on the language, its sounds and its rhythms.[17] Only unadorned language could touch the core of what he wanted to say.

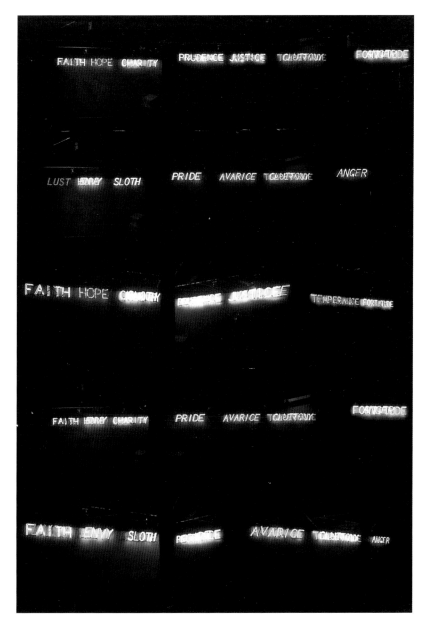

Seven Virtues and Seven Vices. 1983

To Nauman and to Beckett, art is primarily a direct, concrete experience in the here and now. This unites two artists in whose work sound and music are almost always in the foreground or background – Minimal Music. Minimal musicians understandably see a forerunner in Beckett, and it is clear why Morton Feldman dedicated a piece to him. By the same token, Steve Reich's music has inspired Nauman. In 1929 Beckett characterised the work of his admired James Joyce and implicitly his own work, too, in these terms: 'His writing is not *about something, it is that something itself*.' [19] This stance is epitomised in his novels and his plays for the stage, radio and television, which offer the reader or theatre-goer an experience first and foremost instead of a linear story. Language's plastic quality is exploited to the utmost, with images as concrete metaphors. [20]

As a budding artist, Nauman was impressed by Frank Stella's early paintings. Stella's artistic creed, 'What you see is what you see', opened the door to Minimal Art. Nauman gave this direct visual confrontation with a work a more personal touch. He compared the visual impact with a purely physical one: 'Like getting hit in the back of the neck'. [21]

Neither Nauman nor Beckett is given to undue subtlety. Both create representations and images which trigger reactions ranging from amazement to shock. Art as a direct experience, without embellishment, attests to a firm belief in its eloquence. It needs virtually no commentary. Beckett was even less forthcoming than Nauman when it came to explanations. Asked who Godot was, he replied: 'If I knew, I would have said so in the play.' [22]

III. CONSCIOUSNESS OF THE SUBJECT AND THE HUMAN CONDITION

What is the identity of the work of art, what is the artist's identity, and to what extent do they overlap? This ambiguity, inherent in the dialectic of life and art, is particularly evident in *Art Make-Up, Nos. 1-4*, 1967-1968. The theme is the artist's disappearance in the work of art, caused by his applying stage make-up. Beckett describes a similar problem of identity: 'Physically speaking it seemed to me I was now becoming rapidly unrecognisable. And when I passed my hands over my face, in a characteristic and now more than ever pardonable gesture, the face my hands felt was not my face any more, and the hands my face felt were my hands no longer.' [23] Physical changes reveal the I's intrinsic character more clearly.

Nauman's work is characterised by a wide variety of media and forms of expression. As in Beckett's work, no clearly defined style is apparent, no recognisable handwriting or conventional idiom with all the attendant aesthetic and emotional connotations. That explains his renunciation of art as style: 'Art is interesting to me when it ceases to function as art – when what we know as painting stops being painting, (...)'. [18] That is why he adopted a language other than his native one, just as Beckett adopted a 'foreign' language. The bare, sparse material of language, installation, film, video and sculpture precludes the stylistic effects of 'aesthetic' art.

Nauman reconnoitres his territory, demarcating it by keeping his distance, by objectifying himself, for instance in the form of a *Self-Portrait as a Fountain*, 1966, that cliché of public art. Subjectivity and objectivity are played out against each other ironically here, just as in the inordinately vertical elongation of his surname, functioning as a signature, in the form of a neon advertisement: *My Last Name Exaggerated Fourteen Times Vertically*, 1967.

The crisis of the I is the alpha and omega of Beckett's novels. In the beginning is 'I', the narrator narrated, whose identity it is hard to establish, who may not be identified with the artist himself, despite a certain biographical relationship. At the beginning of the novel the I is insistently postulated as I: 34 times on the first page of *Molloy*, 31 times on the first page of *Malone Dies* and 21 times on the first page of *The Unnamable*. I in search of I in the twilight zone of consciousness: 'Where now? Who now? When now? Unquestioning. I, say I. Unbelieving. Questions, hypothesis, call them that.' And a little further on: 'I seem to speak, it is not I, about me, it is not about me. These few general remarks to begin with.' 24

The subject can be divided into different subjects which perceive the world from different angles and are themselves perceived from every angle. Reflected subjects, as in an optical labyrinth. The I's I-dentity constantly shifts in the course of the trilogy *Molloy, Malone Dies* and *The Unnamable*. The narrating subjects are interchangeable, each turning into another, becoming unnamable. Beckett's oeuvre is riddled with such I-metamorphoses whose identity cannot be established. On stage, in the play *I not I*, is an illuminated mouth from which a stream of words issues. Whenever the voice threatens to utter the word 'I', it shouts: 'No!... she!... SHE!' 25

The I divides in Nauman's work as well. He once had a dream in which he met an enigmatic *Doppelgänger* in an enclosed space. The encounter inspired *Dream Passage (Version 1)*, 1983, an architectural installation of corridors ending in a centrally situated, yellow and green-lit room. The I, during its wanderings through the realm of consciousness, can change into the third person, into he or she. Nauman gave one of his rare public performances in the Whitney Museum of American Art in 1969, together with Meredith Monk and Nauman's former wife Judy. He also worked with a performer in

Tony Sinking into the Floor, Face Up and Face Down, 1973. In 1970 he himself vanished from his performances and reappeared in 1990, as performer in *Raw Material—BRRR*. From 1985 on he did so more often in video works, starting with *Good Boy, Bad Boy*, recruiting performers from his own circle.

IV. THE HUMAN BODY AS AN INSTRUMENT OF CONSCIOUSNESS

The body as subject is the perfect instrument for experiencing, examining and portraying the human condition. It is, throughout Nauman's and Beckett's work, the subject's basic point of departure. Its activities, motions, exercises and experiences are registered in minute detail, permitting the reader or spectator to share the experience.

Thrown upon his own resources, that was how Nauman started off as an artist with sparse means at his disposal: 'Alone in his studio, with only himself as a reference, he began to measure his surroundings in terms of his own body; he grew increasingly interested in its reifications and applied its function of sitting, standing, pacing and the like in his performances.' 26

High on the list of artistic procedures which Nauman drew up in 1966 are physical attributes and activities such as appearance and skin, gestures, footprints, vocal quality. In his San Francisco studio he subjected the human body to a laboratory-like examination. Later, when he moved to New Mexico, he took in the horizon too, where he recognised the same existential loneliness as his own as an artist: 'I am sympathetic to the frontier spirit, because as an artist you feel that you're on your own, you function by yourself. ... You are the first one there, and if you can't figure it out, there is no one to help you.' 27 Molloy undergoes the opposite development. After attempting to overstep the frontiers of his expanded region, he comes to the conclusion that change is not possible: 'But now I do not wander any more, anywhere any more, and indeed I scarcely stir at all, and yet nothing is changed. And the confines of my room, of my bed, of my body, are as remote from me as were those of my region, in the days of my splendour.' 28

Nauman's early work, sculptures and performances alike, are characterised by an obsession with physical attributes and activities. By that token it is akin to *Molloy* and *The Unnamable*, in which Beckett subjects the body

Dream Passage (Version I). 1983

to a thorough examination, describing every part of it in detail: the senses, notably the ear, eye, taste, smell,[29] followed by the head, hands, arms and again the head,[30] or a knee that refuses to bend.[31] He at last turns to the physical interaction of various parts of the body such as hands, knees, the soles of the feet, rump, palms.[32] There are also references to proportion, for example an enlarged knee, a telescopic view of the narrator's own body.[33]

Following this exposition of physical parts, the various functions are developed in the manner of a musical motif, in countless variations. With a kind of scientific precision,

Nauman examines variants of body language: applying make-up, grimacing, pulling funny faces, pinching, bouncing the testicles, picking the nose, rubbing the eye, cleaning out the ear. Exercises are endlessly repeated with slight variations in the studio: pacing, walking, turning, dancing, bouncing, stamping, rising. Similarly, Beckett dwells at length on postures such as sitting, drooping between his crutches, lying down, lying on different sides,[34] jumping, rising, levitating, walking, slumping, falling down,[35] lying down, sitting cross-legged, standing or sitting, then lying down and getting up,[36] rolling over,[37] flinging the arms up in the air, shaking, throwing, swaying,[38] jumping, lying on the back, on the stomach.[39] He is also fascinated by obsessive behaviour such as 'the finger in the nose, the scratching of the balls, digital emunction and the peripatetic piss.'[40]

The enlarged knee in Nauman's sculpture *Six Inches of My Knee Extended to Six Feet*, 1967, has its parallel in *Molloy*: 'That my knees are enormous, that I still get up from time to time, these are things that do not seem at first to signify anything in particular.'[41] A simple mathematical formula serves to enlarge inches into feet. The use of mathematical structures in Nauman's work is illustrated by the projection of three-dimensional figures on to the body: a cylinder or a sphere. In a performance of 1969, *Untitled*, two dancers perform the following exercises: A.) Body as Cylinder, and B.) Body as Sphere.

One of the narrating subjects in *The Unnamable* also considers these stereometric models: 'And after all, why a ball, rather than something else, and why big? Why not a cylinder, a small cylinder?'[42] Rolling over like a sphere or ball is then described. Or, in earlier passages in *Molloy* and *Malone Dies*, like a cylinder.[43] Rolling over is also the theme of one of Nauman's unperformed performances. For this, in 1970-1971, he built a *Performance Parallelogram (Rolling) (Performance Piece with Mirrors)*, a platform with a mirrored headboard at each end, on which a performer was supposed to roll round an imaginary centre.

Nauman's performances are inspired by passages in works by Samuel Beckett that describe similarly repetitive and meaningless activities.[44] The characters in *Waiting for Godot* do seemingly pointless exercises in order to relieve the boredom of waiting. There is something of a comical music-hall act about them:

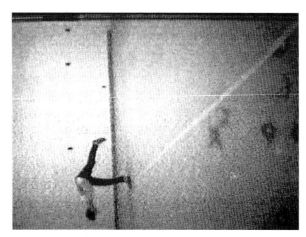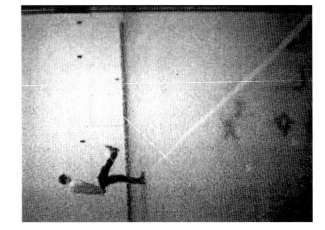

Slow Angle Walk (Beckett Walk). 1968

Estragon: What shall we do now?
Vladimir: While waiting.
Estragon: While waiting.
           (Silence)
Vladimir: We could do our exercises.
Estragon: Our movements.
Vladimir: Our elevations.
Estragon: Our relaxations.
Vladimir: Our elongations.
Estragon: Our relaxations.
Vladimir: To warm us up.
Estragon: To calm us down.
Vladimir: Off we go.
           (Vladimir hops from one foot to the other.
           Estragon imitates him.) [45]

This may be pointless from a metaphysical point of view, but as Moran in *Molloy* says: '... to see yourself doing the same thing endlessly over and over again fills you with satisfaction.' [46]

Moving or pacing or even dancing is a leitmotif throughout Beckett's oeuvre and in Nauman's early performances. Walking, or not walking, not in a straight line but swaying, drifting, turning, tottering, stumbling, leaning, falling, standing, all with the utmost difficulty due to lameness, with or without a cane, even crawling and rolling, are described over and over again by Beckett. It is essentially the theme of Molloy's odyssey towards his mother. [47]

By the same token, Nauman's *Slow Angle Walk (Beckett Walk)* of 1968 alludes explicitly to the strange steps and gaits which are analysed in such detail in *Molloy*. The camera, placed on its side, records movements directly inspired by passages in Beckett's book. Stiff-legged, the performer – Nauman himself – moves criss-cross through the studio, ignoring the logic of the straight line, echoing the three-page description of how Molloy hobbles on his crutch, his leg stiff, his knee straight, taking frequent rests. 'For I didn't know which foot to land on when I came down. Let us try and get

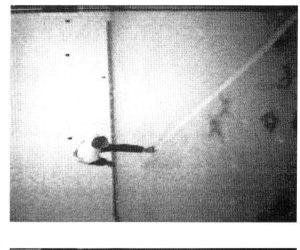

this dilemma clear. Follow me carefully. The stiff leg hurt me, admittedly, I mean the old stiff leg, and it was the other which I normally used as a pivot, or prop.'[48] His progress is therefore extremely slow: 'Some days I advanced no more than thirty or forty paces.'[49] A straight line which turns out to be a circle prompts the converse experiment.[50] Crawling like a reptile, he manages fifteen paces a day, describing a circle or polygon in the hope of advancing in a straight line.[51]

The mathematical and geometrical orientation in both Beckett's and Nauman's work is apparent in the formulation of certain problems, notably those which cannot be solved. Nauman refers to the old puzzle of squaring the circle, which was solved when somebody proved that it was impossible.[52] Molloy describes how he moved sixteen pebbles (four in each pocket) around, transferring the first from the right pocket of his coat to his mouth, then in turn to the left pocket of his coat, the left pocket of his trousers, the right pocket of his trousers and so forth, until he had sucked each pebble. Having considered all the permutations, he comes to

the conclusion that his self-imposed task is impossible, even though he has sixteen pockets. Not entirely satisfactory, perhaps: 'But however imperfect my own solution was, I was pleased at having found it all alone, yes, quite pleased.'[53]

Seeking, finding and defining the centre is an equally serious problem to Beckett, a problem that Nauman also addresses. It accounts for the labyrinthine structure often found in their work. The maze of perspex compartments for rats in Nauman's *Learned Helplessness in Rats (Rock and Roll Drummer)*, 1988, is an example. Virtually the entire oeuvre of Beckett is a linguistic labyrinth whose centre is hard to find. 'It comes to the same thing as far as discerning its limits is concerned. I like to think I occupy the centre, but nothing is less certain. In a sense I would be better off at the circumference, since my eyes are always fixed in the same direction. But I am certainly not at the circumference.'[54]

Defining the centre is a veritable obsession for Hamm in his wheelchair (*Endgame*):[55]

Hamm: Back to my place!
      (Clov pushes chair back to centre.)
      Is that my place?
Clov: Yes, that's your place.
Hamm: Am I right in the centre?
Clov: I'll measure it.
Hamm: More or Less! More or less!
Clov: (moving chair slightly)
      There!
Hamm: I'm more or less in the centre?
Clov: I'd say so.
Hamm: You'd say so! Put me right in the centre!
Clov: I'll go and get the tape.
Hamm: Roughly! Roughly!
      (Clov moves the chair slightly)
      Bang in the centre!
Clov: There!
      (Pause)

Hamm goes on to say that he feels he is too far to the left, to the right, to the front, to the back. Later, he wants a telescope to find the centre.

The Centre plays a role in Nauman's sculptures too. It is an illuminated void in *Lighted Center Piece*, 1967-1968, its exact position indeterminate. It is unreachable in *Double Steel Cage Piece*, 1974, of which Nauman said: 'You couldn't get into the middle of the room.'[56]

V. COMMUNICATION OR NOT, TILL DEATH ENSUES

To communicate or not to communicate, that is the great question of the human condition. Remarks of the 'pick-that-pencil-up' type have nothing to do with art for Nauman. He is only interested when language departs from its conventional text, forgetting its lines, so to speak. He is interested in its collapse: 'I think the point where language starts to break down as a useful tool for communication is the same edge where poetry or art occurs. Attention then shifts towards the sound quality of language and towards its poetic aspects. But when text becomes too unconventional, it is no longer possible to communicate.'[57]

Nauman's series of video works focusing on communication and sound reached new heights in his *World Peace (Projected)*, 1995, and *World Peace (Received)*, 1995. These two variations on one and

the same theme are each other's ideal complements, one version being projected on four walls, the other received on five monitors. This tallies perfectly with the idea of speaking as transmission and listening as reception, the basic activity of communication. The mingled sound of the five voices is a kind of musical language which has assumed polyphonic form:

> *I'll talk (to you),*
> *You'll listen (to me),*
> *You'll talk (to me),*
> *I'll listen (to you),*
> *I'll talk (to them),*
> *They'll listen (to me)*

World Peace is the epitome of rhythmic sound, comparable with Beckett's sonorous prose. Asked about the deeper meaning of his work, the writer answered: 'My work is a matter of fundamental sounds (no joke intended) made as fully as possible, and I accept responsibility for nothing else.'[58]

Molloy listens to language in its purest form as sound, albeit coupled with the painful loss of meaning. 'Yes, the words I heard, and heard distinctly, having quite a sensitive ear, were heard a first time, then a second, and often even a third, as pure sounds, free of all meaning, and this is probably one of the reasons why conversation was unspeakably painful to me. And the words I uttered myself, and which must nearly always have gone with an effort of the intelligence, were often to me as the buzzing of an insect.'[59] The alternation of sound and silence is a significant element of the flow of language in *Molloy*, *Malone Dies* and *The Unnamable*. They hear all the noises of the world,[60] the complex dance of the humming bees,[61] howls finally fading into silence. The dialogue of the two protagonists in *Waiting for Godot*, like the polyphony of *World Peace*, is music to the ear:

Estragon: All the dead voices.
Vladimir: They make a noise like wings.
Estragon: Like leaves.
Vladimir: Like sand.
Estragon: Like leaves.[62]

Language is abused as a weapon of power in authoritarian situations. In Beckett too. Riding his bicycle, Molloy is stopped by a policeman and given a stern talking-to.[63] In the architectural installation *Get Out of My Mind, Get Out of This Room*, 1968, Nauman's taped

Human Nature/Life Death/Knows Doesn't Know. 1983

voice shouts, growls and groans the command with such ferocity that people are intimidated. In *Molloy*, too, Moran has to obey his master's voice: 'Yes, it is rather an ambiguous voice and not always easy to follow, in its reasoning and decrees. But I follow it none the less, more or less, I follow it in this sense, that I know what it means, and this sense, that I do what it tells me.' [64]

Situations in which an invisible voice issues orders occur repeatedly in Beckett's plays. Moreover, there is often something of the clown or mime about his person-ages. In *Act Without Words I*, 1956 – for one mime – set in the blinding light of a desert, the actor does not heed verbal commands but obeys whistled signals coming in turn from the right, left and above. [65] *Shit in Your Hat–Head on a Chair*, 1990, stages violence in the guise of vaudeville. A wooden chair with a wax head is suspended in front of a screen with a slide projection of a female mime who carries out the crazy orders of an invisible voice from the wings: 'Put your hat on the table. Put your head on your head. Put your hand on your head with your head on your hat', etc.

The absence of language, total silence, is even more frightening and violent. The protagonist in *Catastrophe*, dedicated to Vaclav Havel, is a motionless, speechless object on a black cube on the stage. It is a doll, moulded by the director into the shape he has in mind, although at the end of the piece it defies instructions by briefly lifting its head. [66]

It is the beginning of the end when the inability to communicate becomes the most extreme form of non-communication: violence leading to complete isolation – to death, when emotion run riot leads to destruction. It can start with a conversation. In the second chapter of *Molloy*, Jacques Moran has an exchange with a vague person who crosses his path one evening. The outcome: 'He thrust his hand at me. I have an idea I told him once again to get out of my way. I can still see the hand coming towards me, pallid, opening and closing. As if self-propelled. I do not know what happened then. But a little later, perhaps a long time later, I found him stretched on the ground, his head in a pulp.' [67]

The human condition begins and ends with birth and death. It is hence not surprising that these two frontiers of life are leitmotifs in the work of Nauman and Beckett. The theme of death, that great taboo of modernity and its utopianism, runs through Nauman's oeuvre like a black

thread. It is explicitly visible in neon pieces like the monosyllabic *Eat/Death*, 1972, the key work *Human Nature/Life Death*, 1983, the masterly *One Hundred Live and Die* of 1984 and *Sex and Death*, 1985. It also pervades the sculptures consisting of suspended wax heads which resembling skulls, or the taxidermic animals suggesting anything but life. The coffin-like space of *Audio-Video Underground Chamber*, 1972-1974, 'a sealed concrete chamber, buried two and one-half meters deep in the backyard of the owner's house' [68] is a reference to the grave.

Like this chamber of death, the later architectural installations sometimes have the claustrophobic character of a funeral vault. The same mood was conveyed by *Model for Room with My Soul Left Out, Room That Does Not Care*, 1984. The project, installed in the Leo Castelli Gallery in New York, consisted of six long passages, one of them vertical, leading to a central room. The absent soul of the title suggests a deathliness that is reinforced by the yellow light. The enclosed space generates a feeling of disorientation, loss and isolation.

By contrast, holograms exhibited by Nauman in 1969 put critic Peter Schjeldahl in mind of a womb: 'In the gallery, one approached in semi-darkness a tilted plane of frosted glass on a stand and – voilà! – there was Nauman, seen in close-up as if through a green-tinted window or the glass wall of an aquarium... his limbs drawn up and wildly contorted before him, his long hair awry, looking like a baby in mid-tantrum.' [69] Nauman as an unborn child. Space can acquire connotations of both the grave and the cradle, both death and birth.

Malone Dies and *Endgame* are about dying and death. To Beckett, language is so real that it, too, is marked by death. *Beckett's Dying Words*, so to speak. [70] The burden of his tale is that it would be better never to have been born, for life is consciousness and conscious-ness is pain. Total oblivion or Nothingness, the great Void, are preferable to life. This accounts for his reluc-tance to begin. 'The best would be not to begin. But I have to begin. That is to say, I have to go on.' [71] Man is doomed to live. The writer's only escape is language, for it can incorporate death. Birth and death are close together in Beckett's work. The womb or the grave as the beginning and end of man, of life, of art. It is a frequently oppressive space, a space which can be both womb and coffin. The room in which Malone lies dying is also a tight fit: 'Perhaps after all I am in a kind of vault and this space which I take to be the street is in reality

Raw Material—OK, OK, OK. 1990

no more than a wide trench or ditch with other vaults opening on it.' [72]

Before him, Molloy, his *alter ego*, had also landed in a narrow ditch at the end of his life. After imagining his hostess had buried her parrot in its cage, Molloy muses: 'Me too if I had stayed, she would have buried. If I had her address I'd write to her, to come and bury me. I fell asleep. I woke up in bed, in my skin.' [73]
Cage, grave, bed and skin are equivalent here. The room is equivalent to the womb. 'The ceiling rises and falls, rises and falls, rhythmically as when I was a foetus.' [74] But the tide is running out for the I: 'I am being given, if I may venture the expression, birth into death, such is my impression. The feet are clear already of the great cunt of existence. Favourable presentation, I trust. My head will be the last to die.' It all ends with the I falling silent: 'I shall say I no more'. [75]

Ending the end: e, d, c, b, a. Five, four, three, two, one. No more rhythm, no more sound, no word, no letter, no number. The rest is silent as the grave.

Double Steel Cage Piece. 1974

NOTES

1. Marcel Duchamp and V. Halberstadt, *L'opposition et les cases conjuguées sont réconciliées*, L'Echiquier-Edmond Lancel, Brussels, 1932.
2. Samuel Beckett, *Molloy* in *Molloy. Malone Dies. The Unnamable. Three Novels by Samuel Beckett*, Grove Press, New York, 1977, p. 171.
3. Samuel Beckett, *Waiting for Godot* in *The Complete Dramatic Works*, Faber & Faber, London and Boston, 1990, pp. 11, 88.
4. James Knowlson, *Damned to Fame. The Life of Samuel Beckett*, Bloomsbury, London, 1996, p. 378.
5. *Ibid.*, p. 479.
6. *Molloy* in *M.M.U.*, *op. cit.*, 1977, pp. 92, 176.
7. Martin Esslin, *The Theatre of the Absurd*, Penguin Books, London, 1980, p. 45.
8. Samuel Beckett, *Die Welt und die Hose*, trans. from French by Erika Tophoven-Schöningh, Suhrkamp, Frankfurt am Main, 1990, p. 36.
9. Joan Simon, 'Breaking the Silence. An Interview with Bruce Nauman', *Art in America 76*, New York, No. 9, September 1988, p.148.
10. Nauman in a letter to Konrad Fischer in Joan Simon (ed.) *Bruce Nauman*, exhibition catalogue and catalogue raisonné, Walker Art Center, Minneapolis, 1994, p. 261, no. 229.
11. J. Knowlson, *op. cit.*, 1996, p. 536.
12. Hugh Kenner, *A Reader's Guide to Samuel Beckett*, Syracuse University Press, New York, 1996, p. 180.
13. Joan Simon, *Bruce Nauman*, catalogue raisonné, 1994, p. 264, no. 237.
14. Dante, *The Divine Commedy*, Italian/English, trans. by Kenneth MacKenzie.
15. Coosje van Bruggen, *Bruce Nauman*, Rizzoli, New York, 1988, p. 7.
16. Martin Esslin, 'Telling It How It Is: Beckett and the Mass Media' in Joseph H. Smith (ed.) *The World of Samuel Beckett*, The John Hopkins University Press, Baltimore and London, 1991, p. 209.
17. J. Knowlson, *op. cit.*, 1996, p. 357.
18. Christopher Cordes, 'Talking with Bruce Nauman: An Interview' in *Bruce Nauman, Prints 1970-1989. A catalogue raisonné by Christopher Cordes*, Castelli Graphics, Lorence Monk Gallery, New York, Donald Young Gallery, Chicago, 1989, p. 25.
19. M. Esslin in J.H. Smith (ed.), *op. cit.*, 1991, p. 207.
20. *Ibid.*, p. 210.
21. J. Simon, *op. cit.*, 1988, p. 142.
22. M. Esslin, *op. cit.*, 1980, p. 45.
23. *Molloy*, *op. cit.*, 1977, p. 170.
24. *The Unnamable* in *M.M.U.*, *op. cit.*, 1977, p. 291.
25. Samuel Beckett, *The Complete Dramatic Works*, Faber and Faber, London and Boston, 1986, p. 382.
26. C. van Bruggen, *op. cit.*, 1988, p. 108.
27. *Ibid.*, p. 106.
28. *Molloy*, *op. cit.*, 1977, p. 66.
29. *Ibid.*, pp. 19, 49-50, 139.
30. *Molloy*, *op. cit.*, 1977, p. 49-50.
31. *Ibid.*, pp. 19, 49-50, 139.
32. *The Unnamable*, *op. cit.*, 1977, pp. 304-306.
33. *Malone Dies* in *M.M.U.*, *op. cit.*, 1977, p. 234.
34. *Molloy*, *op. cit.*, 1977, pp. 22-23, 48, 54, 140, 153.
35. *Ibid.*
36. *Ibid.*
37. *Ibid.*
38. *Ibid.*
39. *Ibid.*

40. *Ibid.*, p. 25.

41. *Ibid.*, p. 62.

42. *The Unnamable*, *op. cit.*, 1977, p. 305.

43. *Molloy*, *op. cit.*, 1977.

44. See Neal Benezra in J. Simon, *op. cit.*, 1994, p. 25.

45. *Waiting for Godot*, *op. cit.*, 1990, p. 71 (see note 3).

46. *Molloy*, *op. cit.*, 1977, p. 134.

47. *Molloy*, *op. cit.*, 1977.

48. *Ibid.*, pp. 76-78. See also pp. 82-83, 85, 90.

49. *Ibid.*

50. *Ibid.*

51. *Ibid.*

52. J. Simon, *op. cit.*, 1988, p.143.

53. *Molloy*, *op. cit.*, 1977, pp. 69-74.

54. *The Unnamable*, *op. cit.*, 1977, p. 295.

55. *Endgame* in Samuel Beckett, *The Complete Dramatic Works*,
    op. cit., 1990, p. 105 (see note 3).

56. J. Simon, *Bruce Nauman*, catalogue raisonné, 1994, p. 262, no. 233.

57. C. Cordes, *op. cit.*, 1989, pp. 42-43 (see note 18).

58. Beckett after Esslin in J.H. Smith (ed.), *op. cit.*, 1991, p. 206 (see note 16).

59. *Molloy*, *op. cit.*, 1977, p. 50.

60. *Malone Dies*, *op. cit.*, 1977.

61. *Molloy*, *op. cit.*, 1977, p. 132.

62. *Waiting for Godot*, *op. cit.*, 1990, p. 58.

63. *Molloy*, *op. cit.*, 1977.

64. *Molloy*, *op. cit.*, 1977, p. 132.

65. *Catastrophe* in Samuel Beckett, *The Complete Dramatic Works*,
    op. cit., 1990, pp. 455-461 (see note 3).

66. *Ibid.*

67. *Molloy*, *op. cit.*, 1977, pp. 151-152.

68. J. Simon, *Bruce Nauman*, catalogue raisonné, 1994, p. 262, no. 230.

69. Schjeldahl in J. Simon, *ibid.*, p. 236, no. 155.

70. Christopher Ricks, *Beckett's Dying Words*, Oxford University Press,
    New York, 1995.

71. *The Unnamable*, *op. cit.*, 1977, p. 292.

72. *Malone Dies*, *op. cit.*, 1977, p. 219.

73. *Molloy*, *op. cit.*, 1977, p. 38.

74. *Ibid.*, p. 238.

75. *Malone Dies*, *op. cit.*, 1977, p. 38.

Translated from Dutch by Ruth Koenig

Meredith Monk.

HEART

BEAT

AND SILENCE

Interview with Meredith Monk by Christine van Assche

Paris, November 1996

Christine van Assche: When did you meet Bruce Nauman? How did you collaborate?
Meredith Monk: I first met Bruce briefly in 1968 in San Francisco but I knew him best around 1970. Bruce, Richard Serra and I were in an arts festival in Santa Barbara where we were all doing presentations. I asked them both to participate in mine, so we spent some time together.

C.v.A.: I'm preparing a show for the Pompidou Center on Bruce Nauman's work (...) It won't be a retrospective like the one made in the States. This show will try to approach the musicality of his work: the way he deals with the rhythm, the sounds, the relations between sound/text, image, the repetitions, the inversions, etc. We will be showing sound installations, audiovisual installations, but also neons, drawings, photographs. Does this seem to you to be a coherent point of view?
M.M.: It's really interesting to examine Bruce's work from a musical vantage point. I think that he has always been interested in music: rock and roll and jazz too. Even when he uses silence, it's part of the experience. His work is multi-dimensional. I feel very close to him in that way. I think we both try to work with many layers of perception in each piece.

C.v.A.: During the end of the 1960s and beginning of the 1970s, Bruce Nauman was testing simple gestures (walking, turning in a square, etc.), simple attitudes, in a closed space. Did he ever perform in public? Did he work in theaters? He works more in his studio.
M.M.: I'm not sure how many of his own pieces he performed in public but he did perform in the presentation with me in 1970. Even though I was primarily working on site-specific performances at that time, I recall that this presentation was in a theater. I had recently presented *Juice: a theater cantata in 3 installments* (at the Guggenheim Museum, the Minor Lathan Playhouse and the House Loft in New York) so I decided to perform material excerpted from that work. This consisted of a combination of short a cappella vocal pieces; movement and gestural phrases and jew's harp ('guimbarde') solos forming the continuity of the presentation. Then as a counterpoint, I asked Bruce and Richard to intermittently perform physical actions which would alter or break into that continuity. I knew that they were both interested in the body as a sculptural element so I thought that they would enjoy working on the project. We agreed on the activities that they would perform. Bruce would carefully line himself up with the edge of the stage and fall off at

any time; get back up and line himself at the edge again. Richard would twirl himself in the wings until he got totally dizzy and then stumble onto the stage. He could also lift me up and put me down anywhere he wanted while I continued on with my material. Apparently, the result was pretty funny, as you can imagine – a little like the Three Stooges. I had painted myself red from head to toe and wore a red bandanna, big red combat boots; a red undershirt and red painted *Lederhosen*. I remember Bruce wearing a white T-shirt and jeans and Richard wearing jeans and a white undershirt. I wish we had a videotape of the piece.

C.v.A.: I think Bruce's work has a real sense of musicality. More than any other visual artist of his generation, his work, even the drawings and the texts, are based on musicality. Do you think he has a musical method?
M.M.: I think that he has a musical sense. I remember participating in a piece of his that had a fascinating musical dimension. It was performed in the second floor gallery of the Whitney in the spring of 1969 [1]. Bruce, his wife at the time, and I stood with our backs to three corners of the room. Our task was to fall backwards against the corner of the wall, stand back up, fall again, stand back up, like that, for an hour. That was the piece. The thumping sounds of the falls and the rhythmic and visual configurations kept varying because each of us fell in a different way and at different intervals. Thinking about the piece now, the idea seems very musical.

C.v.A.: There was no metric system?
M.M.: No, no meter at all. Each person was free to fall and stand up again whenever he or she wanted. The result was a little bit like a percussion piece, like a drum track, but not metrical.

C.v.A.: In the 1960s and 1970s, the rhythm of his work was binary, metrical. In the 1980s and 1990s, the musicality is more complex and implicates the notion of multiplicity. What do you think of this?
M.M.: In the late 1960s and early 1970s, a lot of people were trying to get back to some fundamental principles. The minimalist aesthetic was prominent and different people were exploring reduction in different ways. I think Bruce's falling piece that I spoke of is a very interesting example – that one could make a performance piece based only on one idea, one activity and the result could be lively and compelling. In sound, one fundamental principle is heartbeat. I think Bruce

liked rock and roll a lot and that kind of music has a very strong metrical, heartbeat kind of base. So dealing with metre seems like getting back to a very basic issue.

C.v.A.: How did he change later, in the 1980s and 1990s? Was he influenced by other types of music, less repetitive, more complex?

M.M.: You said that he loves jazz. In jazz, you would have a much more complex, free rhythmical situation. And certainly if you listen to Coltrane (who you say is one of Bruce's favorite composers and musicians), the textures are incredibly rich and complex, so it's really going very much in another direction from straight metre. I would say that one aspect has to do with breath-length phrases; what you can get out of one cycle of breath. Perhaps the physical, visceral aspect of that kind of phrasing was inspiring to Bruce. But, you know, talking about how he evolved from one kind of musicality to another is just conjecture on our part. The best person to answer these questions is Bruce. How did you first find out that he really loved Coltrane's music?

C.v.A.: I read an interview that he gave in the 1980s for the American Archives [2] in which he talks about some correspondances with other artists. He also made a piece called *John Coltrane Piece* which is quite mysterious. It is an aluminum stone which is supposed to lay on the ground on an empty space – which has a hidden face. What is his relationship to repetitive music, to Steve Reich's music for instance?

M.M.: As I said before, generally there was an impulse to get back to very essential kinds of forms and to eliminate what seemed to be excess. I think that a lot of people in the visual art world were in a dialectical relationship with the Abstract Expressionist kind of impulse. In performance, there was a dialogue with the psychological theater and dance of the 1950s. And in music, it was much more a matter of getting away from the European model, which was theme, development, climax, denouement and recapitulation. The impulse of musicians in the 1960s and 1970s was to find a less linear form. So there were many people working in their own particular ways to go beyond the traditional methods of doing things. Bruce was part of this wave of activity.

C.v.A.: Were there many collaborations in the 1970s between artists coming from different fields?

M.M.: In the beginning of the 1960s, there was a community of people coming from many disciplines who questioned the parameters of their individual disciplines. This was the Judson Dance Theater and Judson Poet's Theater period (1961-65). There were many visual artists involved with this. Poets and painters and sculptors were making dances, dancers were using words and creating sculpture. Everybody was quite involved in just trying to, in a sense, break down the barriers between forms, collaborate in different ways and stretch the definitions of these forms. It was the period of Happenings – Allan Kaprow, Dick Higgings, Jim Dine, Claes Oldenburg, Carolee Schneeman (to name a few) who came from visual backgrounds dealing with a time art. Overall, it was a very fertile period. Bruce and I come from the same generation and while I started working a little earlier than Bruce, I think that by the time each of us came […], the community did not have the same cohesiveness. But, in a sense the resonance and energy generated by all that activity had spread and had been felt in the art world. So even if you were not in that generation, you still felt that things had been opened up.

For me, coming to New York at that time (1964) was a real affirmation. As a student at Sarah Lawrence College, I had been trying to combine my vocal work with visual images and movement and develop a new performance form which wove these things together. I had glimpses of how to do this and made many pieces while I was still there but it was very encouraging to come to New York and actually feel that I wasn't some crazy person having this idea. It was stimulating to enter that sort of atmosphere.

I would imagine that Bruce encountered in New York a very different concept of what was being taught in art school. Some of the most beautiful dance works were being done by visual artists. I'm thinking of Robert Morris' *Waterman Switch* which was a stunning piece. Performers were more sensitive to plastic elements and visual artists had to contend with the element of time. But I think that Bruce, coming from another generation, was probably already thinking about time right from the beginning. So I would say that that goes right back to your musical idea.

C.v.A.: Bruce Nauman had at some point in his education a mathematical training. The logical system in his work is very different from a structure you may find in visual arts.

Juice: a Theater Cantata in Three Installments. 1969
Photograph © Peter Moore/VAGA, New York and DACS, London 1998

Meredith Monk, Bruce Nauman, Richard Serra. Santa Barbara Arts Festival. 1970

M.M.: That's very interesting because it's something that is not immediately apparent in his work. If you see someone like Sol LeWitt, you think this is someone dealing with mathematical principles. There are other artists that I would think of as artists/mathematicians. Actually what I like is that you don't see that in Bruce's work.

C.v.A.: No, you don't see it, but I think it's in the structure.
M.M.: It's in the background, that's what I like, it's not in the foreground. It's very interesting. Something that you might want to explore is the kind of relationship that exists between mathematics and music in Bruce's work. The math is very hidden and the theme of hiding seems to be very much part of his basic strategy.

C.v.A.: Do you think there was any kind of relationship with Cage or Cage's music? He was also opening the field between visual arts and music?
M.M. I don't think that there was any way during that period that anyone could fail to be aware of John Cage and what he was doing. There were people who were thinking along similar lines and others who were working in opposition.

C.v.A.: Did you know him?
M.M.: Yes I did. I knew him more towards the end of his life. I first met him in 1975 when I performed my music for one of Merce Cunningham's *Events*. Then in the mid-1980s, I sang a work of his, *Aria*, in a series of concerts in upstate New York. Before one of the concerts, he came to my house and cooked some mushrooms that he had picked that day. I cooked up some vegetables from my garden and some brown rice and had the pleasure of having a meal with him.

I'm really glad that I was able to have that experience and a few others with him during that period. I found him totally inspiring as a human being. Just a wonderful spirit. I learned about how one could remain open and delight in the moment. I don't know whether Bruce would have had that much contact with him or not.

C.v.A.: I don't think so, he has not talked about him as a big influence.
M.M.: John was a large presence during the early 1960s. He proposed a spirit of inquiry; a spirit of being very open to anything. I think for our generation, beginning when we did, John's ideas became part of our legacy and yet we could choose to be influenced by them, to ignore them, or to work in opposition to them. Nevertheless, I don't think that there was a much more expansive world of possibilities than there had been before John Cage. He made a gigantic contribution.

C.v.A.: What do you think of the new generation?
M.M.: I like what's going on in this generation. I think that the 1980s was a difficult period – values went a bit askew. I think that now because of the economic situation, young people are really coming back to the idea of doing work out of love. There is not a built-in assumption of monetary reward. That might come but that's not the reason for doing it. I think that's a very important value. Sometimes during a hard period, things can open up – you can be very inventive when you don't necessarily have everything. A lot of good energy is coming back into the art world. The people that really needed to do work are continuing to do work and the people that were just doing it for other

Meredith Monk.

reasons are not. It's a question of inner strength and endurance. It's part of the process to want to continue no matter how that also defines you. I think you end up defining your work and your life that way as well.

C.v.A.: What do you appreciate about Bruce Nauman's work?
M.M.: What I appreciate about Bruce's work is his imagination, his honesty, his multiplicity of means, the way he balances playfulness and pain. The mystery and underlying sense of dread in many of his pieces resonates powerfully with our contemporary experience. And yet there is always a sense of irony, of laconic humor.

Bruce is not afraid to reveal his process; to say 'Look, I'm in a transitional period. My ideas are in formation and I'm going to share that with you through my work'. As a reflection of the true nature of reality (which is always changing), I find that very affirming.

NOTES

1. This performance took place at the Whitney Museum of American Art in New York, as part of the exhibition
   Anti-Illusion: Procedures/Materials, in which his first corridor piece was also exhibited.
2. Michele De Angelus, 'Bruce Nauman Interviews, 1980 27 May–30 May', Archives of American Art, Smithsonian Institution,
   Washington D.C., 1980. *Cf. infra*, p. 120.

Marcia Tucker

PHE N A U M A N OLOGY

Bouncing Two Balls Between the Floor and Ceiling with Changing Rhythms. 1967-68

Experience shows that human beings
are not passive components in adaptive systems.
Their responses commonly manifest themselves
as acts of personal creation.

René Dubos, *Man Adapting*

Since his first provocative New York exhibition at the Castelli Gallery in 1968, Nauman's work has become increasingly complex. We are no longer able to take refuge in art-historical analogies to Duchampian esthetics or reference to visual affinities with the work of Johns, Oldenburg, or 'process' art. Nauman's roughly-built acoustical and performance corridors; his elusive camera/monitor pieces; his unenterable channels of air current; 'dance' pieces and slow-motion single image films – all seem to defy our habitual esthetic expectations. To encounter one of these pieces is to experience basic phenomena that have been isolated, inverted, taken out of context, or progressively destroyed.

Nauman does not represent or interpret phenomena, such as sound, light, movement, or temperature, but uses them as the basic material of his new work. Our responses to the situations he sets up are not purely physical, however. Man alone among animals is able to symbolize, to respond not only to the direct effect of a stimulus on his body, but to a symbolic interpretation of it. This interpretation (and its emotional or psychological corollaries) is conditioned by all other experiences a person has had, and which he involuntarily brings to bear on every new situation. Each person will, therefore, respond to the physical experience of Nauman's work in a different way.

Nauman carefully constructs his pieces to create a specific physical situation. Although he is no longer interested in ways of making art nor in the 'interpretation' of a made object, he feels it is still important that a piece be neither over- nor under-refined. In this way focus can be directed to the experience and our response to it, rather than to the object itself.

The structures of sound and movement as a basic function of human behavior and communication are the phenomena which provide not only the artist, but the linguist, the anthropologist, the philosopher, and the social scientist with the sources of our knowledge of man. These are Nauman's concerns, and he sees his art as more closely related to man's nature than to the nature of art. This attitude is evidenced by his evolution from the making of objects and the recording of activities, to his present concern with manipulations of phenomena.

He has utilized progressively intricate 'extensions' of the human body, the same extensions that man has evolved in order to live, to communicate, and to adapt to his environment. They range from writing which extends language and the telephone which extends the voice, to complicated mechanisms like the computer, allowing memory and calculation far beyond the capacity of any human source.

Because Nauman's earlier work consists of visual puns, verbal plays, and manipulations of non-art materials, the intent of this work largely resides in the objects themselves. Recently, by dealing with the ways things are experienced instead of how they are made or perceived, the intent of the work is realized only through the physical involvement of the spectator. To this end, Nauman has investigated a wide variety of modes of communication, each of which is increasingly complex in the responses it is capable of effecting. They include language (both spoken and written); non-verbal sounds, both natural (breathing, walking) and artificial (clapping, making music); physical gesture (facial expressions, body manipulations, dance); and the extension of any or all of these by artificial or technological means.

Our bodies are necessary to the experience of any phenomenon. It is characteristic of Nauman's work that he has always used his own body and its activities as both the subject and object of his pieces. He has made casts from it (*From Hand to Mouth, Neon Templates of the Left Half of My Body Taken at Ten-Inch Intervals*, etc.) and manipulated it (in earlier performances using his body in relation to a

T-bar or neon tube, as well as in the holograms). He has made video tapes of his own activities (*Bouncing Balls in the Studio*) and films of parts of his body being acted upon; *Bouncing Balls* and *Black Balls* are slow-motion films of Nauman's testicles moving and being painted black. He has questioned, in various pieces, his behavior as an artist and his attitudes toward himself as such. He has contorted his body and face to the limits of physical action as well as representation. By making audiotapes of himself

Bouncing Two Balls Between the Floor and Ceiling with Changing Rhythms. 1967-68

clapping, breathing, whispering and playing the violin, he has also explored a range of noises made and perceived by his own body.

This concern with physical self is not simple artistic egocentrism, but use of the body to transform intimate subjectivity into objective demonstration. Man is the perceiver and the perceived; he acts and is acted upon; he is the sensor and the sensed. His behavior constitutes a dialectical interchange with the world he

occupies. Merleau-Ponty, in *The Structure of Behavior*, stresses that man *is*, in fact, his body, despite the essential ambiguity of its being at once lived from the inside and observed from the outside. Nauman has used himself in this way as a prototypical subject for the pieces. These works are meant, essentially, to be encountered privately by one person at a time. Where earlier the artist was the subject and object of recorded situations, now it is the spectator who becomes both the actor and observer of his own activity.

Ordinarily we are unable to experience both things simultaneously – at least, not without a mirror and an extraordinary degree of self-consciousness. At the Nicholas Wilder Gallery in Los Angeles Nauman set up a series of wallboard panels running parallel along the length of the gallery. Cameras and videotape monitors were set up in such a way that a person walking the length of one corridor and turning into the next would see himself on a monitor only as he turned the corner. The space set up is longer and narrower than most spaces we find or make for ourselves. The corridors therefore occupy an ambiguous and uncomfortable realm between too much space, which creates feelings of isolation and disorientation, and too little space, which causes cramping and tension. In this case, both are experienced simultaneously. At the same time, the image on the screen further disorients the viewer because he sees himself at a distance, from below and behind. He is prevented from being intimate with himself because

In Nauman's slow-motion films, he uses uncut footage, taken from an unchanging vantage point. In them, a repeated simple change occurs in the object itself, while the way we perceive it does not change. *Bouncing in the Corner*, *Bouncing Balls* and similar films confound our experience of time by a transference of the functions usually assigned to objects and phenomena.

 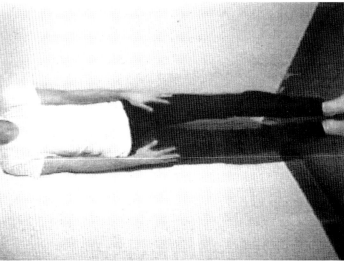

Bouncing in the Corner, N° 2: Upside Down. 1969

he is not even allowed to meet his image head-on. Ordinary experience of the space between man and his image is the frontal, 12 to 16 inch space we normally allow when looking into a mirror.

Like most of his work, this situation does not deal with a concept of space, but with the sensation of it. Its effect goes beyond that of a purely physiological reaction to become a highly charged emotional experience. It is similar in feeling to the impact of seeing, but not immediately recognizing yourself in the reflective surface of a store window as you pass it.

Other pieces deal more specifically with the physiological and emotional effects of time. Even according to the most stringent scientific analyses of time, pure (or absolute) time cannot be measured, because every lapse of time must be connected with some process in order to be perceived. We define time, therefore, according to our experience of it. When looking at a static object, the phenomenon of time, of *how* we perceive something, can be separated from *what* we are looking at, which does not change.

The performance pieces, which Nauman says have duration, but no specific time, operate in a similar fashion. For example, two dance proposals require a performer to work on one exercise for ten to fourteen days before giving an hour-long performance of it. One process involves the use of the body as a cylinder, in which the dancer lies along the junction of wall and floor facing into the angle formed by them. He straightens and lengthens the body through its center into the angle. A second piece uses the body as a sphere, curled into a corner. The dancer attempts to compress his body toward the central point of the sphere, and then toward the corner. Changes in movement during the performance would be barely perceptible to the audience, but the discrepancy between our normal expectation of how long it takes to perform or perceive a given activity, and Nauman's distension of that time, creates extreme tension.

Other kinds of tension resulting from the physiological effect of changes in pressure on the auditory system are used by Nauman. One such piece is an acoustically panelled corridor whose two walls converge. Another is a parallel, staggered group of 8-foot acoustical panels to be walked between. Nauman has pointed out an analogous situation existing in nature, when certain winds or approaching storms can create even minute pressure changes in the atmosphere, which are said to account for widespread emotional instability and increased suicide rates in a given area.

Even a long time ago, when I was painting, I could get to a point where everything worked except for one part of the painting which was a mess, and I couldn't figure out what do with it. One way was to remove that part of the painting. The other way was to make that the important part of the painting; that always ended up the most interesting.

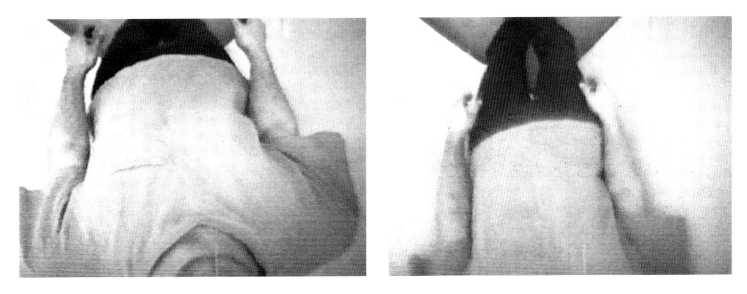

The 'emotional overload' that he is interested in can be partly accounted for in these kinds of terms, but is also due, in a less definable way, to how much of his own ideas and feelings he has been able to incorporate into the work — to how personal it is. For him, this quality is essential, even if it is impossible to measure or evaluate.

*I think when you attempt to engage people that way — emotionally — in what you're doing, then it's difficult because you never know if you succeed or not, or to what extent. In other words, it's easier to be professional, because then you can step outside the situation. When you bring things to a personal level then you're just much less sure whether people can accept what's presented.**

Since the emotional responses to each piece differ according to the receptor, it is almost impossible to name them; loneliness, delight, anxiety, surprise, frustration, serenity and other private feelings provide the sensory poetry of this work.

The artist's concern with making the 'difficult' aspect of a work its focus need not be seen as perversity or artistic sadism, but as a viable working method. For example, Nauman has stated that art generally adds information to a situation, and that it seems reasonable to also make art by removing information from a situation. In fact, sensory deprivation experiments have shown that only the essential information needed to identify a thing tends to be picked up from a surrounding group of stimuli.

One of a group of pieces operating on this principle consists of an empty sealed room and an accessible room. An oscillating picture of the open room and its occupants (if any) is projected onto a monitor in the sealed room. Spectators witness only the video tape of the closed space, rather than the expected image of themselves. The elimination of extraneous material here clarifies the work's intent by making its focus immediately apprehensible.

Mixing up two kinds of information which are similar but not quite the same is still another means of effecting sensory dislocation. For

Dance or Exercise on the Perimeter of a Square. 1967-1968

instance, at Galleria Sperone in Turin last year Nauman made a piece in which touching one wall of the gallery produced the sound of that touch on another wall. He relates this phenomenon to the use of skew lines in mathematics, where two non-parallel lines are situated in relation to each other in space, but never meet.

If you make the lines very close – he says – it's the point at which you get to an optical illusion. Even though you understand how it works, it works every time. It's sort of the way I felt about how these pieces worked. Touching and hearing later, there were two kinds of information that occurred that were very close. You couldn't quite separate them, and you couldn't quite put them together. And so the experience has to do with that confusion that occurs. It's very hard to understand why that turns out to be a complete experience, but it does.

Another method used by Nauman in *Second Poem Piece* is to radically alter the sentence 'YOU MAY NOT WANT TO SCREW HERE' by progressive removal of words. Differences in the degree of information, and changes in our emotional response to each line occur immediately upon reading (i.e. participating in) the work. By removing semantic information until the words 'YOU WANT' are left, the degree of emotive content is increased.

In the audiotapes of breathing, pacing, clapping and playing violin scales, sounds are differentiated from 'noises' by periodicity, which arouses the expectation of pattern in the listener. Intent is thereby revealed through rhythmic structuring. In another tape, he whispers over and over, 'GET OUT OF THE ROOM. GET OUT OF MY MIND'. This highly charged message, delivered regularly and repeatedly, confuses us because we generally associate repetitive messages with a low expressive content.

In a performance at the Whitney Museum last year [1969], a similar situation was structured by using an abrupt, emotionally charged movement. Nauman, his wife Judy, and Meredith Monk each stood about a foot away from respective corners and bounced the upper part of their bodies into them repeatedly for an hour. In both kinds of work, Nauman is also interested in how a movement or sound becomes an exercise, how an exercise becomes a performance, and how specific responses to the performance can be controlled.

In some informal and unpublished notes entitled *Withdrawal as an Art Form*, Nauman describes a diverse group of phenomena and possible methods for manipulating them. He is involved with the amplification and deprivation of sensory data; with an examination of physical and psychological responses to simple situations which yield clearly experienceable phenomena; with our responses to extreme or controlled situations, voluntary and involuntary defense mechanisms, and biological rhythms.

Among his notes, there is a plan for a piece which is, at present, impossible to execute:

A person enters and lives in a room for a long time – a period of years or a lifetime. One wall of the room mirrors the room but from the opposite side; that is, the image room has the same left-right orientation as the real room. Standing facing the image, one sees oneself from the back in the image room, standing facing a wall. There should be no progression of images; that can be controlled by adjusting the kind of information the sensor would use and the kind the mirror wall would put out. After a period of time, the time in the mirror room begins to fall behind the real time – until after a number of years, the person would no longer recognize his relationship to his mirrored image. (He would no longer relate to his mirrored image or a delay of his own time.)

This piece, he says, is related to a dream which he had a long time ago, and could only be done eventually with the aid of a vast computer network.

The experience of such a room, were it possible to build, would slowly alter the way in which we, as human beings, know ourselves in relation to the world we inhabit. If what we know of the world is the sum of our perceptions, and our physical, emotional and intellectual reactions to our environment, then to effectively manipulate these factors is to effect a virtual change in that world.

Nauman's work continues to explore these possibilities. Like the mirror piece, the computer and the dream exemplify the polarities of man's nature, and consequently of his art.

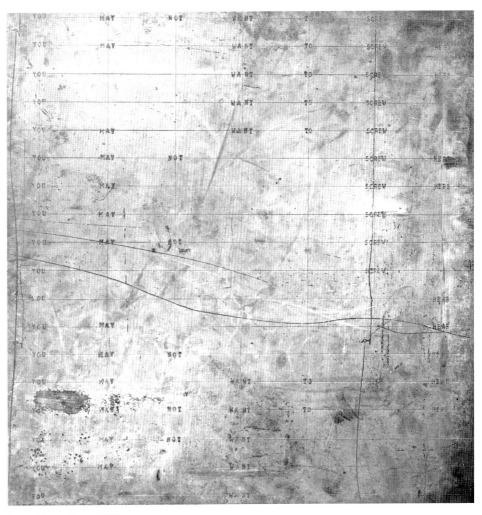

Second Poem Piece. 1969

* All statements by Bruce Nauman are taken from taped interviews with the author made during August 1970.

This article appeared in *Artforum*, 9, New York, December 1970, no. 4, pp. 38–44.

Willoughby Sharp

INTERVIEW

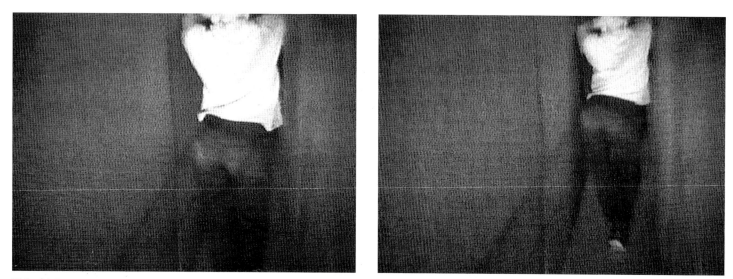

Walk with Contrapposto. 1968

During the first week of May 1970, Nauman made a V-shaped corridor piece
at San Jose State College, California.
The photographs document the execution of this work,
and the following discussion was videotaped in the College's studio
on May 7 and later edited in collaboration with the artist.

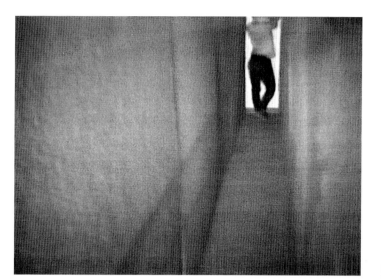

Willoughby Sharp: How did you arrive at the San Jose piece, did it grow out of your *Performance Corridor*?

Bruce Nauman: Yes, because the first pieces that were at all like it were just corridors that ended at a wall and then made into a V. Then I put in another V and finally I put in the mirror.

W.S.: Why did you decide to use it that way?
B.N.: The mirror?

W.S.: No, the change in the interior, the second V.
B.N.: When the corridors had to do with sound damping, the wall relied on soundproofing material which altered the sound in the corridor and also caused pressure on your ears, which is what I was really interested in: pressure changes that occurred while you were passing by the material. And then one thing to do was to make a V. When you are at the open end of the V there's not too much effect, but as you walk into the V the pressure increases quite a bit, it's very claustrophobic…

W.S.: Pressure is also felt on the spectator's own body. Does that come from your ears?
B.N.: It has a lot to do with just your ears.

W.S.: So space is felt with one's ears?
B.N.: Yeah, that's right.

W.S.: The light inside had a particularly soft quality which really got to my body. How did you control the light that way?
B.N.: Because the piece goes to the ceiling, all of the light is reflected into the two entrances, so it's very indirect light.

W.S.: Well, I noticed that the exterior wall started just the other side of one of the light fixtures recessed in the ceiling. Was the piece carefully planned to block off that light?
B.N.: No. I built it so that there wouldn't be any lights in the space. The light in there is more or less accidental.

W.S.: When I walked inside, the mirror cut off my head and the shock of seeing myself headless was a strong part of the piece. But if a shorter person is standing close to the mirror, he can

see his face. Are these differences important?
B.N.: Yes. When I put the mirror in the first time, it was six feet tall, which was half as high as the ceiling. That was too high – you couldn't feel the space behind the mirror at the apex of the V. So I cut it off to a little less than five and a half feet, which is just below my eye level.

W.S.: Then you adjusted the piece after experiencing it. Do you also make that kind of adjustment while you're constructing the piece?
B.N.: Yeah, I first made that piece in my studio.

W.S.: So you knew what you were dealing with in terms of space.
B.N.: Yes, but it was much more crude in the studio.

W.S.: It's really hard to know what I felt in there, but somehow it brought me closer to myself. From your own experience of being in there, how would you say it affects you?
B.N.: Well, the corridors that you walk down are two feet wide at the beginning and they narrow down to about sixteen inches. So going into it is

Pacing Upside Down. 1968

easy, because there is enough space around you for you not to be aware of the walls too much until you start to walk down the corridor. Then the walls are closer and force you to be aware of your body. It can be a very self-conscious kind of experience.

W.S.: So you find yourself in a situation where you are really put up against yourself.
B.N.: Yes, and still the interest – since you are looking into the mirror and seeing out of the other corridor – the visual interest is pretty strong and it's centered somewhere else; it's either in the mirror or looking beyond the mirror into the end of the V.

W.S.: Some people don't see over the top of the mirror into the end of the V.
B.N.: Well, if you are shorter than I am and you see your whole self in the mirror, then you probably wouldn't look over the mirror, so that's really difficult to… If the mirror is too short, it doesn't work either because you look over the mirror; you just see your feet in the mirror, and the bottom of the corridor. So the piece is effectively limited to people who are built somewhat like I am.

W.S.: Then the size of the spectator plays a role in the success of the piece.

B.N.: A big person couldn't go in at all.

W.S.: Right. I didn't get a chance to see your last Wilder show. How does the San Jose corridor piece compare with the ones at Wilder?
B.N.: Well, there were parts of the Wilder piece that you could experience immediately, but the thing was so large and complicated that I think it took much longer to grasp.

W.S.: Do you think this piece is more successful?
B.N.: No, just more immediate.

W.S.: What relation do these corridor pieces have to your recent videotape works like *Come*?
B.N.: It's really like the corridor pieces only without the corridors. I tried to do something similar, but using television cameras and monitors, and masking parts of the lenses on the cameras… If one camera is at one end of the room and the monitor is at the other, then the camera lens can be masked so that an image appears maybe on a third or a quarter of the screen. The camera is sometimes turned on its side, sometimes upside down, and that creates a corridor between the camera and the monitor. You can walk in it and see yourself from the back, but it's hard to stay in the picture because you can't line anything up, especially if the camera is not pointing at the

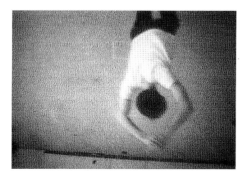

monitor. Then you have to watch the monitor to stay in the picture and at the same time stay in the line of the camera.

W.S.: How did you decide on the title, *Come*?
B.N.: I don't remember.

W.S.: Have you finished those slow motion films of gauze in your mouth and painting your body?
B.N.: Yeah.

W.S.: Could you talk about some of them?
B.N.: There were four films in which the frame speed varied between a thousand frames a second and four thousand frames a second, depending on how large an area I was trying to photograph and what light I could get. In one I was making a face, in another I had about four or five yards of gauze in my mouth which I pulled out very slowly. There were two others, one of which was called *Black Balls*. I put black makeup on my testicles. The other was called *Bouncing Balls* and it was just bouncing testicles.

W.S.: How long are they?
B.N.: Four hundred feet of film, that runs for about ten minutes. They take from six to twelve seconds to shoot, depending on the frame speed. The action is really slowed down a lot.

Sometimes it is so slow that you don't really see any motion but you sort of notice the thing is different from time to time.

W.S.: Do they have color in the system?
B.N.: You can shoot color, but the film speed is not so fast. I suppose you could push it. I just shot black and white.

W.S.: And there is a fourth one?
B.N.: That's four.

W.S.: Do these films stimulate you to work further in that direction with the same equipment?
B.N.: Not yet. It was pretty much something I wanted to do and just did.

W.S.: I know it often happens that you do certain things in one medium, then you do something similar in another medium. How does that come about? Is it because you cannot take a project further at a particular moment?
B.N.: Originally a lot of the things that turned into videotapes and films were performances. At the time no one was really interested in presenting them, so I made them into films. No one was interested in that either, so the film is really a record of the performance. After I had made a few films I changed to videotape, just because it

was easier for me to get at the time. The camera work became a bit more important, although the camera was stationary in the first ones…

W.S.: Were these the films of bouncing balls?

B.N.: Yeah. The videotapes I did after those films were related, but the camera was often turned on its side or upside down, or a wide angle lens was used for distortion… As I became more aware of what happens in the recording medium I would make little alterations. Then I went back and did the performance, and after that…

W.S.: Which performance?

B.N.: The one at the Whitney during the *Anti-Illusion* show in '69. I had already made a video-tape of it, bouncing in the corner for an hour. At the Whitney the performance was by three people, instead of just myself, and after that I tried to make pieces where other people could be involved in the performance situation, individuals.

W.S.: Why did you find that desirable?

B.N.: It makes it possible for me to make a more… it's difficult for me to perform, and it takes a long time for me to need to perform. And doing it once is enough. I wouldn't want to do it the next day or for a week, or even do the same performance again. So if I can make a situation where someone else has to do what I would do, that is satisfactory. Quite a lot of these pieces have to do with creating a very strict kind of environment or situation so that even if the performer doesn't know anything about me or the work that goes into the piece, he will still be able to do something similar to what I would do.

W.S.: Some of the works must be stimulated by a desire to experience particular kinds of situations. Just to see how they feel. Are you doing the work basically for yourself?

B.N.: Yes. it is going into the studio and doing whatever I'm interested in doing, and then trying to find a way to present it so that other people could do it too without having too much explanation.

W.S.: The concern for the body seems stronger now than when we did the *Arts Magazine* interview.

B.N.: Well, the first time I really talked to any-body about body awareness was in the summer of 1968. Meredith Monk was in San Francisco.

She had thought about or seen some of my work and recognized it. An awareness of your-self comes from a certain amount of activity and you can't get it from just thinking about yourself. You do exercises, you have certain kinds of awarenesses that you don't have if you read books. So the films and some of the pieces that I did after that for videotapes were specifically about doing exercises in balance. I thought of them as dance problems without being a dancer, being interested in the kinds of tension that arise when you try to balance and can't. Or do something for a long time and get tired. In one of those first films, the violin film, I played the violin as long as I could. I don't know how to play the violin, so it was hard, playing on all four strings as fast as I could for as long as I could. I had ten minutes of film and ran about seven minutes of it before I got tired and had to stop and rest a little bit and then finish it.

W.S.: But you could have gone on longer than the ten minutes?

B.N.: I would have had to stop and rest more often. My fingers got very tired and I couldn't hold the violin any more.

W.S.: What you are saying in effect is that in 1968 the idea of working with calisthenics and body movements seemed far removed from sculptural concerns. Would you say that those boundaries and the distance between them has dissolved to a certain extent?

B.N.: Yes, it seems to have gotten a lot smaller.

W.S.: What you have done has widened the possibilities for sculpture to the point where you can't isolate video works and say, they aren't sculpture.

B.N.: It is only in the last year that I have been able to bring them together.

W.S.: How do you mean?

B.N.: Well, even last year it seemed pretty clear that some of the things I did were either performance or recorded performance activities, and others were sculptural – and it is only recently that I have been able to make the two cross or meet in some way.

W.S.: In which works have they met?

B.N.: The ones we have been talking about.

The first one was really the corridor, the piece with two walls that was originally a prop in my studio for a videotape in which I walked up and down the corridor in a stylized way for an hour. At the Whitney *Anti-Illusion* show I presented the prop as a piece, called *Performance Corridor*. It was twenty inches wide and twenty feet long, so a lot of strange things happened to anybody who walked into it… just like walking in a very narrow hallway.

W.S.: You had been doing a lot of walking around in the studio. When did you start thinking about using corridors?
B.N.: Well, I don't really remember the choice that led me to… I had made a tape of walking, of pacing, and another tape called *Rhythmic Stamping in the Studio* which was basically a sound problem, but videotaped… I was just walking around the studio stamping in various rhythms.

W.S.: Did you want the sound to be in sync?
B.N.: The sound was in sync on that one. In the first violin film the sound is out of sync, but you really don't know it until the end of the film. I don't remember whether the sound or the picture stops first.

W.S.: I think you stop playing the violin but the sound goes on.
B.N.: The sound is fast and distorted and loud, and you can't tell until all at once… it is a strange kind of feeling.

W.S.: Is the film of the two bouncing balls in the square out of sync? Did you play with the sync on that?
B.N.: No. I started out in sync but there again, it is a wild track, so as the tape stretches and tightens it goes in and out of sync. I more or less wanted it to be in sync but I just didn't have the equipment and the patience to do it.

W.S.: What do you think of it?
B.N.: It was alright. There's one thing that I can't remember – I think I cut it out of some of the prints and left it in others. At a certain point I had two balls going and I was running around all the time trying to catch them. Sometimes they would hit something on the floor or the ceiling and go off into the corner and hit together.

Finally I lost track of them both. I picked up one of the balls and just threw it against the wall. I was really mad.

W.S.: Why?
B.N.: Because I was losing control of the game. I was trying to keep the rhythm going, to have the balls bounce once on the floor and once on the ceiling and then catch them, or twice on the floor and once on the ceiling. There was rhythm going and when I lost it that ended the film. My idea at the time was that the film should have no beginning or end: one should be able to come in at any time and nothing would change. All the films were supposed to be like that, because they all dealt with ongoing activities. So did almost all of the videotapes, only they were longer, they went on for an hour or so. There is much more a feeling of being able to come in or leave at any time.

W.S.: So you didn't want the film to come to an end.
B.N. I would prefer that it went on forever.

W.S.: What kind of practice did you have for those films? Did you play the violin to see what sound you were going to get?
B.N.: I probably had the violin around for a month or two before I made the film.

W.S.: Did you get it because you were going to use it, or did it just come into you life?
B.N.: I think I bought it for about fifteen dollars. It just seemed like a thing to have. I play other instruments, but I never played the violin and during the period of time that I had it before the film I started diddling around with it.

W.S.: When did you decide that it might be nice to use it?
B.N.: Well, I started to think about it once I had the violin and I tried one or two things. One thing I was interested in was playing… I wanted to set up a problem where it wouldn't matter whether I knew how to play the violin or not. What I did was to play as fast as I could on all four strings with the violin tuned D.E.A.D. I thought it would just be a lot of noise, but it turned out to be musically very interesting. It is a very tense piece. The other idea I had was to play two notes very close together so that you

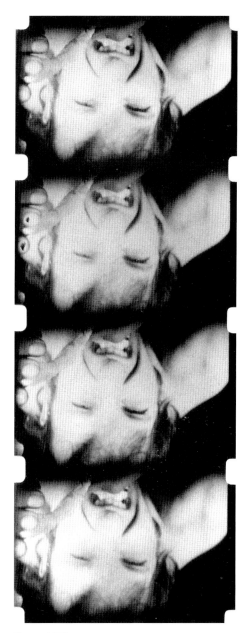

Gauze. 1969

Going Around the Corner Piece. 1970

tired, or if you are honestly trying to balance on one foot for a long time, there has to be a certain sympathetic response in someone who is watching you. It is a kind of body response, they feel that foot and that tension. But many things that you could do would be really boring, so it depends a lot on what you choose, how you set up the problem in the first place. Somehow you have to program it to be interesting.

W.S.: So you reject many ideas on aesthetic grounds.
B.N.: Besides you make mistakes, so it doesn't all come out.

W.S.: Do you ever see one of your films and then decide that you don't want to show it to anyone?
B.N.: Oh yeah. I have thrown a lot of things away.

W.S.: What percentage do you destroy?
B.N.: Gee, I don't know.

W.S.: Does it happen frequently?
B.N.: Oh, pretty often. Maybe half the time.

W.S.: On what grounds? Could you explain a piece that you finally rejected?
B.N.: I couldn't remember. I can't remember any of the other film problems.

W.S.: You did mention that you threw one film away, or you weren't sure. Which one was that?
B.N.: I think we mentioned one, but it wasn't necessarily a film. For the videotapes it is harder to say, because I had the equipment in the studio. With the films I would work over an idea until there was something that I wanted to do, then I would rent the equipment for a day or two. So I was more likely to have a specific idea of what I wanted to do. With the videotapes I had the equipment in the studio for almost a year; I could make test tapes and look at them, watch myself on the monitor or have somebody else

could hear the beats in the harmonics. I did some tapes of that but I never filmed it. Or maybe I did film it while I was walking around the studio playing. The film was called *Walking Around the Studio Playing a Note on the Violin.* The camera was set up near the center of the studio facing one wall, but I walked all around the studio, so often there was no one in the picture, just the studio wall and the sound of the footsteps and the violin.

W.S.: I saw most of these four films about a week ago at the School of Visual Arts – I liked them even better the second time I saw them. You made a simple, repetitive activity seem very important.
B.N.: I guess we talked about this before, about being an amateur and being able to do anything. If you really believe in what you're doing and do it as well as you can, then there will be a certain amount of tension – if you are honestly getting

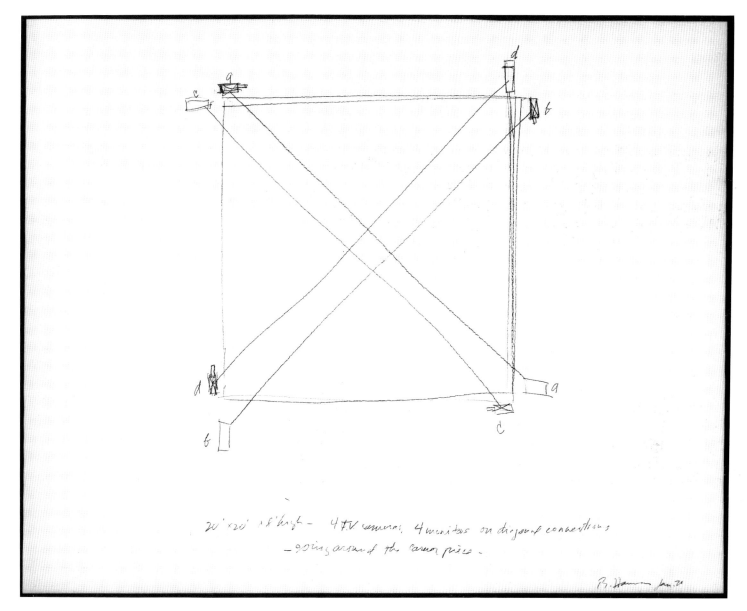

Going Around the Corner Piece. 1970

there to help. Lots of times I would do a whole performance or tape a whole hour and then change it.

W.S.: Edit?
B.N.: I don't think I would ever edit but I would redo the whole thing if I didn't like it. Often I would do the same performance but change the camera placement and so on.

W.S.: In the film of the bouncing balls, it looks as if the camera was just placed there. How carefully did you set up the camera in that film?
B.N. It was set up to show an area of the studio.

W.S.: With a certain definite cut off point.
B.N.: Yeah. It had a lot to do with the lenses I had — I was limited to the three standard lenses. I was using the widest angle lens on the camera.

W.S.: But take the film in which you do a dance step around two squares of masking tape on the floor. The near side of the outermost square is cut off. Now that was obviously deliberate. You knew you weren't getting the nearest line on the film and that your feet wouldn't be seen when you came along that line. Do you remember why you made that decision?

Indoor/Outdoor. 1972

B.N.: No, I don't remember. It was just better that way.

W.S.: Did you try it out so that both squares were completely visible?
B.N.: I don't remember. It's been a long time.

W.S.: How much time did you spend setting up the camera?
B.N.: I don't know. Sometimes it really takes a long time, and other times it's just obvious how it must be done.

W.S.: Did you consider using a video system in the San Jose piece?
B.N.: Well, in this piece the mirror takes the place of any video element. In most of the pieces with closed circuit video, the closed circuit functions as a kind of electronic mirror.

W.S.: So you are really throwing the spectator back on himself. That's interesting. I hadn't realized the similarity between the mirror and the video image before. Is there a natural extension into video from a certain situation, such as this piece? Or didn't you even consider that?
B.N.: I didn't consider it. The mirror allows you to see some place that you didn't think you could see. In other words you are seeing around the corner. Some of the video pieces have to do with seeing yourself go around a corner, or seeing a room that you know you can't get into like one where the television camera is set on an oscillating mount in a sealed room.

W.S.: That was at the Wilder show, wasn't it?
B.N.: Yes. The camera looks at the whole room; you can see the monitor picture of it, but you can't go into the room and there is a strange kind or removal. You are denied access to that room – you can see exactly what is going on and when you are there but you can never get to that place.

W.S.: People felt they were being deprived of something.
B.N.: It is very strange to explain what that is. It becomes easier to make a picture of the pieces or to describe what the elements are, but it becomes much more difficult to explain what happens when you experience them. I was

trying to explain that to somebody the other night. It had to do with going up the stairs in the dark, when you think there is one more step and you take the step, but you are already at the top and have the funny… or going down the stairs and expecting there to be another step, but you are already at the bottom. It seems that you always have that jolt and it really throws you off. I think that when these pieces work they do that too. Something happens that you didn't expect and it happens every time. You know why, and what's going on but you just keep doing the same thing. It is very curious.

W.S.: The Wilder piece was quite complicated.
B.N.: It is hard to understand. The easiest part of the piece to get into was a corridor thirty-four feet long and twenty-five inches wide. There was a television camera at the outside entrance, and the picture was at the other end. There was another picture inside too but that's irrelevant to this part of it. When you walked into the corridor, you had to go in about ten feet before you appeared on the television screen that was still twenty feet away from you. I used a wide angle lens, which disturbed the distance even more. The camera was ten feet up, so that when you did see yourself on the screen, it was from the back, from above and behind, which was quite different from the way you normally saw yourself or the way you experienced the corridor around yourself. When you realized that you were on the screen, being in the corridor was like stepping off a cliff or down into a hole. It was like the bottom step thing – it was really a very strong experience. You knew what had happened because you could see all of the equipment and what was going on, yet you had the same experience every time you walked in. There was no way to avoid having it.

W.S.: Would you like to do something for network TV?
B.N.: I'd like CBS to give me an hour on my terms. I'd like to do color work which I haven't done yet because of the expense involved. I haven't been strongly motivated to either. I suppose if I really wanted to I could hustle it somehow. But if it became available to me I would like to use color. Some people in Europe have been able to use it. I forget who. A Dutch artist did something called the *Television as a Fireplace*.

Apparently a fire was broadcast on the screen for fifteen minutes or so. All you saw was the fire.

W.S.: Right. Jan Dibbets did that last New Year's Eve.
B.N.: In Holland all the stations are government-owned. The European television setup is much lower-keyed than the American, so time is not as valuable as it is here. It is a little easier to do things like that, but it's still difficult.

W.S.: Do you see that as a goal? It seems to me that one of the reasons for working with video-tape is that the work can get out to far more people so that obviously CBS…
B.N.: I would… I'm not interested in making compromises in order to do that, although I still want to do it. I would like to have an hour or half an hour to present some boring material.

W.S.: Do you feel that you could subvert television, change it?
B.N.: I'm not really interested in actively spending my time trying to get those people to let me use their time. If time was offered to me I would use it, and I would want to do things my way. But to take the trouble to do whatever one has to do…

W.S.: What I meant specifically was that if the new art is going to be significant for a larger segment of the culture, working with videotape gives you the means to help bring that about.
B.N.: Oh, I think it is not… although there would be a wider audience. But I would still want to have my time available and have only four people watching the piece, just because of what I could do with equipment that I wouldn't have access to otherwise.

W.S.: So there really isn't a strong desire to change the existing level of communication.
B.N.: No.

W.S.: Then we come back to where we ended the last time: who is your art for?
B.N.: To keep me busy.

This article appeared in *Avalanche*, New York, winter 1971, no. 2, pp. 22-31.

KEEP TAKING IT

Good Boy, Bad Boy. 1985

APART

The following interview is an excerpt from a one-hour conversation
recorded by René Pulfer on 12 July at the Videowochen im Wenkenpark
in Riehen near Basel, where Bruce Nauman's video installation
Good Boy, Bad Boy, 1985 was shown.

Chris Dercon: I have the impression that *Violent Incident* [1] is much like the Punch and Judy-pieces [2]. There is also that kind of distant look, like in the neon-sculptures.

Bruce Nauman: In *Good Boy, Bad Boy* the two people are looking directly at you, so you have contact. It is much more personal. In *Violent Incident*, the image, the activity is something you're looking at from a distance, it's been recorded, the camera is moving, it's further away.

C.D.: What does it mean for you 'looking at a distance'?

B.N.: The space, the psychological and physical distance between the activity going on and the eye of the viewer. In *Good Boy, Bad Boy* the eye-contact is always there, we're looking straight. They are looking straight in the camera, or straight out of the television. So when you pay attention, you have this very immediate contact.

C.D.: It strikes me that in *Good Boy, Bad Boy* the frontal look is completely different from the contact in the neon pieces and *Violent Incident*.

B.N.: *Violent Incident* is observing, so that the distance is like an activity where you're a voyeur somehow, only connected because you happened to pass it. *Good Boy, Bad Boy* is addressed to you.

Also the idea with the television, the image being almost life-size, with only the head, makes a much more immediate, direct connection. And the idea that the words were spoken information was important.

C.D.: Is it direct speech? Does it say 'you'?

B.N.: Well, it does sometimes. It says 'I, we, you... '. It involves you by talking to you. 'I was a good boy – you were a good boy.' It is not a conversation, you are not allowed to talk, but you are involved because someone uses that

form of address. In all of these neon pieces and in *Violent Incident* as well, you're not asked to participate, you're involved only through the intensity of the light or the sound or whatever...

C.D.: It is 'he, she, and it'?
B.N.: Right, it's the third person.

C.D.: Were you thinking about the video monitor as a piece of furniture?

B.N.: In a sense, yes, as something that was just there. From the earliest tapes that I did, coming in a certain sense from some of Andy Warhol's films. They just go on and on and on, you can watch them or you can not watch them. Maybe one's showing already and you come in and watch for a while and you can leave and come back and eight hours later it's still going on. I liked that idea very much, it also comes from some of the music that I was interested in at that time. The early Phil Glass pieces and La Monte Young, whose idea was that music was something that was there. I liked that very much, that kind of way of structuring time. So part of it is not just an interest in the content, the image, but the way of filling a space and taking up time.

C.D.: Something I was wondering about in *Good Boy, Bad Boy* was that the black man takes only about 15 minutes, while the white woman takes 16 minutes, and the image of the man turns to black, while she talks one more minute.

B.N.: They go through the sequence five times, and the first time is supposed to be completely flat, a neutral delivery. Then it's supposed to become more animated and by the fifth recitation, they were very angry and very intense, so it took her a little bit longer to do it than it took him. If you let the tapes play, they become out of sequence, which I like; they're together but not really. After a while she's at the end and he's at

the beginning or vice-versa. It goes through these different possibilities of how they can relate to each other, which I like.

C.D.: The words they are using – are they found words?

B.N.: I made a list and there are more things that could have been added. But I just picked a hundred phrases. It's an arbitrary number. Stop with a hundred and start over.

C.D.: Why are you making lists? Can you make a narrative based upon information?

B.N.: Yeah, I mean 'can'. It's making lists, I do it a lot, a lot of artists do, for example Carl Andre. A lot of poems are really lists, lists of possibilities.

C.D.: The British filmmaker Peter Greenaway stated in *Artforum*: 'Why shouldn't you make a narrative based upon information.' [3] This also struck me in your work. The narrative in *Good Boy, Bad Boy* and in *Violent Incident* actually comes out of information. But it's also a kind of breaking up: a sabotage of the hegemony of information.

B.N.: Yes. When I first did performances a long time ago, they were about a list of the possibilities of making some kind of movements: standing, leaning, sitting, lying... and making a list of what appeared to be discrete movements. When I did the performances, I found that certain positions seemed to have powerful emotional connections and others were just changes and didn't make any sense. So it was interesting to me to take these lists and then see which ones seemed to have some resonance and which didn't. The lists start out being arbitrary and then they begin to organize themselves or I can organize them into what then really becomes a narrative structure.

But it was initially a way of finding a beginning and an ending to an activity, to a film, a tape, a performance.

C.D.: I would say even the neon pieces work that way, the flashing-up, flashing-out also seems like a list.

B.N.: Yes, of possibilities. It becomes a way of covering all the possibilities without really having to make a list.

For instance, it would be really complicated in the case of a neon piece like Welcome (Shaking Hands) because it takes 10 or 15 minutes to run through the whole thing. The programming would be very complicated if I said 'I want to see all the possibilities of these two figures.' But by making this very simple program of one being slightly faster than the other, there is a randomness that covers all the possibilities.

C.D.: In the winter of 1968-1969, your biography in the catalogue of the Kunstmuseum Basel says: 'Bruce Nauman is very busy making video tapes.'

B.N.: Yes, I made about twelve tapes, I think.

C.D.: But before that – you made films?

B.N.: The films were basically the same as the tapes. It has also to do with the availability of equipment. When I was living in San Francisco, there were a lot of filmmakers. When I moved to the east coast, I didn't know any filmmakers. It was hard to get equipment. Then Sony video-equipment started to be fairly inexpensive. I was living outside of New York City, so it was very easy to work on the video tapes. I didn't have to rely on film labs getting equipment and giving it back, things like that…

C.D.: Didn't you have any problems with the 'milky image' of the black & white porter-pack?

B.N.: Well, it seemed okay for the work I was doing. You just have to think in terms of the image you're going to get. I didn't need a highly resolved image. At that time, I was interested in the ambiguous quality of the image. The work isn't autobiographical. It isn't really about me. When I was doing it, it was mostly with images of myself but almost every image is either upside down or the head doesn't show at all or it's only the back. So it was only important to have an image of a human figure, even if I was using myself at the time. A little bit later, when I started using other people, it was easier if there was a face, because it was an actor, an actor being someone who is not anyone.

C.D.: Vito Acconci said: 'Film is like landscape and silence – while video is close-up and sound.' Did you also find that it was something completely different?

B.N.: Video is a much more 'private' kind of communication. Generally, it's what one person does. You sit and have contact with a television set, as opposed to a film, where generally a lot of people go and the image is very large; it's more of a common experience.

C.D.: You were working a lot with the scale of the video image in your corridor pieces.

B.N.: Yes, and at that time, I was thinking a lot about the connection between public and private experiences. I think it came from working in the studio. You work alone in the studio, and then the work goes out into a public situation. How do people deal with that? It's different when someone comes to my studio and sees my work. I mean you have those experiences by yourself as opposed to coming to a museum, where there are going to be a lot of other people around. So you tend to try an experience with art, but protect yourself in some way. You have to learn to shut yourself away from the rest of the public.

So in those corridor pieces which were about the connection between public and private experience, the video helps the private part even though it's a public situation. The way you watch television is a private kind of experience. But it's beginning to break down in those sports events where you now have a large screen.

C.D.: Back to the earlier period, because I think it had a bearing on Violent Incident, what was your idea about sound?

B.N.: It is just the sound that comes from the activity of making the tape, such as a scraping of the feet. Some of the tapes did have a voice sound, things that were spoken to the camera.

C.D.: Did you speak to the camera or to the monitor? You were working with a closed-circuit installation.

B.N.: I remember in some cases I spoke to or looked at the camera. In Slow Angle Walk (Beckett Walk) or Stamping in the Studio, I was interested in the location of the camera in one situation. Part of the activity takes places within the range of the camera, and part of it out of the range of the camera. You can see that the room is larger and the only contact you have is the sound of the activity, and then finally the figure comes back into the range of the camera. I like that idea too, the activity goes on the camera, in the sense of observing but you can't see everything, so it misses parts.

C.D.: About 1968 – you were very interested in the works and writings of Merce Cunningham. Was the dance-world, for example what happened in the Judson Dance Church, important for you?

B.N.: Yes. I didn't know much about it, because I was on the west coast and that is very far away. But I knew about Merce Cunningham and about the writings of John Cage and I had heard some of his works. It had to do with the attitude involved in transforming normal activity into a formal presentation, which Merce was doing with dance and John Cage was doing with music. So knowing about it was even more important than seeing it. One thing came up over and over again in the interview with Coosje van Bruggen.[4] I would tell her about something that had been very important to me, in terms of how to structure a performance or some art activity and she would say: 'Oh, but it wasn't like that.' I said: 'It's the way I remember it.' So she calls what I did 'a creative misreading or a creative misunderstanding.'

C.D.: You were saying that you didn't have the video-equipment yourself. Leo Castelli gave the equipment and then you used it and Richard Serra, Keith Sonnier used it. So it was passed from one artist to another?

B.N.: Yes.

C.D.: Did Castelli commission video works?

B.N.: No, I was asked to do video tapes and so I asked Leo: 'Can we buy this equipment or rent it?' I didn't have any money at that time, so he said: 'Sure.' The gallery owned the equipment and we all used it.

C.D.: Why was everybody so interested?

B.N.: Richard Serra had made some films and he liked the directness of video. He'd been working with a filmmaker to have somebody that understood the technical stuff. Some was just novelty, but video made it very easy to get an idea down quickly.

Good Boy, Bad Boy. 1985

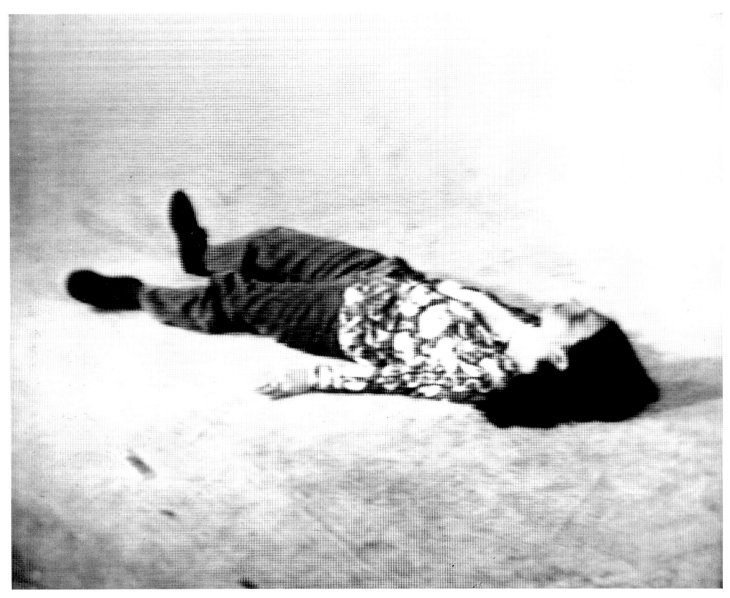

Elke Allowing the Floor to Rise Up over Her, Face Up. 1973

C.D.: You never wanted to work with color, when once the black and white got off?

B.N.: Not for a long time, it was very difficult. The equipment was much more expensive. By that time I had made a first group of video tapes, then I didn't make any tapes for a long time. By the time I made the next tapes, I did use color, it was much easier. I made a couple of tapes, called *Tony Sinking into the Floor, Face Up and Face Down* and *Elke Allowing the Floor to Rise Up over Her, Face Up*. I used some actors for that, not myself. And it was done in a professional studio with somebody else operating the cameras, so I became the director. Before that, I did a few here, in Europe, two or three, in Holland at the Van Abbe Museum in Eindhoven.

C.D.: One of your earliest environmental pieces or sculpture pieces involving video is the piece at the Wide White Space Gallery in Antwerp. There you used a video camera which was relaying the underground of the garden to the gallery space. Was that the first time you used a closed-circuit installation?

B.N.: No, the first one was an installation in Los Angeles, in Nicholas Wilder's gallery (1970). It was actually a combination of five or six different corridors. The one piece that's still around a lot is the one called the *Video Corridor*. In that case, there are two television monitors at the end of a corridor that you can enter. One of the monitors shows constantly a video tape of the empty corridor. Then a camera is installed high above the entrance to the corridor with a connection to the monitor at the closed end of the corridor. There is a wide-angle lens on the camera. So as you walk down the corridor, the camera is above you and behind you. As you walk towards the monitor,

Stamping in the Studio. 1968

towards your own image, your image is yourself from the back. So as you're walking towards your image, you're getting further from the camera. So on the monitor, you're walking away from yourself, and the closer you try to get, the further you get from the camera, the further you're from yourself. It's a very strange kind of situation. That was the first closed circuit. In that same installation, one part of the gallery was completely closed off. There was a camera mounted high in a corner and it kept going back and forth, and then that monitor was out in the gallery so you could see the empty space just panning back and forth across the empty space.

C.D.: The *Video Corridor* and especially the piece in the Wide White Space Gallery also had something to do with a negation of volume. The inside is going to be the outside and the outside is going to be the inside which you already hinted at in your early sculptures.
B.N.: A lot of sculptures did have to do with an intentional question or confusion about which is the inside and which is the outside.

C.D.: Hadn't you any problems with the opaqueness of the video image?
B.N.: It's only giving you information, you can't participate, but it is the nature of how television works. It is opaque, it only gives you, you can't

give back. You can't participate. I like that. To every rule, I also try to find the opposite, to reverse it. There's the real space and there's the picture of the real space which is something else – in a sense, there are two kinds of information, the real information that you have being near walls, in a space, in an enclosure, and other bits of information which are a more intellectual way of dealing with the world. What interested me was the experience of putting those two pieces of information together: physical inform- ation and visual or intellectual information. The experience lies in the tension between the two, of not being able to put them together.

C.D.: Did you do any other video-installations or sculptures involving video after 1970?
B.N.: I had a couple of proposals for public situations, but they were never accepted, so they weren't made.

C.D.: What kind of proposals?
B.N.: For train stations or subway stations. Pictures of inside from the outside, or showing people at another stop, it could have been the same place but they weren't quite the same people. Some of the installations involved going around the corner, so that you could see what was happening there. You would see maybe somebody else leaving the space, but you could never see yourself leaving or entering it.

C.D.: Why, after almost 15 years, did you sud- denly want to make another tape (*Good Boy, Bad Boy*)?
B.N.: I think it's because I had this information that I was writing. I didn't want to make a neon- sign. I didn't know what to do with it, really. I could write it and publish it, print it or what- ever… It took a long time to decide to do it, but I finally did it as a video. I had thought about doing it as a performance in some way, but I have never felt comfortable with performance.

And video seemed to finally be one way to do it. It was very interesting for me when we made the tapes. I used professional actors. The man had done mostly live, stage acting, so he was much more generous and more open in his acting. She had done a lot of television acting, mostly daytime, like commercials and some soap-opera acting. So a lot of her acting is from her face. She didn't use her hands much and I liked that difference. What interests me is the line between others. Because they are actors, it's not auto- biographical, it's not real anger, but pretending to be angry and they are pretty good at it, but maybe not really convincing. I like all these different levels, knowing and not knowing quite how to take the situation, how to relate to it.

C.D.: That's also what happens in the neon- sculptures in a way.
B.N.: Yes.

C.D.: The idea of 'contour' is interesting in this context, too. There is much more fiction in 'contour' than in actual action. This also applies to the *Neon Templates of the Left Half of My Body Taken at Ten-Inch Intervals*.
B.N.: Yes, it's a completely artificial idea. I'm taking something apart in a very arbitrary way.

C.D.: Why is there a shift in the sequence of the images in *Violent Incident*? You see for example, action 2 / action 1 and then action 2 again twice. [5]
B.N.: It makes it more formal. Again to go through the possibilities. First of all reversing the

roles of the man and the woman. That gives you a lot of different possibilities at the same time. Then the slow-motion, changing the colors. There is one whole part on the tape that's just rehearsals. The man that was actually helping do the direction is talking to the woman carrying the camera. So they're walking through it and he's saying: 'Now the chair!' He's breaking the action apart even more: 'chair – goose! – yell! – throw the cocktail! – slap! – take the knife! – stab! – fall down! – finish!' It takes eighteen seconds to do the activity correctly and then 45 seconds to do it when you take it apart and talk about it. I liked all this, keep taking it apart, taking it apart.

C.D.: Do you have any other video projects?
B.N.: I'm not sure but I think I'd like to do some- thing similar to this last tape, only using people dressed as clowns.

C.D.: Why clowns?
B.N.: It just struck me hearing these people that are actors that you could add another level of unreality. Putting someone in a clown-suit is changing the context. It's like the clowns in a circus who are not always funny. Having people that are supposed to be amusing or humorous act in a violent way can add to the violence. I hadn't thought through this very much. Maybe it's like Japanese theatre. There is a mask, and having a figure behind the mask is more threat- ening than an angry person. Because there's something you don't know and you're never going to find out.

NOTES

1. *Violent Incident*,1986, video installation, with 12 monitors.
2. *Punch and Judy: Kick in the Groin, Slap in the Face*, 1985, neon sculpture.
3. Stuart Morgan, 'Breaking the Contract: A Conversation with Peter Greenaway', *Artforum*, no. 3, New York, November 1983, pp. 46–50.
4. Coosje van Bruggen, *Bruce Nauman*, Rizzoli, New York, 1988.
5. *Violent Incident: Man-Woman Segment*, 1986, video installation, 12 monitors.

This article appeared in *Parkett*, Zurich/New York, September 1986, no. 10, pp. 54–69.

Violent Incident. 1986

An interview by Joan Simon

BREAKING

Pay Attention. 1973

THE SILENCE

Reflecting on two decades of his own work,
Nauman discloses some verbal and visual ties
between his recent political allegories
and his earlier use of puns, body parts and space.

(...) The heterogeneity of Nauman's early work not only challenged the purity of Minimal or Late-Formalist sculpture, but it also demonstrated Nauman's characteristic attitude toward art-making, which often treats linguistic fragments and material issues as interchangeable. (...) During 1965–66 Nauman produced his first fiberglass pieces and performances based on simple procedures and body movements. (...) In the 1970s, Nauman's work shifted from the body and elements in the studio to quasi-architectural installations (including many corridor pieces) which often incorporated sound or video. (...) Nauman's 1980s work focuses increasing attention on social and political subject matter. (...)

Bruce Nauman: There is a tendency to clutter things up, to try to make sure people know something is art, when all that's necessary is to present it, to leave it alone. I think the hardest thing to do is to present an idea in the most straightforward way.

What I tend to do is see something, then re-make it and re-make it and re-make it and try every possible way of re-making it. If I'm persistent enough, I get back to where I started. I think it was Jasper Johns who said, 'Sometimes it's necessary to state the obvious.'

Still, how to proceed is always the mystery. I remember at one point thinking that some day I would figure out how you do this, how you do art – like, 'What's the procedure here, folks?' – and then it wouldn't be such a struggle anymore. Later, I realized it was never going to be like that, it was always going to be a struggle. I realized I would never have a specific process; I would have to re-invent it, over and over again. That was really depressing.

After all, it was hard work; it was a painful struggle and tough. I didn't want to have to go through all that every time. But of course you do

have to continually re-discover and re-decide, and it's awful. It's just an awful thing to have to do.

On the other hand, that's what's interesting about making art, and why it's worth doing: it's never going to be the same, there is no method. If I stop and try to look at how I got the last piece done, it doesn't help me with the next one.

Joan Simon: What do you think about when you're working on a piece?
Bruce Nauman: I think about Lenny Tristano a lot. Do you know who he was? Lenny Tristano was a blind pianist, one of the original – or maybe second generation – bebop guys. He's on a lot of the best early bebop records. When Lenny played well, he hit you hard and he kept going until he finished. Then he just quit. You didn't get any introduction, you didn't get any tail – you just got full intensity for 2 minutes or 20 minutes or whatever. It would be like taking the middle out of Coltrane – just the hardest, toughest part of it. That was all you got.

From the beginning I was trying to see if I could make art that did that. Art that was just there all at once. Like getting hit in the face with a baseball bat. Or better, like getting hit in the back of the neck. You never see it coming; it just knocks you down. I like that idea very much: the kind of intensity that doesn't give you any trace of whether you're going to like it or not.

J.S.: In trying to capture that sort of intensity over the past 20 or so years you've worked in just about every medium: film, video, sound, neon, installation, performance, photography, holography, sculpture, drawing – but not painting. You gave that up very early on. Why?
B.N.: When I was in school I was a painter. And I went back and forth a couple of times. But basically I couldn't function as a painter. Painting is one of those things I never quite made sense of. I just couldn't see how to proceed as a painter.

It seemed that if I didn't think of myself as a painter, then it would be possible to continue.

It still puzzles me how I made decisions in those days about what was possible and what wasn't. I ended up drawing on music and dance and literature, using thoughts and ideas from other fields to help me continue to work. In that sense, the early work which seems to have all kinds of materials and ideas in it, seemed very simple to make because it wasn't coming from looking at sculpture or painting.

J.S.: That doesn't sound simple.
B.N.: No, I don't mean that it was simple to do the work. But it was simple in that in the '60s you didn't have to pick just one medium. There didn't seem to be any problem with using different kinds of materials – shifting from photographs to dance to performance to video-tapes. It seemed very straightforward to use all those different ways of expressing ideas or presenting material. You could make neon signs, you could make written pieces, you could make jokes about parts of the body or casting things, or whatever.

J.S.: Do you see your work as part of a continuum with other art or other artists?
B.N.: Sure there are connections, though not in any direct way. It's not that there is someone in particular you emulate. But you do see other artists asking the same kinds of questions and responding with some kind of integrity.

There's a kind of restraint and morality in Johns. It isn't specific, I don't know how to describe it, but it's there, I feel it's there. It's less there, but still important, in Duchamp. Or in Man Ray, who also interests me. Maybe the morality I sense in Man Ray has to do with the fact that while he made his living as a fashion photographer, his art works tended to be jokes – stupid jokes. The whole idea of Dada was that you

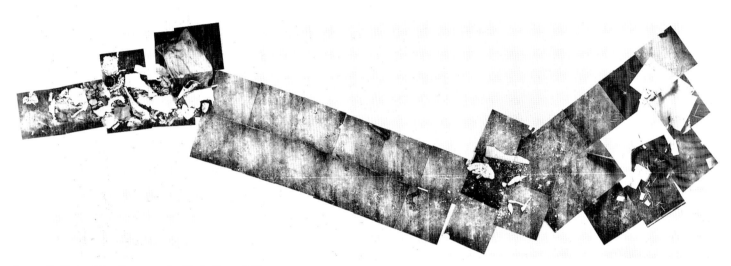

Composite Photo of Two Messes on the Studio Floor. 1967

didn't have to make your living with your art; so that generation could be more provocative with less risk. Then there is the particularly American idea about morality that has to do with the artist as workman. Many artists used to feel all right about making a living with their art because they identified with the working class. Some still do. I mean, I do, and I think Richard Serra does.

J.S.: No matter how jokey or stylistically diverse or visually dazzling your works are, they always have an ethical side, a moral force.
B.N.: I do see art that way. Art ought to have a moral value, a moral stance, a position. I'm not sure where that belief comes from. In part it just comes from growing up where I grew up and from my parents and family. And from the time I spent in San Francisco going to the Art Institute, and before that in Wisconsin. From my days at the University of Wisconsin, the teachers I remember were older guys – they wouldn't let women into teaching easily – and they were all WPA guys [1]. They were socialists and they had points to make that were not only moral and political, but also ethical. Wisconsin was one of

the last socialist states, and in the '50s, when I lived there and went to high school there, Milwaukee still had a socialist mayor. So there were a lot of people who thought art had a function beyond being beautiful – that it had a social reason to exist.

EARLY WORK

J.S.: What David Whitney wrote about your *Composite Photo of Two Messes on the Studio Floor*, 1967 – that 'it is a direct statement on how the artist lives, works and thinks' – could apply in general to the variety of works you made in your San Francisco studio from 1966-68.
B.N.: I did some pieces that started out just being visual puns. Since these needed body parts in them, I cast parts of a body and assembled them or presented them with a title. There was also the idea that if I was in the studio, whatever I was doing was art. Pacing around, for example. How do you organize that to present it as art? Well, first I filmed it. Then I video-taped it. Then I complicated it by turning the

camera upside down or sideways, or organizing my pacing to various sounds.

In a lot of the early work I was concerned with ideas about inside and outside and front and back – how to turn them around and confuse them. Take the *Window or Wall Sign* – you know, the neon piece that says, 'The true artist helps the world by revealing mystic truths.' That idea occurred to me because of the studio I had in San Francisco at the time. It had been a grocery store, and in the window there was still a beer sign which you read from the outside. From the inside, of course, it was backwards. So when I did the earliest neon pieces, they were intended to be seen through the window one way and from the inside another way, confusing the message by reversing the image.

J.S.: Isn't your interest in inverting ideas, in showing what's 'not there', and in solving – or at least revealing – 'impossible' problems related in part to your training as a mathematician?
B.N.: I was interested in the logic and structure of math and especially how you could turn that logic inside out. I was fascinated by mathematical problems, particularly the one called 'squaring the circle'. You know, for hundreds of years mathematicians tried to find a geometrical way of finding a square equal in area to a circle – a formula where you could construct one from the other. At some point in the 19th century, a mathematician – I can't remember his name – proved it can't be done. His approach was to step outside the problem. Rather than struggling inside the problem, by stepping outside of it, he showed that it was not possible to do it at all.

Standing outside and looking at how something gets done, or doesn't get done, is really fascinating and curious. If I can manage to get outside of a problem a little bit and watch myself having a hard time, then I can see what I'm going to do – it makes it possible. It works.

Henry Moore Bound to Fail. 1967-70

J.S.: A number of early pieces specifically capture what's 'not there'. I'm thinking about the casts of 'invisible spaces': the space between two crates on the floor, for example, or the 'negative' space under a chair.
B.N.: Casting the space under a chair was the sculptural version of de Kooning's statement: 'When you paint a chair, you should paint the space between the rungs, not the chair itself.' I was thinking like that: about leftovers and negative spaces.

J.S.: But your idea of negative space is very different from the sculptor's traditional problem of locating an object in space or introducing space into a solid form.

Art Make-Up, N°1: White. 1967

B.N.: Negative space for me is thinking about the underside and the backside of things. In casting, I always like the parting lines and the seams – things that help to locate the structure of an object, but in the finished sculpture usually get removed. These things help to determine the scale of the work and the weight of the material. Both what's inside and what's outside determine our physical, physiological and psychological responses – how we look at an object.

J.S.: The whole idea of the visual puns, works like *Henry Moore Bound to Fail* and *From Hand to Mouth*, complicates this notion of how we look at an object. They are similar to ready-mades. On the one hand, they translate words or phrases into concrete form – in a sense literalizing them. On the other hand, they are essentially linguistic plays, which means abstracting them. I'm curious about the thought process that went into conceiving those works. For instance, how did *From Hand to Mouth* come about?

B.N.: In that case, the cast was of someone else, not of myself as has generally been assumed – but that doesn't really matter. It was just supposed to be a visual pun, or a picture of a visual pun.

I first made *From Hand to Mouth* as a drawing – actually there were two or three different drawings – just the idea of drawing 'from hand to mouth'. But I couldn't figure out exactly how to make the drawing. My first idea was to have a hand in the mouth with some kind of connection – a bar, or some kind of mechanical connection. I finally realized that the most straightforward way to present the idea would be to cast that entire section of the body. Since I couldn't cast myself, I used my wife as the model.

I worked with the most accurate casting material I could find, something called 'moulage'. I found the stuff at some police shop. You know, they used it to cast tire prints and things like that. It's actually a very delicate casting process; you could pick up fingerprints in the dust with it. The moulage is a kind of gel you heat up. Because it's warm when you apply it to a body, it opens up all the pores – it picks up all that, even the hairs. But it sets like five-day-old Jell-O. You have to put plaster or something over the

back of it to make it hold its shape. Then I made the wax cast, which became very super-realistic – hyper-realistic. You could see things you don't normally see – or think about – on people's skin.

J.S.: All your work seems to depend not only on this kind of tactile precision, but also on a kind of incompleteness – a fragmentariness, a sense of becoming. As a result, your pieces accrue all sorts of meaning over time. With *From Hand to Mouth* – completed over 20 years ago – what other meanings have occurred to you?
B.N.: Well, it's funny you should ask that, because not long ago I read this book in which a character goes to funeral homes or morgues, and uses this moulage stuff on people and makes plaster casts – death masks – for their families. I had no idea that this was a profession. But it turns out that this moulage is a very old, traditional kind of material, and was often used this way. But it just connects up in a strange sort of way with my more recent work, since over the past several years I have been involved with both the idea of death and dying and the idea of masking the figure.

MASKS AND GAMES

J.S.: An early example of masking the figure – your figure, to be precise – was your 1969 film *Art Make-Up*.
B.N.: That film – which was also later a videotape – has a rather simple story behind it. About 20 years ago – this was in '66 and '67 – I was living in San Francisco, and I had access to a lot of film equipment. There were a lot of underground filmmakers there at that time and I knew a bunch of those guys. And since everybody was broke, I could rent pretty good 16mm equipment for $5 or $6 a day – essentially the cost of gas to bring it over. So I set up this *Art Make-Up* film.

Of course, you put on makeup before you film in the movies. In my case, putting on the makeup became the activity. I started with four colors. I just put one on over the other, so that by the time the last one went on it was almost black. I started with white. Then red on the white, which came out pink; then green on top of that, which came out gray; then something very black on top of that.

One thing which hadn't occurred to me when I was making the film was that when you take a solid color of makeup – no matter what color – it flattens the image of the face on film. The flatness itself was another kind of mask.

J.S.: The whole idea of the mask, of abstracting a personality, of simultaneously presenting and denying a self, is a recurring concern in your work.

B.N.: I think there is a need to present yourself. To present yourself through your work is obviously part of being an artist. If you don't want people to see that self, you put on makeup. But artists are always interested in some level of communication. Some artists need lots, some don't. You spend all of this time in the studio and then when you do present the work, there is a kind of self-exposure that is threatening. It's a dangerous situation and I think that what I was doing, and what I am going to do and what most of us probably do, is to use the tension between what you tell and what you don't tell as part of the work. What is given *and* what is withheld become the work. You could say that if you make a statement it eliminates the options; on the other hand if you're a logician, the opposite immediately becomes a possibility. I try to make work that leaves options, or is open-ended in some way.

J.S.: The tenor of that withholding – actually controlling the content or subject – changed significantly when you stopped performing and began to allow the viewer to participate in some of your works. I'm thinking of the architectural installations, in particular the very narrow corridor pieces. In one of them, the viewer who could deal with walking down such a long claustrophobic passage would approach a video monitor on which were seen disconcerting and usually 'invisible' glimpses of his or her own back.

B.N.: The first corridor pieces were about having someone else do the performance. But the problem for me was to find a way to restrict the situation so that the performance turned out to be the one I had in mind. In a way, it was about control. I didn't want somebody else's idea of what could be done.

There was a period in American art, in the '60s, when artists presented parts of works, so that people could arrange them. Bob Morris did some pieces like that, and Oyvind Fahlstrom did those political-coloring-book-like things with magnets that could be rearranged. But it was very hard for me to give up that much control. The problem with that approach is that it turns art into game playing. In fact, at that time, a number of artists were talking about art as though it were some kind of game you could play. I think I mistrusted that idea.

Of course, there is a kind of logic and structure in art-making that you can see as game-playing. But game-playing doesn't involve any responsibility – any moral responsibility – and I think that being an artist does involve moral responsibility. With a game you just follow the rules. But art is like cheating – it involves inverting the rules or taking the game apart and changing it. In games like football or baseball cheating is allowed to a certain extent. In hockey breaking the rules turns into fighting – you can't do that in a bar and get away with it. But the rules change. It can only go so far and then real life steps in. This year warrants were issued to arrest hockey players; two minutes in the penalty box wasn't enough. It's been taken out of the game situation.

J.S.: Nevertheless, many of your works take as their starting point very specific children's games.

B.N.: When I take the game, I take it out of context and apply it to moral or political situations. Or I load it emotionally in a way that it is not supposed to be loaded. For instance, the *Hanged Man* neon piece (1985) derives from the children's spelling game. If you spell the word, you win; if you can't spell the word in a certain number of tries, then the stick figure of the hanged man is drawn line by line with each wrong guess. You finally lose the game if you complete the figure – if you hang the man.

With my version of the hanged man, first of all, I took away the part about being allowed to participate. In my piece you're not allowed to participate – the parts of the figure are put into place without you. The neon 'lines' flash on and off in a programmed sequence. And then the game doesn't end. Once the figure is complete, the whole picture starts to be recreated again. Then I added the bit about having an erection or ejaculation when you're hanged. I really don't know if it's a myth or not.

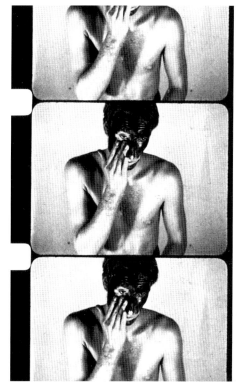

Art Make-Up, Nº4: Black. 1967-68

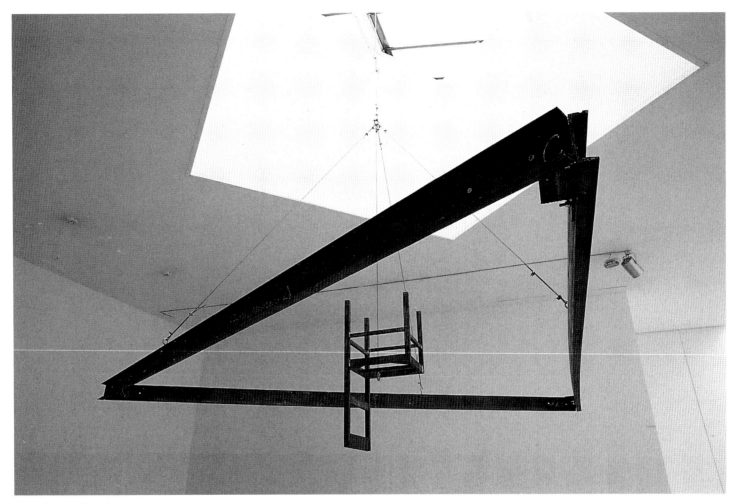

South America Triangle. 1981

I've also used the children's game 'musical chairs' a number of times. The simplest version was *Musical Chair (Studio Piece)* in 1983, which has a chair hanging at the outside edge of a circumference of suspended steel Xs. So, when the Xs swing or the chair swings, they bang into each other and actually make noise − make music. But of course it was more than that because musical chairs is also a cruel game. Somebody is always left out. The first one to be excluded always feels terrible. That kid doesn't get to play anymore, has nothing to do, has to stand in the corner or whatever.

LARGE-SCALE SCULPTURE

J.S.: There seems to be something particularly ominous about your use of chairs − both in this and other works. Why a chair? What does it mean to you?

B.N.: The chair becomes a symbol for a figure − a stand-in for the figure. A chair is used, it is functional; but it is also symbolic. Think of the electric chair, or that chair they put you in when the police shine the lights on you. Because your imagination is left to deal with that isolation, the image becomes more powerful, in the same way that the murder offstage can be more powerful than if it took place right in front of you. The symbol is more powerful.

I first began to work with the idea of a chair with that cast of the space underneath a chair − that was in the '60s. And I remember, when I think back to that time, a chair Beuys did with a wedge of suet on the seat. I think he may have hung it on the wall. I'm not sure. In any case, it was a chair that was pretending it was a chair − it didn't work. You couldn't sit in it because of that wedge of grease or fat or whatever it was − it filled up the space you would sit in. Also, I'm particularly interested in the idea of hanging a chair on the wall. It was a Shaker idea, you know. They had peg boards that ran around the wall, so they could pick up all the furniture and keep the floors clean. The chairs didn't have to be on the floor to function.

In 1981, when I was making *South American Triangle*, I had been thinking about having something hanging for quite a long time. The *Last Studio Piece*, which was made in the late '70s when I was still living in Pasadena, was made from parts of two other pieces – plaster semicircles that look like a cloverleaf and a large square – and I finally just stuck them together. I just put one on top of the other and a metal plate in between and hung it all from the ceiling. That was the first time I used a hanging element. I was working at the same time on the 'underground tunnel pieces.' These models for tunnels I imagined floating underground in the dirt. The same ideas and procedures, the same kind of image, whether something was suspended in water, in earth, in air.

J.S.: *South American Triangle* in a certain sense continues these ideas of game-playing, suspension, inside and outside, and the chair as a stand-in for the figure. In this case though, we're talking about a big steel sculpture hanging from the ceiling, with the chair isolated and suspended upside-down in the middle of the steel barrier. This seems considerably more aggressive than the earlier work, though the content is still covert, an extremely private meditation. But the title hints at its subject matter and begins to explicate its intense emotional and political presence. I'm wondering what your thoughts were when you were making this piece?
B.N.: When I moved to New Mexico and was in Pecos in '79, I was thinking about a piece that had to do with political torture. I was reading V.S. Naipaul's stories about South America and Central America, including *The Return of Eva Peron* and especially *The Killings in Trinidad* – that's the one that made the biggest impression on me. Reading the Naipaul clarified things for me and helped me continue. It helped me to name names, to name things. But it didn't help me to make the piece. It didn't help me to figure out how the bolts went on. It just gave me encouragement.

At first, I thought of using a chair that would somehow become the figure: torturing a

chair and hanging it up or strapping it down, something like that. And then torture has to take place in a room (or at least I was thinking in terms of it taking place in a room), but I couldn't figure out how to build a room and how to put the chair in it. Well, I'd made a number of works that had to do with triangles, like rooms in different shapes. I find triangles really uncomfortable, disconcerting kinds of spaces. There is no comfortable place to stay inside them or outside them. It's not like a circle or square that gives you security.

So, in the end, for *South American Triangle*, I decided that I would just suspend the chair and then hang a triangle around it. My original idea was that the chair would swing and bang into the sides of the triangle and make lots of noise. But then when I built it so that the chair hung low enough to swing into the triangle, it was too low. It didn't look right, so I ended up raising it. The triangle became a barrier to approaching the chair from the outside.

Again, it becomes something you can't get to. There is a lot of anger generated when there are things you can't get to. That's part of the content of the work – and also the genesis of the piece. Anger and frustration are two very strong feelings of motivation for me. They get me into the studio, get me to do the work.

J.S.: That sense of frustration and anger also becomes the viewer's problem in approaching and making sense of your work, especially a piece as disturbing as *South American Triangle*. One critic, Robert Storr, said recently, 'Unlike settling into the reassuring "armchair" of Matisse's painting, to take one's seat in Nauman's art is to risk falling on one's head…'
B.N.: I know there are artists who function in relation to beauty – who try to make beautiful things. They are moved by beautiful things and they see that as their role: to provide or make beautiful things for other people. I don't work that way. Part of it has to do with an idea of beauty. Sunsets, flowers, landscapes: these kinds of things don't move me to do anything. I just want to leave them alone. My work comes out of being frustrated about the human condition. And about how people refuse to understand other people. And about how people can be cruel to each other. It's not that I think I can change that, but it's just such a frustrating part of human history.

RECENT VIDEOS

J.S.: Recently, you've returned to video for the first time since the late '60s. In *Violent Incident*, 1986, you not only moved from 'silents' to 'talkies', but you also used actors for the first time. Nevertheless, the video seems to pick right up on issues you've explored from the beginning. The chair is a central element in the action and the whole tape centers on a cruel joke. Again there is this persistent tension between humor and cruelty.
B.N.: *Violent Incident* begins with what is supposed to be a joke – but it's a mean joke. A chair is pulled out from under someone who is starting to sit down. It intentionally embarrasses someone and triggers the action. But let me describe how it got into its present form. I started with a scenario, a sequence of events which was this: two people come to a table that's set for dinner with plates, cocktails, flowers. The man holds the woman's chair for her as she sits down. But as she sits down, he pulls the chair out from under her and she falls on the floor. He turns around to pick up the chair, and as he bends over, she's standing up, and she gooses him. He turns around and yells at her – calls her names. She grabs the cocktail glass and throws the drink in his face. He slaps her, she knees him in the groin and, as he's doubling over, he grabs a knife from the table. They struggle and both of them end up on the floor.

Now this action takes all of about 18 seconds. But then it's repeated three more times: the man and woman exchange roles, then the scene is played by two men and then by two women. The images are aggressive, the characters are physically aggressive, the language is abusive. The scripting, having the characters act out these roles and the repetition all build on that aggressive tension.

J.S.: Sound is a medium you've explored since your earliest studio performances, films and audiotapes. The hostile overlayering of angry noises contributes enormously to the tension of *Violent Incident*.
B.N.: It's similar with the neon pieces that have transformers, buzzing and clicking and what not; in some places I've installed them, people are disturbed by these sounds. They want them to be completely quiet. There is an immediacy

Clown Torture. 1987

and an intrusiveness about sound that you can't avoid.

So with *Violent Incident*, which is shown on 12 monitors at the same time, the sound works differently for each installation. At one museum, when it was in the middle of the show, you heard the sound before you actually got to the piece. And the sound followed you around after you left it. It's kind of funny the way *Violent Incident* was installed at the Whitechapel. Because it was in a separate room, the sound was baffled; you only got the higher tones. So the main thing you heard throughout the museum was 'Asshole!'.

J.S.: That's sort of the subliminal version of a very aggressive sound piece you used to install invisibly in empty rooms, isn't it?
B.N.: You mean the piece that said, 'Get out of

the room, get out of my mind'? That piece is still amazingly powerful to me. It's really stuck in my mind. And it's really a frightening piece. I haven't heard it for a few years, but the last time I did I was impressed with how strong it was. And I think that it is one of those pieces that I can go back to. I don't know where it came from or how I managed to do it because it's so simple and straightforward.

J.S.: How did that come about?
B.N.: Well, I had made a tape of sounds in the studio. And the tape says over and over again, 'Get out of the room, get out of my mind'. I said it a lot of different ways: I changed my voice and distorted it, I yelled it and growled it and grunted it. Then, the piece was installed with the speakers built into the walls, so that when you went into this small room — 10 feet square or something — you could hear the sound, but there was no one there. You couldn't see where the sound was coming from. Other times, we just stuck the speakers in the corners of the room and played the tape — like when the walls were too hard to build into. But it seemed to work about as well either way. Either way it was a very powerful piece. It's like a print I did that says, 'Pay attention motherfuckers' (1973). You know, it's so angry it scares people.

J.S.: Your most recent videotapes feature clowns. I can see a connection to the *Art Make-Up* film we talked about, but why did you use such theatrical clowns?
B.N.: I got interested in the idea of the clown first of all because there is a mask, and it becomes an abstracted idea of a person. It's not anyone in particular, see, it's just an idea of a person. And for this reason, because clowns are abstract in some sense, they become very disconcerting. You, I, one, we can't make contact with them. It's hard to make any contact with an idea or an abstraction. Also, when you think

114

about vaudeville clowns or circus clowns, there is a lot of cruelty and meanness. You couldn't get away with that without makeup. People wouldn't put up with it, it's too mean. But in the circus it's okay, it's still funny. Then, there's the history of the unhappy clown: they're anonymous, they lead secret lives. There is a fairly high suicide rate among clowns. Did you know that?

J.S.: No, I didn't. But it seems that rather than alluding to this melancholic or tragic side of the clown persona the video emphasizes the different types of masks, the historically specific genres of clowns or clown costumes.

B.N.: With the clown videotape, there are four different clown costumes: one of them is the Emmett Kelly dumb clown; one is the old French Baroque clown (I guess it's French); one is a sort of traditional polka-dot, red-haired, oversize-shoed clown; and one is a jester. The jester and the Baroque type are the oldest, but they are pretty recognizable types. They were picked because they have a historical reference, but they are still anonymous. They become masks, they don't become individuals. They don't become anyone you know, they become clowns.

J.S.: In your tape *Clown Torture*, 1987, the clowns don't act like clowns. For one thing, they're not mute. You have the clowns tell stories. Or, I should say, each of the clowns repeats the same story.

B.N.: Each clown has to tell a story while supporting himself on one leg with the other leg crossed, in such a way that it looks like he is imitating sitting down. So there is the physical tension of watching someone balance while trying to do something else – in this case, tell a story. The takes vary because at some point the clown gets tired and falls over. Then I would stop the tape. Each of the four clowns starts from the beginning, tells the story about 15 times or so, falls over and then the next clown starts.

Clown Torture. 1987

This circular kind of story, for me, goes back to Warhol films that really have no beginning or end. You could walk in at any time, leave, come back again and the figure was still asleep, or whatever. The circularity is also a lot like La Monte Young's idea about music. The music is always going on. You just happen to come in at the part he's playing that day. It's a way of structuring something so that you don't have to make a story.

J.S.: What's the story the clowns tell?

B.N.: 'It was a dark and stormy night. Three men were sitting around a campfire. One of the men said, "Tell us a story, Jack." And Jack said, "It was a dark and stormy night. Three men were sitting around a campfire. One of the men said, "Tell us a story, Jack." And Jack said, "It was a dark and stormy night…"'

NOTE

1. Workingmen's Party of America

This text is an excerpt from interviews with Nauman for the film, *Four Artists: Robert Ryman, Eva Hesse, Bruce Nauman, Susan Rothenberg* (Michael Blackwood Productions, 1988). The interviews were recorded in January 1987 while Nauman was installing a retrospective of his work at the Whitechapel Art Gallery in London. Simultaneously, a retrospective of Nauman's drawings, organized by the Kunstmuseum Basel, toured Europe and was later shown in the U.S.

This article appeared in *Art in America*, 76, New York, September 1988, no. 9, pp. 140–203.

An Interview by Tony Oursler

Bruce Nauman. 1992

WAYS

OF SEEING

THE WARPED VISION
OF BRUCE NAUMAN

Bruce Nauman has had such a profound effect on a particular sensibility, a way of seeing, examining and even questioning things, that those who are prone to think and wonder in those ways cannot help but rate him as one of the most significant influences on their lives. It's not Nauman's fault, of course, but much of the work he did, from the late '60s to the present, has really warped a lot of viewers. A visit to the Nauman exhibition, at the Museum of Modern Art, should go far in illustrating not only why this seminal body of conceptual gestures has been so influential, but how and who it has so deeply affected. While so much of what he has addressed, particularly his personal meditations on the body, has become central to the discourse of contemporary art, it is the fluidity with which he moves through such diverse mediums that is so amazing. His extremely experimental efforts in performance art, sculpture, installation, language, video and a variety of representational alternatives, from holograms to neon, have provided a wealth of potent images and fertile ground for the imaginations of many contemporary artists. Beyond the obvious laudable aspects of bringing this relatively obscure Californian conceptualist into the public eye, there is also the fortuitous timing of a major touring retrospective of Nauman's work over the past 30 years – just when a younger generation of artists, whose vision owes much to Nauman's creative practices, are beginning to receive critical attention. A lot of what we like in artists such as Kiki Smith, Mike Kelley or Matthew Barney has to do with what they liked about Nauman. This certainly holds true for artist Tony Oursler, who was granted a rare interview with Nauman by phone from his New Mexico ranch.

Carlos McCormick

Tony Oursler: Do you ever get artist's block?

Bruce Nauman: Yeah, several times. Somewhere in the early or middle '70s I had a really serious one – the first one I'd ever really had. It was pretty scary, because you start thinking, 'Well, now what am I going to do? I'll have to get a job.' It lasted maybe six months. When I started working (again), the work didn't really change much from the work I did before. I still have kind of long ones from time to time.

T.O.: Did putting together your retrospective make you go back in time and think about all of the stuff that you hadn't really had to think about in a long time?

B.N.: I guess so. I'm not sure why, because some of the work I couldn't really relate to anymore at all. I couldn't even figure out why I did it or put myself in that kind of situation in any way; and other work was kind of interesting to look at because the thoughts appear in the work continually.

T.O.: What pieces did you have no connection with?

B.N.: I think the early fiberglass pieces and the rubber pieces. I could kind of remember why I did them and what I was thinking about, but it's not work that interests me anymore. In fact, I told them if they're going to put it in the show, then they're totally responsible for figuring it out, because I can't.

T.O.: What does it feel like to have this huge block of stuff, which is somehow representing you personally, out there moving around?

B.N.: After a time, you train yourself that once the work is out of the studio, it's up to somebody else how it gets shown and where it gets shown. You can't spend all your time being responsible for how the work goes out in the world, so you do have to let go. What happens is that it starts to become overbearing and I catch myself getting frustrated and angry about the situation. Then I see that it's taken over, and then I can let go.

T.O.: You mentioned anger. I've been doing a lot of work with various ways that people relate to emotions and trying to put that in the work as a kind of barometer, which is something I've always found interesting in your work. Is a lot of it motivated by emotional states that you get in?

B.N.: I think so, although I'm always puzzled by this myself – trying to figure out where work comes from, what gets you to go and try and do work, what gets you in the studio. Roy Lichtenstein, when he first started doing comic-book paintings, said he didn't know what else to do. I just have to do something, so I do something and it might be really stupid, but I just can't think of anything else to do. Sometimes it even gets put aside because it's such a stupid idea, but oftentimes when I go back to it, it has a lot of power because it was created totally out of the need to make something.

T.O.: And then sometimes other works of yours seem very methodical.

B.N.: Yeah, I think I have to have work that is really justifiable and has reasons. I suppose that's the stuff that appears to be more methodical. Then you get caught up in that too much, then you think, 'Gee, this is so self-important and so serious.' You need to be able to be stupid and make mistakes, too.

T.O.: Speaking of being stupid, do you watch television at all?

B.N.: Not a huge amount. [My wife] Susan likes to watch Seinfeld because it's her connection to New York. So that works. But if I watch it too often I get really annoyed with it. I used to like to watch baseball, but we don't have baseball anymore. But I like to lie on the couch on Saturday or Sunday afternoon and fall asleep in front of some sort of ball game. It doesn't seem to matter if it was baseball or football or whatever, I could always fall asleep. It was kind of nice.

T.O.: I was wondering: If you were, say, 25, a woman and just got out of art school, what kind of work would you be making?

B.N.: I don't see why I wouldn't be doing the work I'm doing now. I remember saying many years ago to a friend that I wish I had spent more time hiking in the mountains when I was younger. Like I said, 'When I was 18, I should have been doing that stuff.' He said, 'Well, what the fuck are you talking about? Why can't you do that now?' It's just a stupid thing – of course I can do that now. So I did. Maybe if you're not a well-known artist, if you don't have the opportunity to show work, you might not do certain kinds of work. I've always felt that I've worked with whatever money's been available and whatever equipment's been available. You just do the work. Using those things as an excuse, like 'I haven't got the money or the equipment or the room', are bad excuses for not doing work.

T.O.: You've always been attracted to using new technologies.

B.N.: When I did the holograms, that was probably the most advanced I've ever gotten in terms of new technology. In general, I think I just use stuff that's there. Sometimes you push a little bit, but not too much. It gets too expensive or too hard to find, then it's just not interesting. But I was interested in having an object but not having an object, the 3-D stuff. It's not gotten any easier for anyone to do that sort of work since that time.

T.O.: I have a really off question: Do you have any beliefs or experiences with UFOs?

B.N.: I've never had any experience. But there are people here [in New Mexico] who believe in them and think that they have a landing piece where they actually go into the mountain. I've always been kind of curious about how I'd react if confronted with a being of some sort – if I'd be scared shitless or curious. I'm just waiting to see, I guess.

This article first appeared in Paper Magazine, New York, April 1995, vol. II, no. 10, p. 104.

Clown with Video Surveillance. 1986

Michele De Angelus

INTERVIEW

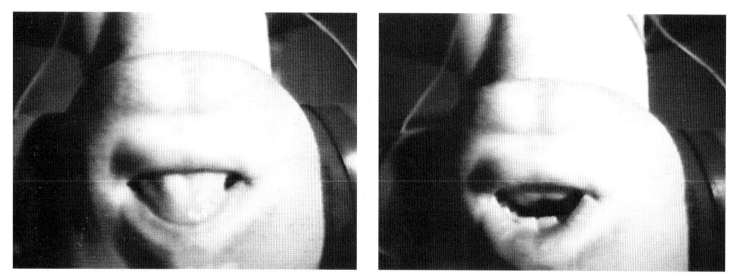

Lip-Sync. 1969

Extracts from an interview that took place
at the artist's home in Pecos, New Mexico,
from 27 to 30 May 1980.

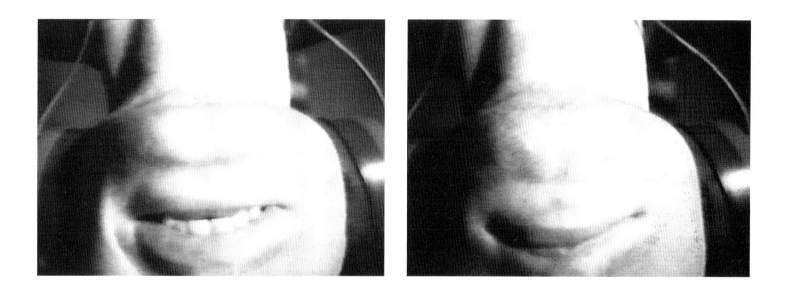

EDUCATION. MUSIC AND MATHEMATICS

Michele De Angelus: Were you interested generally in classical music, and what I sort of call contemporary classical, even in high school? That's pretty extraordinary.
Bruce Nauman: But also folk music.

M.D.A.: What kind of music did you study, I mean, what were the directions of the teachers that you chose?
B.N.: Well, the most serious studying that I did was when I was being a guitarist; I had a good teacher and, I guess what happened, when I finally left and went off to college, well, I had played the bass in a polka band in high school, because, you know, in that part of the country, we'd play at weddings and stuff like that. So I started playing with a dance band in college, and eventually started playing with jazz groups, which was much more interesting, and kind of made a lot of money through college with that. Somehow the thing that's the most interesting

about my career or whatever is all that time having thought that maybe I was going to be an engineer or something and finally [—] I think the tendency was always toward something more pure than a practicing engineer, was to be a mathematician or a physicist, I don't know why or where that comes from. And certainly wanting to be an engineer is in some ways because my father was an engineer, but also the vocational stuff then, that was okay, I could do math. But I feel it even in my work now, I don't know what you call it, abstract, or tendency towards abstraction, or intellectual.

M.D.A.: Cognition.
B.N.: Something like that, that made me want to be a mathematician not an engineer. More interested in the structure of mathematics than solving problems in math, which I suppose is a little bit more philosophical than the practical in that sense.

ART AND EXPERIMENTAL MUSIC

M.D.A.: Was there anybody whose work you were seeing at that time that was important to you?
B.N.: No. I think that what was important more than the work and other artists, was the number of musicians I knew that I'd known before, but most of them were living on the East Coast, Phil Glass, and Steve Reich, and I knew La Monte Young's music although I'd never known him, but I used to spend time with him at the studio.

M.D.A.: How did you meet them? You said you knew them before you went to New York?
B.N.: La Monte Young and Steve Reich are from the West Coat. Steve is a friend of Bill Wiley's and I met him through Bill. I think they had done some projects together. Also I'd met Meredith Monk on the West Coast. I've forgotten why she was out there. I met her at a party and talked to her for a little bit, and then when I got to the East Coast I was still doing some performance.

One time I did a performance at the Whitney and I got nervous and decided I needed some professional in the group and asked her to work with me. After that, I worked with her once or twice at different places. But I think those were really important, because you do, you call yourself an artist or a painter or sculptor or whatever and then you do performance or make things or music, but you can get away with a lot by not putting it into the field of music and calling it a dance. (…) There's a lot of *naïveté* which lets you do things, but at the same time maybe they're things that have been done or done better, or could stand a little more competence even.

M.D.A.: Did you know Terry Riley?
B.N.: No, I don't know him, but I knew his music also, because I'd seen him perform once or twice.

M.D.A.: What was important to you about what these people were doing, or about their work?
B.N.: Well, I think the sense of structure and time, things that continue. La Monte's idea that the music always went on and it was a performance that it was always available, that it was continuous. There was no beginning and no end.

M.D.A.: What about Phil Glass?
B.N.: Well, a lot of that same feeling was there; a lot of it also went back to two other things, when I was in school as an undergraduate in Wisconsin and still playing music like jazz, I think Coltrane was the person I listened to as much as anybody, and a lot of the music was modal rather than more traditional jazz. That also has that sense that there's no progression, it just goes on and on until you choose to stop. And so I really liked that idea of performance or videotape that went on longer than film, or film that went on in loops and things like that. You could walk in at any point. (…) There's a kind of a tension set up (…). A lot of the films were about dance or exercise problems or repeated movements, as were the performances. You have the repeated action, and at the same time, over a long period of time you have mistakes or at least a chance, changes, and you get tired and all kinds of things happen, so there's a certain tension that you can exploit once you begin to understand how those things function. And a lot of the videotapes were about that. [...]

WORK PROCESS

M.D.A.: A lot of those have to do with position in relation to rooms, it seemed to me. What were you thinking of in doing those?
B.N.: Well, by that time there was, I think, I don't know exactly, but a certain amount of that had to do with my response to the Bob Morris and Don Judd stuff that was in the magazines. Also, I think a really important piece for me, that I'd forgotten about for years and remembered not too long ago, was a show of some kind (…) in San Francisco. There were two pieces of Richard Tuttle's, early pieces. And especially because I knew so few people, I spent a lot of time at the studio kind of reassessing, or assessing, why, why are you an artist and what do you do, and finally that's what the work came out (…) that question, why is anyone an artist and what do artists do. I paced around a lot, so I tried to figure out a way of making that function as the work. And so some of that early work after I got out of school had to do with how I spent my time. I drank a lot of coffee, so those photographs of coffee thrown away, … of hot coffee spilled… […]

M.D.A.: Were you in any way taking on the idea that this wasn't what artists had been doing as art up to that point?
B.N.: No. Well, I think there's always, when you feel you aren't getting a lot of attention anyway, or there's a very small audience that you have, then I think that a certain amount of testing can … I think that you do things to find out if you believe in it in the first place, just like often you'll say things in conversation, just to test, and so you do that. I think a lot of work is done that way, which doesn't make a fake or anything, it's the only way you find out is to do it. So there was a lot of that. I made that neon sign which said, *The True Artist Is an Amazing Luminous Fountain*, and *The True Artist Helps the World by Revealing Mystic Truths*.

M.D.A.: That set of photographs is really interesting to me. That's the first, when I was first finding out about your work that was the first I saw, then I learned about the earlier sculptures, and to me that seems to be about what an artist is in this society. Were you consciously taking on those things?

B.N.: Well, that was the examination, what is the function of an artist. Why am I an artist is the same question. And a lot of the reading that I was doing at that time. I think that I finally realized that the sculpture I had made in college revolved around that reinforcement (a lot of people doing work that was art about art). I needed to work out of a broader social context, and I needed to get more of what I thought and what I knew about it into the work… I was reading, I think a lot of word/visual puns and other pieces come from reading Nabokov. I was reading Wittgenstein's *Philosophical Investigations*, which I think doesn't provide you with anything except a way to question things. You can have an argument and follow it until you find out that it makes sense or doesn't make sense, but it was still useful to me to find out that it didn't go to anywhere or it was wrong.

M.D.A.: The punning pieces, like *Drill Team* and those sorts of things, talk about those.
B.N.: Probably, as much as anything, I did them after I saw the Man Ray show in Los Angeles, I forget when that was. I think I did those around that time, and probably after that. He's an interesting person, but he lacks the cohesiveness and the direct intellectual trail of Duchamp, but in another way he did all of that different stuff and made no apologies for any of it, too…

M.D.A.: He's American; you know, Duchamp comes out of the Cartesian system of thought that is very French.
B.N.: Of course, Man Ray really tried to identify himself with that…

M.D.A.: But he didn't have the basis for it.
B.N.: Also, somehow, it's more working class, if that's, I don't know what his background is, but he also worked as a photographer. Duchamp comes out of a more leisure attitude. There was family money, and then he worked for the Arensbergs for all those years.

John Coltrane Piece. 1968

WORK PROCESS — DIFFERENT MEDIA

M.D.A.: It's interesting to me that if you see those photos in isolation, I didn't connect them at first with your [–] I don't know what you want to call it [–] phenomenological pieces in some of the videotapes and films and the situation that you would set up in the galleries later. I don't know what category to call those things, but they came out of the same processes when you talk about the process that made them. That's interesting. There's a real cohesion there in the development of your work.

B.N.: It feels like it to me. I know it's not always easy, because a lot of connecting steps get left out, things that are not made, or things that don't need to be made, so the evidence isn't always there.

M.D.A.: There are pieces that are really interesting like that, the shelf sinking into the wall, and then you made casts of the spaces underneath. Can you talk about those a little bit?
B.N.: They were from looking at futurist pictures, that interested me. But it was also, by the time I got to the shelf sinking into the wall, I think there was a feeling that I wanted to make, and there were a number of other pieces that were sort of abstract fragments of shelves and things…

Revolving Upside Down. 1968

M.D.A.: That piece at eye level with the curve at the bottom.

B.N.: Yes. Guess it was an excuse to make an object, and I'm not clear exactly, if you don't have the courage to go ahead and just make it, an abstract object, and just stick it on the wall, but somehow to give it a reason or meaning by alluding to something.

M.D.A.: Conceptual process.

B.N.: It was necessary at that time for me to do that in order to make work. I was just sort of tied in a knot and couldn't get anything out and so now there was a reason or excuse so that things could be made. Certainly they needed to be physically, sculpturally interesting to me. I felt that was important, but at the same time, to append a title made me more comfortable.

M.D.A.: What's interesting to me is I see your art as being very involved in, as you say, intellectual, cognitive, philosophical process and explorations, and yet to see you here in your home, where you're involved with building and making a place out of a tough landscape; it seems like New Mexico is a tough place to live.

B.N.: It is.

M.D.A.: And that seems like a very different kind of thing than the intellectual aspect of your art; it's a real contrast.

B.N.: Well, I often have that double process at some point there's always a really strong need to make something, and there's a great deal of satisfaction in it, either art, or cabinet work or whatever, and I lose patience with it after a while too, I'm not good at finishing work. I'd never really say that, I get impatient with finishing work, probably I'm not very good either but I'd hate to say it, because I think also, with the art as well as with the house or anything else, once the idea is clear, I mean it's made far enough so that it's clear what's going on, I'm finished with it, emotionally and mentally, I'm finished with it. I don't care to fuss with it.

M.D.A.: When did your use of holograms begin, when did you get involved with them?

B.N.: That was 1968 or so.

M.D.A.: How did that happen, was it an extension of the photographs?

B.N.: Well, yes, it came out of the performance things, and the idea of making faces was the first group, and we did the photographs making faces. And the idea of being just sort of [–] you can manipulate your body as a dancer would or

even you can manipulate yourself making faces, or social attitudes, things like that. So they were made as photographs first and that wasn't quite satisfactory and then I did some as short films, film loops, and eventually, I don't remember where I came across the idea for one, *Scientific American* or someplace, and found a company to do the work.

M.D.A.: How did that change the quality of the images?
B.N.: Well, they became three-dimensional images. They existed in space (…) they were much more sculptural.

M.D.A.: Did you see those as being self-portraits, essentially, or more about human gesture?
B.N.: Yes, more about human gestures, although I don't know. I've always worked pretty much alone, even in this case where somebody else was making, doing the work. I used myself as the subject matter. I'm not sure if I could or would have at the time used someone else or let somebody else do that much, so I'm not clear about that.

M.D.A.: Would you say that you work predominantly with your own body, though?

B.N.: It's just what was available. And I think because when you're trying to find something out, it's much easier to do, using yourself (…), we were talking the other day abut having somebody else do work for you. You have to make a whole different set of instructions, you have to think about the work: whether it's a performance or having a piece made or something; you have to be able to think about it in a different way. If I have an object fabricated out of steel or something then, I have to know, maybe even more, because you have to tell somebody else everything, more than maybe you have to tell yourself. It's really a lot harder in a certain way.

M.D.A.: Well, after you were in San Francisco, you began pretty quickly, it seemed to me, to start working in ways that were other than object-oriented. Did you do film or video pieces before that portfolio of photographs?
B.N.: No. I think the first film pieces were shortly after that. They were pieces that I had kind of intended as performances, but I didn't know exactly how to go about setting them up as performances. I had access to a guy at the Art Institute that I knew that was a filmmaker, I don't remember his name. He worked in the gallery. I did do one performance piece before that was part of my graduate show at Davis.

Andy Warhol, **Merce.** 1974

M.D.A.: And what was that piece like, or about?
B.N.: Manipulating a fluorescent tube.

M.D.A.: Was that your first interest in light as part of the work?
B.N.: No, I had made some neon work before then. I think I just threw it all away, destroyed it all before I left school and never showed any of that work to anybody outside of the people I knew. But anyway, there was an interest in the use of light.

M.D.A.: Your involvement with all these different media, your work has a lot of different aspects that are other than art: psychology, behavior, phenomenology, do you read extensively in other fields than art?
B.N.: Not extensively, I don't think. I read a lot of stuff, but not programmatically at all. I think the interest in reading comes after the work more, rather than the work coming out of the reading.

M.D.A.: How did you come to video, had you worked with it?
B.N.: No, I hadn't. I think my only familiarity with it was seeing it in store windows, you know, a camera on the sidewalk and you see pictures in the store window. Leo [Castelli] bought the equipment and I used it for about a year and then gave it back to the gallery and then Keith Sonnier used it, Richard Serra used it, everybody got to use it.

THE SPECTATOR

M.D.A.: Talk a little bit about how the spectator, how you wanted the spectator to deal with these pieces.
B.N.: Well, I wasn't interested in a boring situation and I think what was important was that (…), there always was a beginning and an end, but it seemed to me that if it went on long enough, if somebody could come in and watch it, you could give them an hour or a half hour or two hours or whatever, but what I always wanted to be careful about was to have the structure include enough tensions in either random error or getting tired and making a mistake, whatever, that there always was some structure programmed into the event. And I really was interested in tensions, not in the

tension of sitting there for a long time and having nothing change. And I think the pieces that were successful, were successful for those reasons, and the pieces that weren't successful failed because they didn't have enough structure built into them.

M.D.A.: This business of making art out of drinking coffee in your studio or, like, pacing in your studio, these are commonplace human activities, you know. It's not like let's say, the technique of painting or something where that is something that is an art activity as opposed to drinking coffee, which is also a life activity shared by your spectator.
B.N.: But, see, that's where, well, what I might say, is I think that those early Warhol films and what I'd known and seen of Merce Cunningham's dance were important considerations. Because his dance is built up of very normal activities. But again, it's how you structure the experience in order to communicate it. I think that's really important. You can't just make a documentation and present it, because people do it all the time and some of it is boring and some of it will be interesting, and I think that's where the art comes in, the ability to communicate not just a bunch of information, but to make an experience that's more general.

M.D.A.: The neon pieces that come out of your body, the templates from your body, so much of your art does come out of your physical presence and size. How do you think the audience can relate to that? Does it involve an imaginative process of evoking the artist and his presence?
B.N.: No, I think those things were really quite impersonal. I think I used myself as an object; maybe impersonal is the wrong word. I think the attempt is to go from the specific to the general. Maybe it's the same kind of way of making a self-portrait, as Rembrandt made a self-portrait, and a lot of other people, making a self-portrait (…) you're making a painting, but you're also making an examination of yourself and also making a generalization beyond yourself.

M.D.A.: Was that important to you to have people who understood your work, who you were showing with?
B.N.: Yes. Oh, I think those kinds of things probably give you as much encouragement as

anything. And Walter [De Maria] was on the West Coast a long time before he moved to New York. De Maria came out to visit; we went to the track and stuff. But I think that recognition by your peers is really more important than anything else. It was to me at the time and still is.

M.D.A.: I'm curious about the way your work manipulates the spectator. Do you feel any kind of responsibility about that? It's clearly an aim in a lot of the work.
B.N.: Well, maybe at the simplest level, but when I do something that's of interest to me, or the experience of the work is interesting, I don't know, that's confusing [–] well, then I just have to assume that some number of people will, if I've done a good job and made some interesting statement, be interested in that, too. And so I don't in that sense feel that it's a manipulation. I think that, but of course it's real complicated because I'm involved in the whole discovery of the piece and what's left is the piece which I made. I seldom have a lot of interest in it once it's finished; I've done what I set out to do or got someplace and found something out about it. In the end all you can do is trust that my needs and the situation are general enough that other people can become involved in it. And I know they're quite often quite demanding, but I think that's all right, too. (…) I was talking to Peter Schjeldahl, he's a poet and critic, and we were talking about where the work came from and that we both felt that our work came a lot out of frustration and anger. So a lot of the work is about that, frustration and anger, it was the social situation, not so much out of specific personal incidents but out of the world or mores or any cultural dissatisfaction, or disjointedness or something, and it doesn't always appear that way in the work, I think. Somehow it generates work; it generates energy from the work.

INSTALLATION WORK

M.D.A.: What was *Art Make-Up* about?
B.N.: I think I did a tape of it and I did a film of it or there were four separate films, about ten-minute films, I put them all together, I've forgotten the sequence of the colors. In the film there were four different colors, there was white, I put on white makeup, then green and then

purple, and then black. From the waist up, I think, is what the film showed. And I think in the tape it was just two colors, black and white, because it was black and white tape. And I suppose it had whatever social connections it had with skin color and things like that. Also the play on the words 'making up art'.

M.D.A.: Tell me what the *'69 Performance Corner* was.
B.N.: It was a piece, that's when I lived in Southampton, I was doing videotapes in the studio, that's about all I was doing at the time, and I built it as a prop for a particular performance which was taped. When Marcia Tucker had the show at the New Museum, the piece was still in the studio, and I'd had it there for a long time. I'd used it a while and then taken it down, and I'd gotten very used to it and I liked it. But I had never displayed anything like that or showed it. Initially I'd never thought of it as a sculpture or an art object at all, it was a prop.

M.D.A.: What was it exactly?
B.N.: It was just two parallel walls that stuck straight out from the studio wall about twenty feet and about twenty inches apart. I remember it wasn't very big [–] I can remember some bigger ones. I finally just decided it was fine the way it was, it didn't need the performance. I think it was very hard for me to present it with any particular instructions, because I felt, I didn't want people to make their own performance. I wanted to control the situation, and I felt that by giving something as simple and uninflected as that corridor, that I was allowing people a lot more latitude than I was used to.

M.D.A.: And you were uncomfortable with that.
B.N.: Yes, I was very uncomfortable. At the same time, the idea of the dead-end corridor, which I hadn't thought of when I built the piece but I found out about it when it was there, it really appealed to me.

M.D.A.: You used that in other pieces. Can you talk about what they were like?
B.N.: Well, there were a number of corridors that were designed after that. You see, that was the first one. Some of them were to look into, most of them were made to enter, some were a little wider and some were a lot narrower (…) One piece

that the Tate has, has a mirror at the end at a slight angle, which does two things. It makes it look like it's going around a corner, and, because the mirror ends before the top of the wall, it makes the end look like it's twisted. It's very strange, almost an optical illusion.

M.D.A.: That difference between film which to my eye is crisp, obviously, a resolved image, and there's a great deal of depth in it, as compared to video, which is often really grainy and the space is really, it seems to me that there's not very much depth. It's like an intimate image, and then it's right up against the screen. How did that change the nature of your work, or did it?
B.N.: Well, I think it did. And you also have to deal with the fact of the equipment, the monitor, and the television set in the space.

M.D.A.: Did you have a video camera just set up and going, or did you have it connected with a monitor (…)
B.N.: Generally I had it with the monitor, (…) but usually I could see what was going on. You had to be able to, I didn't have anybody else there to keep track, because usually the camera was fixed. I needed to be able to see where I was in the picture and what was going on.

M.D.A.: Isn't that a weird kind of schizophrenia, though, because you were performing for yourself?
B.N.: Well, I used that in one of the corridor pieces. One of the more successful ones was the long corridor that had a live image and a taped image of the empty corridor. The other thing that made it work was that I used a wide-angle lens and it was above and behind you as you walked into the corridors, so you were removed from yourself, sort of doubly removed. Your image of yourself was from above and behind, and as you walked, because the wide-angle lens changes the rate that you're going away from the camera, so as you took a step, you took a double step with your own image. It's a strange feeling.

M.D.A.: It really made you doubt your physical presence. Cameras don't lie. Here I am, I know I'm here but I'm not there. The camera says I'm not here.

B.N.: The feeling that I had about a lot of that work was of going up the stairs in the dark and either having an extra stair that you didn't expect or not having one that you thought was going to be there. That kind of misstep surprises you every time it happens. Even when you knew how those pieces were working, as the camera was always out in front of you, but they seemed to work every time anyway. You couldn't avoid the sensation, which was very curious to me.

M.D.A.: At that point, though, you were making work that was essentially the place where it operated [–] maybe this is true of all of your work [–] (…) because it was the sum of all that in the spectator.
B.N.: Well, I think what you have very obviously in that situation is two kinds of information. You have the information that you've given yourself walking down this space, and then the other information through the camera visually. You have a piece of visual information and a piece of kinetic, or kinesthetic information and they don't line up [–] this idea that you're passing in the dark [–] and I think that the tension is set up by those two kinds of information that you can't ever quite put together. They won't quite fit. That's what the piece is, that stuff that's not coming together.

ART AND POLITICAL RELATIONSHIPS

M.D.A.: What interests you about these situations? It's clearly, the end point is not to create X emotional situation.
B.N.: No, the important thing is the tension, of how to deal with the situation. My intention would be to set it up, so that it is hard to resolve, so that you're always on the edge of one kind of way of relating to the space or another, and you're never quite allowed to do either.

M.D.A: But this art doesn't affect the culture in a larger sense. It's not like social work or something. […]
B.N.: Oh, no. I think that people make a mistake about that. Art can never (…) have any direct political or social impact on culture. But I would think that art is what's used in history; it's what's kind of left. And that's how we view history, as

through art and writing, art in the broad sense: music and writing and all that, (…) you know art is political in the sense that it pokes at the edges of what's accepted or what's acceptable, or because it does investigate why people do art or why people do anything, or how the culture can and should function. I think art's about those things, and art is a very indirect way of pursuing those kinds of thoughts. So the impact has to be indirect, but at the same time I think it can be real. I think it's almost impossible to predict or say what it is, but it certainly doesn't apply to the political situation today or tomorrow, except in an abstract and more general way. I think that with art or philosophy (…), if you think of art as discipline, the people that are interesting are the people that are exploring the structure of the discipline. In that sense they're breaking the discipline down, too, as they're expanding it. They tend to break down what's there. Certainly there are artists who function entirely within the discipline. I would find those people uninteresting. Not that they're not talented or skilled or all those things, but it's not of interest to me. In that sense there's a great deal of confusion, because it doesn't require being able to draw or being able to paint well or know colors, it doesn't require any of those specific things that are in the discipline, to be interesting. On the other hand, if you don't have any skill at all, then you can't communicate, either, so it's an interesting edge between [–] that edge is interesting for those reasons.

Oral History Interview with Bruce Nauman, conducted by Michele De Angelus between 27 May and 30 May 1980, Archives of American Art, Smithsonian Institution.

APPENDICES

LIST OF WORKS

I. Audio-visual installations

Going Around the Corner Piece, 1970
4 wooden panels 305 x 610 cm, 4 video cameras,
4 monitors (b/w, silent)
36 m² (approx.)
Collection Mnam-Cci, Centre Georges Pompidou, Paris, France.

Live-Taped Video Corridor, 1970
Wooden panels, 1 video camera, 2 monitors,
1 video-cassette recorder, 1 videotape U-MATIC (b/w, silent)
366 x 975 x 51 cm (approx.)
Collection Solomon R. Guggenheim Museum,
gift of the Collection Panza (1992), New York, USA.

Indoor/Outdoor, 1972
1 video camera, 1 monitor, 1 microphone, 1 amplifier
(b/w, sound)
Collection Vancouver Art Gallery, gift of Ian Davidson,
Vancouver, Canada.

Good Boy, Bad Boy, 1985
2 monitors with 2 loudspeakers, 2 videodisc players,
2 videodiscs (colour, sound)
Collection Mnam-Cci, Centre Georges Pompidou, Paris, France.

Violent Incident, 1986
12 26-inch monitors with loudspeakers,
4 videodisc players, 4 videodiscs (colour, sound)
Exhibition copy
260 x 267 x 47 cm
Collection Tate Gallery, London, Great Britain.

Clown Torture, 1987
2 video projectors, 2 20-inch monitors, 2 25-inch monitors,
4 loudspeakers, 4 videodiscs (colour, sound)
Exhibition copy
Collection The Art Institute of Chicago, Chicago, USA.

Raw Material—OK, OK, OK, 1990
1 video projector with reverse mechanism, 2 monitors with
loudspeakers, 2 videodisc players, 2 videodiscs (colour, sound)
Exhibition copy
Collection Pamela and Richard Kramlich, San Francisco, USA.

Raw Material with Continuous Shift—OK, OK, OK, 1991
1 video projector with reverse mechanism, 2 monitors with
loudspeakers, 2 videodisc players, 2 videodiscs (colour, sound)
Exhibition copy
Collection Selma and Jos Vandermolen, Ghent, Belgium.

Raw Material with Continuous Shift—MMMM, 1991
1 video projector with reverse mechanism, 2 monitors with
loudspeakers, 2 videodisc players, 2 videodiscs (colour, sound)
Exhibition copy
Private collection, Switzerland.

ANTHRO/SOCIO (Rinde Facing Camera), 1991
3 video projectors, 6 monitors with stereo speakers,
6 videodisc players, 6 videodiscs,
1 amplifier, 2 loudspeakers (colour, sound)
Exhibition copy
Collection Ydessa Hendeles, Toronto, Canada
Courtesy Ydessa Hendeles Art Foundation, Toronto, Canada.

Falls, Pratfalls and Sleights of Hand, 1993
5 video projectors, 1 monitor, 5 videodisc players,
5 loudspeakers with amplifiers, 1 switch,
5 videodiscs (colour, sound)
Exhibition copy
Kunstmuseum Wolfsburg, Wolfsburg, Germany.

Poke in the Eye/Nose/Ear 3/8/94 Edit, 1994
1 videodisc player, 1 video projector,
1 videodisc (colour, silent)
Exhibition copy
Collection Walker Art Center, Minneapolis, USA.

World Peace (Projected), 1996
5 video projectors, 5 videodisc players, 5 videodiscs,
10 loudspeakers, 1 remote control, 1 stool (colour, sound)
Exhibition copy
Bayerische Staatsgemäldesammlungen, Munich
Staatsgalerie moderner Kunst.

II. Film installation

Art Make-Up, N° 1: White, 1967
Art Make-Up, N° 2: Pink, 1967-68
Art Make-Up, N° 3: Green, 1967-68
Art Make-Up, N° 4: Black, 1967-68
4 video projectors, 4 videodiscs (colour, silent)
Exhibition copy (from 16mm film)
Collection Mnam-Cci, Centre Georges Pompidou, Paris, France.

III. Sound installation

Get Out of My Mind, Get Out of This Room, 1968
1 CD player, 2 loudspeakers, 1 CD, 6 mn (on a loop)
Collection Jack and Nell Wendler, London, Great Britain.

IV. Sculpture and installation

First Poem Piece, 1968
Sheet steel, 152.4 x 152.4 x 1.3 cm
Collection Museum Kröller-Müller, Otterlo, The Netherlands.

Consummate Mask of Rock, 1975
Installation and text
8 chalk cubes of 35.6 cm and 8 chalk cubes of 38.1 cm
Typed text, lead pencil and collage on paper, 100 x 50 cm
Courtesy Anthony d'Offay Gallery, London, Great Britain.

V. Neons

None Sing Neon Sign, 1970
Neon tubes, 33 x 61.6 x 3.8 cm
Exhibition copy
Collection Sylvio Perlstein, Antwerp, Belgium.

Raw War, 1970
Neon tubes, 16.5 x 43.5 x 3.8 cm
Exhibition copy
Collection Sylvio Perlstein, Antwerp, Belgium.

Run from Fear, Fun from Rear, 1972
Neon tubes, 20.3 x 116.8 x 5.7 cm and 18.4 x 113 x 5.7 cm
Exhibition copy
Collection Froehlich, Stuttgart, Germany.

Human Nature/Life Death/Knows Doesn't Know, 1983
Neon tubes, 273.1 x 271.8 x 14.6 cm
Exhibition copy
Collection Los Angeles County Museum of Art, Los Angeles, USA,
purchased with funds provided by the Modern and Contemporary
Art Council.

One Hundred Live and Die, 1984
Neon tubes, 299.7 x 335.9 x 53.3 cm
Exhibition copy
Collection Benesse Corporation,
Naoshima Contemporary Art Museum, Kagawa, Japan.

VI. Photographs and photo collages

Composite Photo of Two Messes on the Studio Floor, 1967
Photograph, silver nitrate print, 102.9 x 312.4 cm
Collection Museum of Modern Art, gift of Philip Johnson (1984),
New York, USA.

*Letter to Bill Allan: Three Well-Known Knots
(Square Knot, Bowline and Clove Hitch)*, 1967
3 colour photographs, 9.3 x 16.8 cm; 5 x 7.6 cm; 4.5 x 7.2 cm
Exhibition copy
Collection William Allan Papers, Archives of American Art,
Smithsonian Institution, Washington D.C., USA.

Perfect Balance, 1990
4 colour photo collages, 48.5 x 33.5 cm (each)
Collection Selma and Jos Vandermolen, Ghent, Belgium.

Rinde Spinning, 1992
Photo collage (maquette), colour, 38.3 x 57 cm
Collection Katharina Faerber, Geneva, Switzerland.

VII. Drawings

Love Me Tender, Move Te Lender, 1966
Pencil, 96.5 x 63.5 cm
Collection The Saint Louis Art Museum, gift of
Mr and Mrs Joseph A. Helman, Saint Louis, USA.

Study of Lips, 1967
Pencil, 42.5 x 69 cm
Collection Sylvio Perlstein, Antwerp, Belgium.

LIST OF WORKS

First Poem Piece, 1968
Lead pencil, ink, 70 x 90 x 3.8 cm
Collection Museum Kröller Müller, Otterlo, The Netherlands.

Beckett Walk Diagram II, 1968-69
Black and colour pencil, 41 x 47.3 x 4.4 cm
Courtesy of the artist, Santa Fe, USA.

Going Around the Corner Piece, 1970
Graphite on paper, 58.6 x 73.8 cm
Collection Mnam-Cci, Centre Georges Pompidou, Paris, France.

Elke Allowing the Floor to Rise Up over Her, Face Up, 1973
Pencil, 28 x 21.5 cm
Collection Konrad Fischer, Düsseldorf, Germany.

Tony Sinking into the Floor, Face Up and Face Down, 1973
Pencil, 28 x 21.5 cm
Collection Konrad Fischer, Düsseldorf, Germany.

WHITE ANGER, RED DANGER, YELLOW PERIL, BLACK DEATH, 1984
Pencil and acrylic, 127 x 97 cm
Collection Sylvio Perlstein, Antwerp, Belgium.

Untitled (Haus Esters Installation), 1985
Lead pencil and collage on paper, 71.3 x 89.9 x 5.7 cm
Courtesy of the artist, Santa Fe, USA.

Clown with Video Surveillance, 1986
Watercolour, pencil and collage on paper, 108.6 x 95.9 cm
Courtesy Mr and Mrs Jay Bernstein,
Shoshana Wayne Gallery, USA.

ANTHRO/SOCIO, 1992
Ink, 21.5 x 34 cm
Collection Konrad Fischer, Düsseldorf, Germany.

VIII. Videotapes and films

Bouncing Two Balls Between the Floor and Ceiling with Changing Rhythms, 1967-68
16 mm film, b/w, sound, 10 mn (videodisc copy)
Courtesy Sperone Westwater, New York, USA.

Playing a Note on the Violin While I Walk Around the Studio, 1967-68
16 mm film, b/w, sound, 10 mn (videodisc copy)
Courtesy Sperone Westwater, New York, USA.

Walking in an Exaggerated Manner Around the Perimeter of a Square, 1967-68
16 mm film, b/w, silent, 10 mn (videodisc copy)
Courtesy Sperone Westwater, New York, USA.

Revolving Upside Down, 1968
Videotape, b/w, sound, 10 mn (videodisc copy)
Courtesy Sperone Westwater, New York, USA.

Slow Angle Walk (Beckett Walk), 1968
Videotape, b/w, sound, 60 mn (videodisc copy)
Courtesy Sperone Westwater, New York, USA.

Stamping in the Studio, 1968
Videotape, b/w, sound, 60 mn (videodisc copy)
Courtesy Sperone Westwater, New York, USA.

Walk with Contrapposto, 1968
Videotape, b/w, sound, 60 mn (videodisc copy)
Courtesy Sperone Westwater, New York, USA.

Lip-Sync, 1969
Videotape, b/w, sound, 30 mn (videodisc copy)
Courtesy Sperone Westwater, New York, USA.

Pulling Mouth, 1969
16 mm film, b/w, silent, 8 mn (videodisc copy)
Courtesy Sperone Westwater, New York, USA.

Violin Tuned D E A D, 1969
Videotape, b/w, sound, 60 mn (videodisc copy)
Courtesy Sperone Westwater, New York, USA.

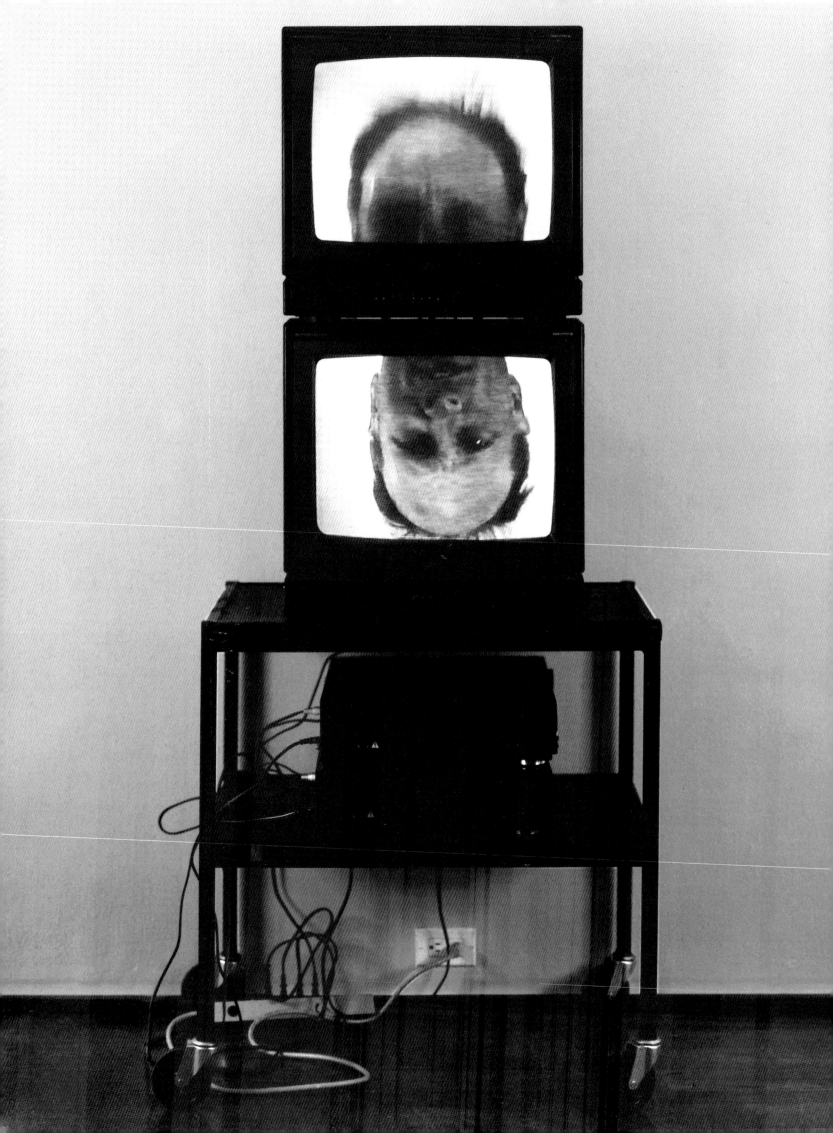

BIOGRAPHY

1941 Born in Fort Wayne, Indiana.

1960 Studied mathematics, physics and art at the University of Wisconsin (Madison).

1964 Studied art at the University of California, Davis. Studied with William T. Wiley and Robert Arneson.

1964-1966 Abandoned painting. Became interested in sculpture, performance and film.
Published *Pictures of a Sculpture in a Room*.
Collaborated on film projects with Robert Nelson and William Allan (1965-66).

1966 Graduated in art at the University of California.
Taught at the Art Institute of San Francisco.
Collaborated with W.T. Wiley.
First solo exhibition at the Nicholas Wilder Gallery, Los Angeles.
Eccentric Abstraction, first group exhibition at the Fischbach Gallery, New York.

1968 Met the choreographer Meredith Monk and the composer Steve Reich.
Discovered the work of John Cage, Merce Cunningham and Karlheinz Stockhausen.
First solo exhibition at the Leo Castelli Gallery, New York.
Travelled in Europe, where he had his first solo exhibition at the Galerie Konrad Fischer, Düsseldorf.

1969 Performance with Judy Nauman and Meredith Monk at the Whitney Museum of American Art, New York,
part of the exhibition *Anti-Illusion: Procedures/Materials*.

1970 Invited by Jasper Johns to conceive the work *Tread*, presented by the Merce Cunningham Dance Company.
Taught at the University of California (Irvine).
At Santa Barbara, he participated with Richard Serra in a performance conceived by Meredith Monk.

1972 *Bruce Nauman: Work from 1965 to 1972*, first solo exhibition in a museum,
co-organised by the Los Angeles County Museum of Art and the Whitney Museum of American Art, New York.

1989 He moved to Galisteo (New Mexico) where he trained horses.

1993-1995 Touring retrospective organised by the Walker Art Center, Minneapolis, in association with the Hirshhorn Museum
and Sculpture Garden, Smithsonian Institution, Washington D.C.; travelled to the Museum of Contemporary Art, Los Angeles,
the Museum of Modern Art, New York, the Museo Nacional Centro de Arte Reina Sofia, Madrid, and the Kunsthaus, Zurich.
Exhibition accompanied by a catalogue raisonné.

SELECTED SOLO EXHIBITIONS

1966 Nicholas Wilder Gallery, Los Angeles.

1968 Leo Castelli Gallery, New York.
Sacramento State College Art Gallery, Sacramento.
6 Day Week: 6 Sound Problems, Galerie Konrad Fischer, Düsseldorf.

1969 Nicholas Wilder Gallery, Los Angeles.
Bruce Nauman: Holograms, Videotapes, and Other Works, Leo Castelli Gallery, New York.
Galerie Ileana Sonnabend, Paris.
Bruce Nauman: Photographs, School of Visual Arts, New York.
Audio/Video Projects, Palley Cellar, San Francisco.

1970 Galerie Konrad Fischer, Düsseldorf.
Galeria Sperone, Turin.
Nicholas Wilder Gallery, Los Angeles.
Untitled: Corridor Piece with Mirror, San Jose State College, San Jose.

1971 Leo Castelli Gallery, New York.
Galerie Ileana Sonnabend, Paris.
Galerie Konrad Fischer, Düsseldorf.
Studies on Holograms, Five Silkscreens and New Lithographs, Betty Gold Fine Modern Prints, Los Angeles.
Left or Standing, Standing or Left Standing, Leo Castelli Gallery, New York.
Galeria Françoise Lambert, Milan.

1972 *Bruce Nauman: 16 mm Filme 1967-1970*, Ursula Wevers, Cologne.
Bruce Nauman: Work from 1965 to 1972, Los Angeles County Museum of Art, Los Angeles,
Whitney Museum of American Art, New York; Kunsthalle, Berne; Städtische Kunsthalle, Düsseldorf;
Stedelijk Van Abbe Museum, Eindhoven; Palazzo Reale, Milan; Contemporary Arts Museum, Houston;
San Francisco Museum of Art, San Francisco.

1973 *Bruce Nauman: Floating Room*, Fine Arts Gallery, University of California, Irvine.
Bruce Nauman: Floating Room, Leo Castelli Gallery, New York.
Flayed Earth/Flayed Self (Skin/Sink), Nicholas Wilder Gallery, Los Angeles.
Image Projection and Displacement (No Promises), Ace Gallery, Vancouver.

1974 *Installation*, Ace Gallery, Vancouver.
Yellow Body, Galerie Konrad Fischer, Düsseldorf.
Yellow Triangular Room, Santa Ana College Art Gallery, Santa Ana.
Wall with Two Fans, Wide White Space, Antwerp.
Galerie Ileana Sonnabend, Paris.

1975 *Bruce Nauman: Cones Cojones*, Leo Castelli Gallery, New York.
Consummate Mask of Rock, Albright-Knox Art Gallery, Buffalo.
Forced Perspective: Open Mind, Closed Mind, Equal Mind, Parallel Mind (Allegory and Symbolism),
Galerie Konrad Fischer, Düsseldorf.

1976 Atholl McBean Gallery, San Francisco Art Institute, San Francisco.
Enforced Perspective. Allegory and Symbolism, Ace Gallery, Vancouver.
White Breathing, UNLV Art Gallery, University of Nevada, Las Vegas.
Consummate Mask of Rock, Sperone Westwater Gallery in collaboration with Leo Castelli Gallery, New York.
Sonia Henie-Niels Onstad Foundation, Oslo.

1978 Leo Castelli Gallery, New York.
InK. Halle für Internationale neue Kunst, Zurich.
1/12 Scale Study in Fiberglass and Plaster for Cast Iron of a Trench and Four Tunnels in Concrete at Full Scale,
Art Gallery, California State University, San Diego.
Wood, Plaster and Steel Works and Cor-Ten Steel Sculpture, Ace Gallery, Vancouver.

1979 Galerie Schmela, Düsseldorf.
Bruce Nauman: An Installation, Portland Center for the Visual Arts, Portland.

1980 Leo Castelli Gallery, New York.
Bruce Nauman: New Sculpture, Hill's Gallery of Contemporary Art, Santa Fe.
North, East, South, South East, Galerie Konrad Fischer, Düsseldorf.
Ink. Halle für Internationale neue Kunst, Zurich.

1981 *Bruce Nauman: 1/12-Scale Models for Underground Pieces*, Albuquerque Museum, Albuquerque.
Stone Sculpture: Enforced Perspective: Allegory and Symbolism, Galeria Ace, Venice.
Bruce Nauman, 1972-1981, Rijksmuseum Kröller-Müller, Otterlo; Staatliche Kunsthalle, Baden-Baden.
Bruce Nauman: New Iron Casting, Plaster, and Drawings, Young Hoffman Gallery, Chicago.
Bruce Nauman: Photo Piece, Window Screen, Hologram, Neon Sculptures, Cast-Iron Sculpture, Drawings 1967-1981,
Galerie Konrad Fischer, Düsseldorf.

1982 *Bruce Nauman: Violins, Violence, Silence*, Leo Castelli Gallery, New York.
Bruce Nauman: Neons, Baltimore Museum of Art, Baltimore.

1983 *Bruce Nauman: Dream Passage, Stadium Piece, Musical Chairs—Drei neue Arbeiten*, Museum Haus Esters, Krefeld.
Hoffnung/Neid, Galerie Konrad Fischer, Düsseldorf.

1984 Hallen für neue Kunst, Schaffhausen.
Bruce Nauman: Recent Neons and Drawings, Daniel Weinberg Gallery, Los Angeles.
Room with My Soul Left Out, Leo Castelli Gallery, New York.
Seven Virtues and Seven Vices; White Anger, Red Anger, Yellow Peril, Black Death, Sperone Westwater Gallery, New York.

1985 *New Work: Neons and Drawings*, Donald Young Gallery, Chicago.
New Neons, Galerie Konrad Fischer, Düsseldorf.
Leo Castelli Gallery, New York.

1986 Galerie Jean Bernier, Athens.
Bruce Nauman : Œuvres sur papier, Galerie Yvon Lambert, Paris.
Bruce Nauman: Drawings/Zeichnungen 1965-1986, Museum für Gegenwartskunst, Basle; Kunsthalle, Tübingen;
Städtisches Kunstmuseum, Bonn; Museum Boymans-van Beuningen, Rotterdam; Kunstraum, Munich;
Badischer Kunstverein, Karlsruhe; Hamburger Kunsthalle, Hamburg; New Museum of Contemporary Art, New York;
Contemporary Arts Museum, Houston; Museum of Contemporary Art, Los Angeles; University of California, Berkeley.
Bruce Nauman, Whitechapel Art Gallery, London; Kunsthalle, Basle; ARC, Musée d'Art Moderne de la Ville de Paris, Paris.

1987 *Bruce Nauman: Neon and Video*, Donald Young Gallery, Chicago.
Daniel Weinberg Gallery, Los Angeles.

1988 *Bruce Nauman: Videos 1965-1986*, Museum of Contemporary Art, Los Angeles.
Galerie Micheline Szwajcer, Antwerp.
Bruce Nauman, Sperone Westwater Gallery, New York.
Bruce Nauman, Collection Mnam-Cci, Centre Georges Pompidou, Paris.

1989 *Bruce Nauman: New Prints*, Sperone Westwater Gallery, New York.
Bruce Nauman: Heads and Bodies, Galerie Konrad Fischer, Düsseldorf.
Bruce Nauman: Prints 1970-1989, Leo Castelli Graphics and Lorence-Monk Gallery, New York.
Bruce Nauman: A Survey, Anthony d'Offay Gallery, London.

1990 *Bruce Nauman: Shadow Puppets and Instructed Mime*, Sperone Westwater Gallery, New York.
Leo Castelli Gallery, New York.
Bruce Nauman: Skulpturen und Installationen 1985-1990, Museum für Gegenwartskunst, Basle;
Städtische Galerie, Städelsches Kunstinstitut, Frankfurt; Musée Cantonal des Beaux-Arts, Lausanne.

1991 *Bruce Nauman, Prints and Multiples*, Thea Westreich, New York; Museum van Hedendaagse Kunst, Ghent;
Douglas Hyde Gallery, Trinity College, Dublin; Museum Boymans-van Beuningen, Rotterdam;
Heiligenkreuzerhof, Hochschule für Angewandte Kunst, Vienna; Institute of Contemporary Arts, London;
City Museum, Stoke on Trent; Tel Aviv Museum of Art, Tel Aviv.
Bruce Nauman–OK OK OK, Portikus, Frankfurt.
Galerie Metropol, Vienna.
Bruce Nauman, Fundación Espai Poblenou, Barcelona.

1992 *Bruce Nauman: Neons*, Anthony d'Offay Gallery, London.
Bruce Nauman, Ydessa Hendeles Art Foundation, Toronto.
Bruce Nauman, Salzburger Kunstverein, Salzburg.

1993 *Bruce Nauman: Light Works*, Steinberg Hall, Washington University Gallery of Art, St Louis.
Bruce Nauman, Museo Nacional Centro de Arte Reina Sofia, Madrid; Walker Art Center, Minneapolis;
Museum of Contemporary Art, Los Angeles; Hirshhorn Museum and Sculpture Garden, Washington D.C.;
Museum of Modern Art, New York.
Shoshana Wayne Gallery, Santa Monica.

1994 *Falls, Pratfalls and Sleights of Hand*, Leo Castelli Gallery, New York.
Prints and Drawings, Leo Castelli Gallery, New York.
Seven Virtues and Seven Vices, Galerie Konrad Fischer, Düsseldorf.
Falls, Pratfalls and Sleights of Hand (Dirty Version), Anthony d'Offay Gallery, London; Galerie Konrad Fischer, Düsseldorf.

1995 *Elliot's Stones*, Museum of Contemporary Art, Chicago.
Falls, Pratfalls and Sleights of Hand (Dirty Version), 1993, Galerie Jean Bernier, Athens.
Bruce Nauman, Kunsthaus Zürich, Zurich.

1996 *Bruce Nauman: Rotating Glass Walls (1970)*, Museum Boymans-van Beuningen, Rotterdam.
Bruce Nauman, Konsthall, Stockholm.
Fifteen Pairs of Hands, White Bronze, "End of the World" with Lloyd Maines, Leo Castelli Gallery, New York.
Video & Sculpture, Sperone Westwater Gallery, New York.

1997 *Bruce Nauman: Shadow Puppet Spinning Head*, Galerie Hauser + Wirth, Zurich.

1997-1998 *Bruce Nauman, 1985-1996: Drawings, Prints, and Related Works*, The Aldrich Museum of Contemporary Art, Ridgefield, Connecticut;
Cleveland Center for Contemporary Art, Ohio.
Bruce Nauman, Casa Masaccio, San Giovanni Valdarno, Florence.

1997-1999 *Bruce Nauman: Image/Texte 1966-1996*, Kunstmuseum Wolfsburg, Wolfsburg; Mnam-Cci, Centre Georges Pompidou, Paris;
Hayward Gallery, London; Nykytaiteen museo/The Museum of Contemporary Art Kiasma, Helsinki.

SELECTED GROUP EXHIBITIONS

1966 *The Slant Step Show*, University Art Gallery, Berkeley, San Francisco.
New Directions: The Tenth SECA Show, San Francisco Museum of Art, San Francisco.
Eccentric Abstraction, Fischbach Gallery, New York.
William Geis and Bruce Nauman, San Francisco Art Institute, San Francisco.

1967 *American Sculpture of the Sixties*, Los Angeles County Museum of Art, Los Angeles; Philadelphia Museum of Art, Philadelphia.

1968 *Dokumenta 4*, Museum Fridericianum, Kassel.
Primary Structure, Minimal Art, Pop Art, Antiform, Galerie Ricke, Kassel.
Prospect 68: Internationale Vorschau auf die Kunst in den Galerien der Avantgarde, Städtische Kunsthalle, Düsseldorf.
Anti-Form, John Gibson Gallery, New York.
Soft Sculpture, American Federation of Arts, New York; Georgia Museum of Art, University of Georgia, Athens;
State University of New York, College of Oswego, Oswego; Cedar Rapids Art Center, Cedar Rapids;
Michigan State University, East Lansing; Andrew Dickinson White Museum of Art, Cornell University, Ithaca.
9 at Leo Castelli, Leo Castelli Gallery, New York.

1969 *Here and Now: An Exhibition of Thirteen Artists*, Steinberg Hall, Washington University Gallery of Art, St Louis.
Thirty-first Biennial of Contemporary American Painting, Corcoran Gallery of Art, Washington D.C.
Repair Show, University Art Gallery, Berkeley University, San Francisco.
Young American Artists, Wide White Space Gallery, Antwerp.
Op Losse Schroeven: Situaties en Cryptostructuren (Square Pegs in Round Holes), Stedelijk Museum, Amsterdam;
Museum Folkwang, Essen.
When Attitudes Become Form: Works—Concepts—Processes—Situations—Information/
Wenn Attitüden Form werden: Werke—Konzepte—Prozesse—Situationen—Information,
Kunsthalle, Berne; Museum Haus Lange, Krefeld; Institute of Contemporary Arts, London.
The Sky's the Limit, University of St. Thomas, Houston.
Anti-Illusion: Procedures/Materials, Whitney Museum of American Art, New York.
Nine Young Artists: Theodoron Awards, Solomon R. Guggenheim Museum, New York.
557, 087, Seattle Art Museum, Seattle, Washington; Vancouver Art Gallery and Student Union Building Gallery,
University of British Columbia, Vancouver.
Konzeption-Conception: Dokumentation einer heutigen Kunstrichtung/Documentation of a to-day's art tendency,
Städtisches Museum, Schloss Morsbroich, Leverkusen.
Drawings, Fort Worth Art Center Museum, Fort Worth.
Art by Telephone, Museum of Contemporary Art, Chicago.
Kompas 4: Westkust USA/West Coast USA, Stedelijk Van Abbe Museum, Eindhoven.
West Coast 1945-1969, Pasadena Art Museum, Pasadena; City Art Museum of St Louis, St Louis;
Art Gallery of Ontario, Toronto; Fort Worth Art Center Museum, Fort Worth.
Time Photography, School of Visual Arts, New York.
Art in Process IV, Contemporary Wing, Finch College Museum of Art, New York.

1970 *String and Rope*, Sidney Janis Gallery, New York.
Kompass: West Coast USA, Museum am Ostwall, Dortmund; Kunsthalle, Berne.
1 Klischee + AntiKlischee: Bildformen der Gegenwart, Neue Galerie, Aachen.
Body Movements, La Jolla Museum of Contemporary Art, La Jolla.
Conceptual Art and Conceptual Aspects, New York Cultural Center, New York
(in collaboration with Farleigh Dickinson University, Rutherford).
Art in the Mind, Allen Memorial Art Museum, Oberlin College, Oberlin.
N Dimensional Space, Finch College Museum of Art, New York.
American Art since 1960, Art Museum, Princeton University, Princeton.
Tokyo Biennale '70: Between Man and Matter, 10th International Art Exhibition of Japan, Tokyo Metropolitan Art Gallery, Tokyo;
Kyoto Municipal Art Museum, Kyoto; Aichi Prefectural Art Gallery, Nagoya; Fukuoka Prefectural Culture House, Fukuoka.
Conceptual Art, Arte Povera, Land Art, Galleria Civica d'Arte Moderna, Turin.

Air, National Gallery of Victoria, Melbourne; Art Gallery of South Australia, Adelaide; Fort Pavilion, Sydney.

Information, Museum of Modern Art, New York.

Holograms and Lasers, Museum of Contemporary Art, Chicago.

Recorded Activities, Moore College of Art, Philadelphia.

Body Works, Breen's Bar, San Francisco.

Looking West 1970, Joslyn Art Museum, Omaha.

Young Bay Area Sculptors, San Francisco Art Institute Gallery, San Francisco.

Against Order: Chance and Art, Institute of Contemporary Art, University of Pennsylvania, Philadelphia.

3–∞: New Multiple Art, Whitechapel Art Gallery, London.

1970 Annual Exhibition of Contemporary American Sculpture, Whitney Museum of American Art, New York.

1971 *Sixth Guggenheim International Exhibition*, Solomon R. Guggenheim Museum, New York.

Multiples: The First Decade, Philadelphia Museum of Art.

Lucht/Kunst, Stedelijk Museum, Amsterdam.

II. Biennale Nürnberg: Was die Schönheit sei, das weiss ich nicht, Kunsthalle, Nuremberg.

Sonsbeek 71, Park Sonsbeek, Arnhem.

¿Kid Stuff?, Albright-Knox Art Gallery, Buffalo, New York.

Amerikansk kunst 1950-70, Louisiana Museum, Humlebaek.

7ème Biennale de Paris, Parc Floral de Vincennes, Paris.

Group Film Exhibition (Jonas, Morris, Nauman, Serra, Sonnier), Leo Castelli Gallery, New York.

The Artist as Filmmaker, Hansen-Fuller Gallery, San Francisco.

11 Los Angeles Artists, Hayward Gallery, London; Palais des Beaux-Arts, Brussels; Akademie der Künste, Berlin.

Prospect '71–Projection, Städtische Kunsthalle, Düsseldorf.

Neon, Diagramma, Milan.

Stedelijk '60-'70: Verzameling 1960-1970, Palais des Beaux-Arts, Brussels.

Oversize Prints, Whitney Museum of American Art, New York.

1972 *1972: USA West Coast*, Hamburger Kunstverein, Hamburg; Kunstverein Hannover, Hanover; Kölnischer Kunstverein, Cologne; Württembergischer Kunstverein, Stuttgart.

Photographic Portraits, Moore College of Art, Philadelphia.

Films by American Artists, Whitney Museum of American Art, New York.

Dokumenta 5, Museum Friedericianum, Kassel.

420 West Broadway at Spoleto Festival: 33 Artists Shown by Leo Castelli, André Emmerich, Sonnabend, John Weber, XV Festival dei due Mondi, Spoleto.

Diagrams and Drawings, Rijksmuseum Kröller-Müller, Otterlo; Kunstverein, Stuttgart; Kunstmuseum, Basle; Kunstmuseum Düsseldorf, Düsseldorf.

Eighteenth National Print Exhibition, Brooklyn Museum, Brooklyn, New York; California Palace of the Legion of Honor, San Francisco.

1973 *3D into 2D: Drawing for Sculpture*, New York Cultural Center, New York.

Amerikanische und Englische Graphik der Gegenwart, Graphische Sammlung, Staatsgalerie, Stuttgart.

Bilder, Objekte, Filme, Konzepte: Werke aus der Sammlung Herbig, Städtische Galerie im Lenbachhaus, Munich.

American Drawings 1963-1973, Whitney Museum of American Art, New York.

Kunst aus Fotografie, Kunstverein Hannover, Hanover.

Group Exhibition, Leo Castelli Gallery, New York.

American Art: Third Quarter Century, Seattle Art Museum Pavilion, Seattle.

Video Tapes by Gallery Artists, Leo Castelli Gallery, New York.

Contemporanea: Incontri Internazionali d'Arte, Parcheggio di Villa Borghese, Rome.

1974 *Artisti della West Coast*, Galeria Françoise Lambert, Milan.

Idea and Image in Recent Art, Art Institute of Chicago, Chicago.

The Ponderosa Collection, Contemporary Arts Center, Cincinnati.

Painting and Sculpture Today 1974, Indianapolis Museum of Art, Indianapolis;

Contemporary Arts Center and Taft Museum, Cincinnati.

Collectors' Video and Projected Art: Artists at Work, Los Angeles County Museum of Art, Los Angeles.

Art Now 74: A Celebration of American Arts, John F. Kennedy Center for the Performing Arts, Washington D.C.

Kunst bleibt Kunst: Project '74, Aspekte internationaler Kunst am Anfang der 70er Jahre,

Kölnischer Kunstverein and Kunsthalle, Cologne.

In Three Dimensions, Leo Castelli Gallery, New York.

1975 *L'Art corporel*, Galerie Stadler, Paris.

Video Art, Institute of Contemporary Art, University of Pennsylvania, Philadelphia; Contemporary Arts Center, Cincinnati;

Museum of Contemporary Art, Chicago; Wadsworth Atheneum, Hartford.

Body Works, Museum of Contemporary Art, Chicago.

Spiralen und Progressionen, Kunstmuseum, Lucerne.

Menace, Museum of Contemporary Art, Chicago.

Functies van Tekenen/Functions of Drawing, Rijksmuseum Kröller-Müller, Otterlo; Kunstmuseum, Basle.

Three L.A. Sculptors: Lloyd Hamrol, George Herms, Bruce Nauman, Los Angeles Institute of Contemporary Art, Los Angeles.

Sculpture: American Directions 1945-1975, National Collection of Fine Arts, Smithsonian Institution, Washington D.C.;

Dallas Museum of Fine Arts, Dallas; New Orleans Museum of Art, New Orleans.

Collector's Choice: Where I've Been—Where I'm Going, Los Angeles Institute of Contemporary Art, Los Angeles.

University of California, Irvine 1965-1975, La Jolla Museum of Contemporary Art, La Jolla.

Autogeography, Whitney Museum of American Art, New York.

1976 *Drawing Now: 1955-1975*, Museum of Modern Art, New York; Kunsthaus Zürich, Zurich; Staatliche Kunsthalle, Baden-Baden;

Graphische Sammlung, Albertina, Vienna; Sonja Henie-Niels Onstad Foundation, Oslo; Tel Aviv Museum, Tel Aviv.

Holografi: det 3-dimensionella mediet, På Kulturhuset, Stockholm.

Seventy-second American Exhibition, Art Institute of Chicago, Chicago.

200 Years of American Sculpture, Whitney Museum of American Art, New York.

Ideas on Paper 1970-76, Renaissance Society at the University of Chicago, Chicago.

Painting and Sculpture in California: The Modern Era, San Francisco Museum of Modern Art, San Francisco;

National Collection of Fine Arts, Smithsonian Institution, Washington D.C.

1977 *1977 Biennial Exhibition, Contemporary American Art*, Whitney Museum of American Art, New York.

Words: A Look at the Use of Language in Art 1967-1977, Whitney Museum of American Art, New York.

Ideas in Sculpture 1965-1977, Renaissance Society at the University of Chicago, Chicago.

Words at Liberty, Museum of Contemporary Art, Chicago.

Dokumenta 6, Museum Fridericianum, Kassel.

Skulptur-Ausstellung in Münster, Westfälisches Landesmuseum für Kunst und Kulturgeschichte, Munster.

A View of a Decade, Museum of Contemporary Art, Chicago.

1978 *Making Faces: The Artist and the Portrait*, Vancouver Art Gallery, Vancouver.

XXXVIII Venice Biennale, Venice.

20th Century American Drawings: Five Years of Acquisitions, Whitney Museum of American Art, New York.

Door beeldhouwers gemaakt/Made by Sculptors, Stedelijk Museum, Amsterdam.

1979 *The Sense of Self: From Self-Portrait to Autobiography*, Independent Curators, Inc., Washington D.C. and New York.

(Exhibition organised for the New Gallery of Contemporary Art, Cleveland).

Wahrnehmungen, Aufzeichnungen, Mitteilungen: Die Erweiterung des Wirklichkeitsbegriffs in der Kunst der 60er und der 70er Jahre, Museum Haus Lange, Krefeld.

Words, Words, Museum Bochum, Bochum; Palazzo Ducale, Genoa.

Images of the Self, Hampshire College Gallery, Amherst.

Great Big Drawing Show, P.S. 1, Institute for Art and Urban Resources, New York.

Verbiage: An Exhibition of Words, Kettle's Yard, Cambridge University, Cambridge.

Contemporary Sculpture: Selections from the Collection of The Museum of Modern Art, Museum of Modern Art, New York.

73rd American Exhibition, Art Institute of Chicago, Chicago.

New Spaces: The Holographer's Vision, Franklin Institute, Philadelphia.

Space/Time/Sound—1970s: A Decade in the Bay Area, San Francisco Museum of Modern Art, San Francisco.

1980 *142 Greene Street Opening Exhibition*, Leo Castelli Gallery, New York.

The New American Filmmakers Series, Whitney Museum of American Art, New York.

Contemporary Art in Southern California, High Museum of Art, Atlanta.

Pier + Ocean, Hayward Gallery, London; Rijksmuseum Kröller-Müller, Otterlo.

Sculpture in California 1975-80, San Diego Museum of Art, San Diego.

XXXIX Venice Biennale, Venice.

Zeichnungen der 50er bis 70er Jahre aus dem Kaiser Wilhelm Museum, Museum Haus Lange, Krefeld.

Architectural Sculpture, Los Angeles Institute of Contemporary Art, Los Angeles.

Artist and Camera, Arts Council of Great Britain; Mappin Art Gallery, Sheffield; City Museum and Art Gallery, Stoke on Trent; Durham Light Infantry Museum and Arts Centre, Durham; City Art Gallery and Museum, Cartwright Hall, Bradford.

Minimal + Conceptual Art aus der Sammlung Panza, Museum für Gegenwartskunst, Basle.

1981 *Kounellis, Merz, Nauman, Serra: Arbeiten um 1968*, Museum Haus Lange, Krefeld.

New Dimensions in Drawing 1950-1980, Aldrich Museum of Contemporary Art, Ridgefield.

Westkunst: Zeitgenössische Kunst seit 1939, Museen der Stadt Köln, Cologne.

Art in Los Angeles: Seventeen Artists in the Sixties, Los Angeles County Museum of Art, Los Angeles.

Neon Fronts: Luminous Art for the Urban Landscape, Washington Project for the Arts, Washington D.C.

Drawing Distinctions: American Drawings of the Seventies, Louisiana Museum, Humlebaek; Kunsthalle, Basle; Städtische Galerie im Lenbachhaus, Munich; Wilhelm Hack Museum, Ludwigshafen.

Variants: Drawings by Contemporary Sculptors, Sewall Art Gallery, Rice University, Houston.

1982 *A Century of Modern Drawing from the Museum of Modern Art, New York*, Museum of Modern Art, New York; British Museum, London; Cleveland Museum of Art, Cleveland; Museum of Fine Arts, Boston.

Arte povera, antiform : sculptures 1966-1969, Capc, Bordeaux.

'60-'80: Attitudes/Concepts/Images, Stedelijk Museum, Amsterdam.

Castelli and His Artists/Twenty-five Years, Aspen Center for the Visual Arts, Aspen; La Jolla Museum of Contemporary Art, La Jolla; Leo Castelli Gallery, New York; Portland Center for the Visual Arts, Portland; Laguna Gloria Art Museum, Austin.

Documenta 7, Museum Fridericianum, Kassel.

Werke aus der Sammlung Crex, Kunsthalle, Basle.

20 American Artists: Sculpture 1982, San Francisco Museum of Modern Art, San Francisco.

Postminimalism, Aldrich Museum of Contemporary Art, Ridgefield.

Sculptors at UC Davis: Past and Present, University of California, Davis.

American Sculpture from the Permanent Collection, Solomon R. Guggenheim Museum, New York.

1983 *Neue Zeichnungen aus dem Kunstmuseum Basel*, Kunstmuseum, Basle; Kunsthalle Tübingen; Neue Galerie, Kassel.

Objects, Structures, Artifice: American Sculpture 1970-1983, SVC Fine Arts Gallery, University of South Florida, Tampa; Center Gallery, Bucknell University, Lewisburg.

De Statua, Stedelijk Van Abbe Museum, Eindhoven.

Video as Attitude, Museum of Fine Arts, Museum of New Mexico, Santa Fe.

American/European Painting and Sculpture (Part I), L.A. Louver, Venice.

1984 *Works on Paper: Graduate Students from UC Davis, 1965-1982*, Memorial Union Gallery, University of California, Davis.

Bruce Nauman/Dennis Oppenheim: Drawings and Models for Albuquerque Commissions, University Art Museum, University of New Mexico, Albuquerque.

20 Jaar Verzameln, Stedelijk Museum, Amsterdam.

A Focus on California: Selections from the Collection, Los Angeles County Museum of Art, Los Angeles.

Content: A Contemporary Focus 1974-1984, Hirshhorn Museum and Sculpture Garden, Smithsonian Institution, Washington D.C.

Gemini G.E.L.: Art and Collaboration, National Gallery of Art, Washington D.C.

L'Architecte est absent: Works from the Collection of Annick and Anton Herbert, Stedelijk Van Abbe Museum, Eindhoven.

Ouverture: Arte Contemporanea, Castello di Rivoli, Turin.

Quartetto: Joseph Beuys, Enzo Cucchi, Luciano Fabro, Bruce Nauman, L'Accademia Foundation, Venice.

1985 *Large Scale Drawings by Sculptors*, Renaissance Society at the University of Chicago, Chicago.

1985 Biennial Exhibition, Whitney Museum of American Art, New York.

The Maximal Implications of the Minimal Line, Edith C. Blum Art Institute, Bard College, Annandale-on-Hudson.

First Exhibition-Dialogue on Contemporary Art in Europe/Primeira Exposição-Diálogo sobre a Arte Contemporânea na Europa, Centro de Arte Moderna Fundação Calouste Gulbenkian, Lisbon.

Die Spirale im menschlichen Leben und in der Natur: eine interdiziplinäre Schau, Museum für Gestaltung, Gewerbemuseum Basel, Basle.

New Work on Paper 3: Robert Morris, Bruce Nauman, James Rosenquist, Robert Ryman, Pat Steir, Robert Wilson, Museum of Modern Art, New York.

Affiliations: Recent Sculpture and Its Antecedents, Whitney Museum of American Art at Champion, Stamford.

Dreissig Jahre durch die Kunst: Museum Haus Lange, 1955-1985, Museum Haus Lange and Museum House Esters, Krefeld.

Ars Medica: Art, Medicine and the Human Condition, Philadelphia Museum of Art, Philadelphia.

Doch Doch, Arensberg Institute, Louvain.

Räume heutiger Zeichnung: Werke aus dem Basler Kupferstichkabinett, Kunstmuseum, Basle; Staatliche Kunsthalle, Baden-Baden; Tel Aviv Museum, Tel Aviv.

1985 Carnegie International, Museum of Art, Carnegie Institute, Pittsburgh.

American Eccentric Abstraction, BlumHelman Gallery, New York.

Vom Zeichnen: Aspekte der Zeichnung 1960-1985, Frankfurter Kunstverein, Frankfurt; Kunstverein, Kassel; Museum moderner Kunst, Vienna.

Transformations in Sculpture: Four Decades of American and European Art, Solomon R. Guggenheim Museum, New York.

Amerikanische Zeichnungen 1930-1980, Städtische Galerie, Städelsche Kunstinstitut, Frankfurt.

An American Renaissance: Painting and Sculpture since 1940, Museum of Art, Fort Lauderdale.

1986 *The Real Big Picture*, Queens Museum, Flushing, New York.

Recent Acquisitions: Richard Artschwager, Eric Fischl, Donald Judd, Bruce Nauman, Martin Puryear, David Salle, Frank Stella, Andy Warhol, Donald Young Gallery, Chicago.

Drawings by Sculptors, Nohra Haime Gallery, New York.

Art from Two Continents, Helander Gallery, Palm Beach.

Personal Environments, Museum of Fine Arts, Museum of New Mexico, Santa Fe.

Works on Paper: Richard Artschwager, Sol LeWitt, Robert Mangold, Bruce Nauman, Donald Young Gallery, Chicago.

Sculpture and Drawings by Sculptors, L.A. Louver, Venice.

Maelstrom: Contemporary Images of Violence, Emily Lowe Gallery, Hofstra University, Hempstead.

Entre la Geometria y el Gesto: Escultura Norteamericana 1965-1975/Between Geometry and Gesture: American Sculpture 1965-1975, Palacio de Velasquez, Madrid.

Sonsbeek '86: International Sculpture, Sonsbeek Foundation, Arnhem.

Chambres d'Amis, Museum van Hedendaagse Kunst, Ghent.

Videowochen im Wenkenpark, Wenkenpark, Basle.

Franz Gertsch und Bruce Nauman, Kunsthalle, Basle.

Lumières : Perception-Projection, Centre International d'Art Contemporain de Montréal, Montreal.

Monumental Drawing: Works by 22 Contemporary Americans, Brooklyn Museum, Brooklyn, New York.

Die Wahlverwandtschaften–Zitate–, (part of "Stierischer Herbst" festival) Grazer Kunstverein and Stadtmuseum Graz, Graz.
Love, Glory and Guns, Allen Memorial Art Museum, Oberlin College, Oberlin.
Lost/Found Language: The Use of Language as Visual or Conceptual Component, Deriving Directly or Indirectly from Popular Culture, Lawrence Gallery, Rosemont College, Rosemont.
The Spiritual in Art: Abstract Painting 1890-1985, Los Angeles County Museum of Art, Los Angeles; Museum of Contemporary Art, Chicago; Haags Gemeentemuseum, The Hague.
Los Angeles 1960-1970, Burnett Miller Gallery, Los Angeles.
Leo Castelli at Gagosian, Larry Gagosian Gallery, Los Angeles.
Lightworks: Works of the Art Using Light as a Medium, University Drill Hall Gallery, Canberra.
Individuals: A Selected History of Contemporary Art 1945-1986, Museum of Contemporary Art at the Temporary Contemporary, Los Angeles.

1987 *About Sculpture*, Anthony d'Offay Gallery, London.
1967: At the Crossroads, Institute of Contemporary Art, University of Pennsylvania, Philadelphia.
Exposition collective : Andre, Flavin, Judd, LeWitt, Nauman, Serra, Galerie Daniel Templon, Paris.
Merce Cunningham and His Collaborators, Lehman College Art Gallery, Bronx, New York.
Corps étrangers, Galerie Yvon Lambert, Paris.
1987 Biennial Exhibition, Whitney Museum of American Art, New York.
Avant-Garde in the Eighties, Los Angeles County Museum of Art, Los Angeles.
L'époque, la mode, la morale, la passion : Aspects de l'art d'aujourd'hui, 1977-1987, Mnam-Cci, Centre Georges Pompidou, Paris.
Photography and Art: Interaction since 1946, Los Angeles County Museum of Art; Museum of Art, Fort Lauderdale; Queens Museum, Flushing, New York; Des Moines Art Center, Des Moines.
Skulptur Projekte in Münster 1987, Westfälisches Landesmuseum für Kunst und Kulturgeschichte, Münster.
Big Drawings, Center for Contemporary Art of Santa Fé, Santa Fe.
Leo Castelli y sus Artistas. XXX Años de Promocion del Arte Contemporaneo, Centro Cultural Arte Contemparaneo, Mexico.
1987 Phoenix Biennial, Phoenix Art Museum, Phoenix.
Neon-Kunst: Bruce Nauman, Richard Serra, Keith Sonnier, Städtisches Museum Abteiberg, Mönchengladbach.
Fifty Years of Collecting: An Anniversary Selection–Sculpture of the Modern Era, Solomon R. Guggenheim Museum, New York.

1988 *Übrigens sterben immer die Anderen: Marcel Duchamp und die Avantgarde seit 1950*, Museum Ludwig, Cologne.
Arte minimal de la Collecíon Panza, Museo Nacional Centro de Arte Reina Sofia, Madrid.
1988: The World of Art Today, Milwaukee Art Museum, Milwaukee.
Zeitlos: Kunst von Heute, Hamburger Bahnhof, Berlin.
Modes of Address: Language in Art since 1960, Whitney Museum of American Art, Downtown at Federal Reserve Plaza, New York.
Carnegie International, Carnegie Museum of Art, Pittsburgh.
Nobody's Fools, De Appel Foundation, Amsterdam.
Identity: Representations of the Self, Whitney Museum of American Art, Downtown at Federal Reserve Plaza, New York.
Three Decades: The Oliver-Hoffman Collection, Museum of Contemporary Art, Chicago.

1989 *Modern Masterworks from the Permanent Collection*, Museum of Fine Arts, Museum of New Mexico, Santa Fe.
Video-Skulptur: retrospektiv und aktuell, 1963-1989, Kölnischer Kunstverein, Kunstation St. Peter and DuMont Kunsthalle, Cologne; Kongresshalle, Berlin; Kunsthaus Zürich, Zurich.
4e Semaine Internationale de Vidéo, Saint-Gervais, Geneva.
Bruce Nauman, Robert Mangold, Saatchi Collection, London.
Open Mind (Gesloten circuits/Closed Circuits), Museum van Hedendaagse Kunst, Ghent.
Wiener Diwan: Sigmund Freud heute, Museum des 20. Jahrhunderts, Vienna.
First Impressions: Early Prints by Forty-six Contemporary Artists, Walker Art Center, Minneapolis; Laguna Gloria Art Museum, Austin; Baltimore Museum of Art, Baltimore; Neuberger Museum, State University of New York, Purchase.
Collection Panza : Richard Long, Bruce Nauman, Musée d'Art Moderne, Saint-Étienne.
Hardware, Museum Boymans-van Beuningen, Rotterdam.

Image World: Art and Media Culture, Whitney Museum of American Art, New York.

Einleuchten, Will, Vorstel & Simul in HH, Deichtorhallen, Hamburg.

L'Art conceptuel : une perspective, Musée d'Art Moderne de la Ville de Paris; Fundación Caixa de Pensions, Madrid; Deichtorhallen, Hamburg; Musée d'Art Contemporain, Montreal.

Bruce Nauman–Robert Gober, Galerie Micheline Szwajcer, Antwerp.

1990 *Time Span: Jenny Holzer, On Kawara, Bruce Nauman, Lawrence Weiner*,
Sala d'Exposicions of the Fundación Caixa de Pensions, Barcelona.

Fragments, Parts, and Wholes: The Body and Culture, White Columns, New York.

The New Sculpture 1965-75: Between Geometry and Gesture, Whitney Museum of American Art, New York;
Museum of Contemporary Art at the Temporary Contemporary, Los Angeles.

Energieen, Stedelijk Museum, Amsterdam.

The Readymade Boomerang: Certain Relations in 20th Century Art: The Eighth Biennale of Sydney,
Art Gallery of New South Wales, Sydney.

Affinities and Intuitions: The Gerald S. Elliott Collection of Contemporary Art, Art Institute of Chicago.

Word as Image: American Art 1960-1990, Milwaukee Art Museum, Milwaukee; Oklahoma City Art Museum, Oklahoma;
Contemporary Arts Museum, Houston.

Un choix d'art minimal dans la collection Panza, Musée d'Art Moderne de la Ville de Paris, Paris.

Figuring the Body, Museum of Fine Arts, Boston.

Life-Size: A Sense of the Real in Recent Art, Israel Museum, Jerusalem.

NEONstücke, Sprengel Museum Hannover, Hanover.

Work in Progress: Arte Internacional en la Colección de la Fundación Caixa de Pensions,
Sala de exposiciones Fundación Caixa de Pensions, Madrid.

1991 *1991 Biennial Exhibition*, Whitney Museum of American Art, New York.

Metropolis–International Art Exhibition Berlin 1991, Martin-Gropius-Bau, Berlin.

Singular Visions: Contemporary Sculpture in New Mexico, Museum of Fine Arts, Museum of New Mexico, Santa Fe.

Nachtregels/Nightlines, Centraal Museum, Utrecht.

Eröffnungsausstellung, Museum für Moderne Kunst, Frankfurt.

Motion and Document–Sequence and Time: Eadweard Muybridge and Contemporary American Photography, Addison Gallery
of American Art, Phillips Academy, Andover; National Museum of American Art, Smithsonian Institution, Washington D.C.;
Long Beach Museum of Art, Long Beach; Henry Art Gallery, University of Washington, Seattle; Wadsworth Atheneum, Hartford;
International Museum of Photography at George Eastman House and Visual Studies Workshop, Rochester.

Beyond the Frame: American Art 1960-1990, Setagaya Art Museum, Tokyo; National Museum of Art, Osaka;
Fukuoka Art Museum, Fukuoka.

Power: Its Myths and Mores in American Art, 1961-1991, Indianapolis Museum of Art, Indianapolis;
Akron Art Museum, Akron; Virginia Museum of Fine Arts, Richmond.

The Interrupted Life, New Museum of Contemporary Art, New York.

Immaterial Objects, Whitney Museum of American Art, Downtown at Federal Reserve Plaza, New York;
Whitney Museum at Champion, Stamford.

Emanuel Hoffmann-Stiftung Basel 1980-1991, Museum für Gegenwartskunst, Basle; Deichtorhallen, Hamburg.

DISLOCATIONS, Museum of Modern Art, New York.

Carnegie International 1991, Carnegie Museum of Art, Pittsburgh.

Paysage intérieur, Rijksmuseum Kröller-Müller, Otterlo.

1992 *Yvon Lambert collectionne*, Musée d'Art Moderne, Villeneuve d'Ascq.

Les extrêmes se touchent : La collection d'art moderne du musée Boymans-van Beuningen Rotterdam, Institut Néerlandais, Paris.

Minima(a)l, Museum van Hedendaagse Kunst, Ghent.

Allegories of Modernism: Contemporary Drawing, Museum of Modern Art, New York.

Marking the Decades: Prints 1960-1990, Baltimore Museum of Art, Baltimore.

Psycho, KunstHall, New York.

Habeas Corpus, Stux Gallery, New York.

Words, Galerie Kukje, Seoul.

Los 80 en la Colección de la Fundación 'la Caixa', Estación Plaza de Armas, Seville.

Bourgeois, Jaar, Kounellis, Solano, Tapies, Nauman, Lelong Gallery, New York.

Nauman, Oppenheim, Serra: Early Works 1968-1971, BlumHelman Warehouse, New York.

Passions and Cultures: Selected Works from the Rivendell Collection, 1967-1991,
Center for Curatorial Studies and Art in Contemporary Culture, Bard College, Annandale-on-Hudson.

Group Sculpture Show, Sperone Westwater Gallery, New York.

15th Anniversary Exhibition, Rhona Hoffman Gallery, Chicago.

Gifts and Acquisitions in Context, Whitney Museum of American Art, New York.

Summer Group Exhibition (Part 1), Leo Castelli Gallery, New York.

Szenenwechsel II, Museum für Moderne Kunst, Frankfurt.

Documenta 9, Museum Fridericianum, Kassel.

Transform: BildObjektSkulptur im 20. Jahrhundert, Kunstmuseum and Kunsthalle, Basle.

Territorium Artis, Kunst- und Ausstellungshalle der Bundesrepublik Deutschland, Bonn.

Schwerpunkt Skulptur, Kaiser Wilhelm Museum, Krefeld.

Re: Framing Cartoons, Wexner Center for the Arts, Ohio State University, Columbus.

Moving Image: Images in Movement: Electronic Art, Zentrum für Kunst und Medientechnologie,
Karlsruhe and Fundación Joan Miró, Barcelona.

Cross Section, World Financial Center, New York.

Tropismes: Colección d'Art Contemporani Fundación 'la Caixa', Centre Cultural Tecla Sala, L'Hospitalet de Llobregat.

Arte–Vanguardia–Empresa, Palacete Embarcadero, Santander.

Summer Group Exhibition (Part II), Leo Castelli Gallery, New York.

*In Through the Out Door: Vito Acconci, Rachel Berwick, Bruce Nauman, Roman Signer, Thom Merrick, Jeffery Wisniewski,
and a Special Project by Sam Samore*, Nordansstad-Skarstedt, New York.

Word and Image, Brooke Alexander Editions, New York.

Both Art and Life: Gemini at 25, Newport Harbor Art Museum, Newport Beach.

Nauman, Serra, Sonnier, Leo Castelli Gallery, New York.

What is Political Anyway?, Borås Konstmuseum, Borås.

Art of New Mexico: 75th Anniversary Exhibition, Museum of Fine Arts, Museum of New Mexico, Santa Fe.

Paysage intérieur, Rijksmuseum Kröller-Müller, Otterlo.

Photography: Expanding the Collection, Whitney Museum of American Art, New York.

Aanwinsten/Acquisitions: 1985-1993, Stedelijk Museum, Amsterdam.

1993 *Gravity and Grace: The Changing Condition of Sculpture 1965-1975*, Hayward Gallery, London.

Un'avventura internazionale: Torino e le arti 1950-1970, Castello di Rivoli, Museo d'Arte Contemporanea, Turin.

På kanten af kaos–nye billeder af werden, Louisiana Museum, Humlebaek.

Amerikanische Kunst im 20. Jahrhundert/American Art in the 20th Century, Martin-Gropius-Bau, Berlin;
Royal Academy of Arts, London.

La Biennale d'art contemporain, Lyons.

Pour la Vie–Gilbert and George, Jeff Koons, Bruce Nauman, Capc, Bordeaux.

Sculpture, Laura Carpenter Fine Arts, Santa Fe.

1994 *Arte Contemporanea della Collezione della Federazione Cooperative Migros*, Museo Cantonale d'Arte, Lugano.
Multiples Dimensions, Centro Cultural de Belem, Lisbon.
Starlight: James Turrell, Maurizio Nannucci, Bruce Nauman, Aarhus Kunstmuseum, Aarhus.
Uma Seleco por Leo Castelli dos Seus Artistas, Renato Magalhars Gouvea, São Paulo.
Self/Made Self/Conscious—Janine Antoni & Bruce Nauman, Museum of Fine Arts, Boston.
The Essential Gesture, The Newport Harbor Art Museum, Newport Beach.

1995 *Facts and Figures—Selections from the Lannan Foundation Collection*, Lannan Foundation, Los Angeles.
Hors Limites, L'Art et la Vie, 1952-1994, Mnam-Cci, Centre Georges Pompidou, Paris.
Light Into Art: From Video to Virtual Reality, Contemporary Arts Center, Cincinnati.
From Acconci to Ryman: American Drawings from the 1970s & 1980s, Kunsthaus Zürich, Zurich.
Figur Natur, Sprengel Museum, Hanover.
Outside The Frame: Performance And The Object, Newhouse Center for Contemporary Art/
Snug Harbor Cultural Center, Staten Island.
Attitudes/Sculptures, Works from 1963 to 1972, Capc, Bordeaux.
SITE Santa Fe, Longing and Belonging: From the Faraway Nearby, Museum of Fine Arts, Santa Fe.
Temporarily Possessed, the Semi-Permanent Collection, The New Museum of Contemporary Art, New York.
1965-1975: Reconsidering the Object of Art, Museum of Contemporary Art at the Temporary Contemporary, Los Angeles.
Soyons Sérieux..., Points de vue sur l'art des années 80-90, Musée d'art moderne, Villeneuve d'Ascq.

1996 *Narcissism, Artists Reflect Themselves*, California Center for the Arts Museum, Escondito.
Reconsidering the Object of Art, Museum of Contemporary Art, Los Angeles.
La Biennale d'art contemporain, Lyons.
Everything that's Interesting is New, The Dakis Joannou Collection, Athens School of Fine Arts "the factory", Athens;
Museum of Modern Art, Copenhagen ; Guggenheim Museum Soho, New York.
L'Informe, mode d'emploi, Mnam-Cci, Centre Georges Pompidou, Paris.
De Beuys à Trockel: Dessins contemporains du Kunstmuseum de Bâle, Mnam-Cci, Centre Georges Pompidou, Paris.
The Froehlich Foundation: German and American Art from Beuys and Warhol, Tate Gallery, London.
L'Art au corps. Le corps exposé de Man Ray à nos jours, M.A.C., Musées de Marseille, Marseilles.

1997 *1997 Biennial Exhibition*, Whitney Museum of American Art, New York.
The Age of Modernism: Art in the 20th Century, Martin-Gropius-Bau, Berlin.
The Hirshhorn Collects: Recent Acquisitions 1992-1996, Hirshhorn Museum and Sculpture Garden, Washington D.C.
4e Biennale de Lyon d'art contemporain, Halle Tony Garnier, Lyons.
Views from Abroad: European Perspectives on American Art 3. American Realities, Whitney Museum of American Art, New York.
Scene of the Crime, UCLA at the Armand Hammer Museum of Art and Cultural Center, Los Angeles.
97 Kwangju Biennale: Unmapping the Earth, Kwangju, Korea.

1997-1998 *Art at Work*, Des Moines Art Center, Iowa.
Sunshine & Noir: Art in L.A., 1960-1997, Louisiana Museum of Modern Art, Humlebaek; Kunstmuseum Wolfsburg, Wolfsburg.
Artists Projects, P. S. 1 Contemporary Art Center, New York.

1998 *Wounds: Between Democracy and Redemption in Contemporary Art*, Moderna Museet, Stockholm.

ARTIST'S BOOKS

Pictures of Sculpture in a Room, edited by the artist, San Francisco, 1965-1966.
Clear Sky, New York, Leo Castelli Gallery, New York, 1967-1968.
Burning Small Fires, editor unknown, San Francisco, 1968.

ARTIST'S WRITINGS

'Bruce Nauman: Notes and Projects', *Artforum*, 9, n°4, New York, Dec. 1970, p. 44.
LAAir, New York, Multiples Inc., 1970.
'Body Works', *Interfunktionen*, n°6, Cologne, Sept. 1971, p. 2-8.
Bruce Nauman: Left or Standing, Standing or Left Standing, Leo Castelli Gallery, New York, 1971.
Bruce Nauman: Floating Room, Leo Castelli Gallery, New York, 1973.
Flayed Earth/Flayed Self (Skin/Sink), Nicholas Wilder Gallery, Los Angeles, 1974.
'Instruction for a Mental Exercise', *Interfunktionen*, n°11, Cologne, 1974, p. 122-124.
Bruce Nauman: Cones/Cojones, Leo Castelli Gallery, New York, 1975.
'False Silences', *Vision*, n°1, Angers, Sept. 1975, p. 44-45.
The Consummate Mask of Rock, Albright-Knox Art Gallery, Buffalo, 1975.
'Violent Incident, 1986', *Parkett*, n°10, Zurich, Sept. 1986, p. 50-53.

INTERVIEWS AND MONOGRAPHS

BRUGGEN (Coosje van), *Bruce Nauman*, Rizzoli, New York, 1988.
BUTTERFIELD (Jan), 'Bruce Nauman: The Center of Yourself', *Arts Magazine*, 49, n°6, New York, Feb. 1975, p. 53-55.
DE ANGELUS (Michele), 'Bruce Nauman Interviews, 1980 May 27-30', *Archives of American Art*, Smithsonian Institution, Washington D.C., 1980.
DERCON (Chris), 'Keep Taking It Apart: A Conversation with Bruce Nauman', *Parkett*, n°10, Zurich, Sept. 1986, p. 54-69.
HOFFMANN (Christine), *Bruce Nauman. Interviews 1966-1988*, German edition, Verlag der Kunst, Amsterdam, 1996.
OURSLER (Tony), 'Ways of Seeing. The Warped Vision of Bruce Nauman', *Paper Magazine*, vol. II, n°10, New York, April 1995, p. 104.
RAFFAELE (Joe) et BAKER (Elizabeth), 'The Way-Out West: Interviews with 4 San Francisco Artists', *Art News*, 66, n°4, New York, summer 1967, p. 38-41, 75-76.
SCIARRA (Lorraine), Unpublished interview, Pomona College, Claremont, 1972.
SHARP (Willoughby), 'Nauman Interview', *Arts Magazine*, 44, n°5, New York, March 1970, p. 22-27.
SHARP (Willoughby), 'Bruce Nauman', *Avalanche*, n°2, New York, winter 1971, p. 22-31.
SIMON (Joan), 'Breaking the Silence: An Interview with Bruce Nauman', *Art in America*, 76, n°9, Sept., New York, 1988, p. 140-149, 203.
SMITH (Bob), 'Bruce Nauman Interview', *Journal* 4, n°2, Institute of Contemporary Art, Los Angeles, spring 1982, p. 35-38.
WALLACE (Ian) et KEZIERE (Russell), 'Bruce Nauman Interviewed', *Vanguard*, n°1, Vancouver, Feb. 1979, p. 15-18.

ARTICLES AND REVIEWS

ADAMS (Brooks), 'The Nauman Phenomenon', *Art and Auction* 13, n°5, Rotterdam, Dec. 1990, p. 118-125.

ALBRIGHT (Thomas), 'Kooky Group "Repair" Show', *San Francisco Chronicle*, San Francisco, 19.03.1969.

'Albright-Knox Buys Area Artists' Work', Buffalo Evening News, Buffalo, 5.03.1976, p. 37.

ANFAM (David), 'Evaluating a Radical Decade', *Art International*, n°12, Lugano, autumn 1990, p. 94-95.

ANTIN (David), 'Another Category: 'Eccentric Abstraction'', *Artforum*, 5, n°3, New York, Nov. 1966, p. 56-57.

ARCHER (Michael) and ALLTHORPE-GUYTON (Marjorie), 'Whitney Move', *Artscribe International*, n°81, London, May 1990.

ARGHIR (Anca), 'Bruce Nauman: Museum Haus Esters, Krefeld', *Das Kunstwerk*, 37, n°1, Stuttgart, Feb. 1984, p. 40-41.

ARMSTRONG (Richard), 'The Avant-Garde: Subtle, Cerebral, Elusive', *Time 92*, n°21, Nov. 1968, p. 70-77.

ARMSTRONG (Richard), 'John Duff, Robert Mangold, Bruce Nauman', *Artforum*, 22, n°1, New York, Sept. 1983, p. 68-69.

ARTNER (Alan G.), 'A Few Vital Questions Dim MCA's View of Its Decade', *Chicago Tribune*, Chicago, 25.09.1977, p. 6.

ARTNER (Alan G.), 'Lively Force is Entrenched in Nauman's Latest Works', *Chicago Tribune*, Chicago, 19.06.1981, p. 12-13.

AUPING (Michael), 'Bruce Nauman's Yellow Triangular Room', *Artweek*, 6, n°9, San Jose, 1.03.1975, p. 5-6.

AUTY (Giles), 'Strange Desires', *Spectator* 262, n°8390, 29.04.1989, p. 39.

AVGIKOS (Jan), 'The New Sculpture 1965-1975: Did It Live up to Its Own Expectations?', *Flash Art*, n°153, Milan, summer 1990, p. 138-139.

BAKER (Elizabeth C.), 'Los Angeles 1971', *Art News*, 70, n°5, New York, Sept. 1971, p. 27-39.

BAKER (Kenneth), 'Bruce Nauman: Castelli Gallery', *Artforum*, 9, n°8, New York, April 1971, p. 77-78.

BAKER (Kenneth), 'Bruce Nauman at Castelli, Sonnabend and Sperone Westwater Fischer', *Art in America*, 65, n°2, New York, March-April 1977, p. 111-112.

BAKER (Kenneth), 'The Saatchi Museum Opens', *Art in America*, 73, n°7, New York, July 1985, p. 23-24.

BAKER (Kenneth), 'Nostalgia for the Postminimal', *San Francisco Chronicle*, San Francisco, 29.04.1990, p.14.

BARNITZ (Jacqueline), 'In the Galleries: Bruce Nauman', *Arts Magazine*, 42, n°5, New York, March 1968, p. 62.

BARRIE (Lita), 'Head Trip: Bruce Nauman at Daniel Weinberg Gallery', *Artweek*, 22, n°6, San Jose, 14.02.1991, p. 1, 20.

BARTER (Ruth), 'Bruce Nauman', *Arts Magazine*, 66, n°6, New York, Feb.1992, p. 93.

BEATTY (Frances), 'Nauman's Art Downtown', *Art World*, 1, n°3, New York, 20.11.1976, p. 9.

BECK (Martin), '... the way he makes you home', *Texte zur Kunst*, 18, Cologne, 1995, p. 156-164.

BELL (Jane), 'Bruce Nauman: Leo Castelli; Sperone Westwater Fischer', *Art News*, 81, n°5, New York, May 1982, p. 168-170.

BENEZRA (Neal), 'Bruce Nauman: Raw Material', *Art Press*, n°184, Paris, October 1993, p. 10-20.

BIRD (Kay), '"Amazing": $100,000 Award from Foundation Impresses Recipient Sculptor', *New Mexican*, Santa Fe, 27.01.1993.

BISCHOFF (Ulrich), 'Halle 6: Objekt Skulptur Installation (Kampfnagelfabrik, Hamburg)', *Pantheon*, 40, n°3, Munich, July-Sept. 1982, p. 239.

BISMARCK (Beatrice von), 'Ein Appell an die Eigenverantwortlichkeit', *Noema*, n°37, Salzburg, Sept.-Oct. 1991, p. 50-53.

BLOEM (Marja), 'La Photographie : Lieu d'une expérience artistique nouvelle', *Art Actuel* in *Skira Annuel*, n°2, Lausanne, 1976, p. 147-149.

BODET (Aude), 'Néon : De l'électricité dans l'art', *Beaux-Arts Magazine*, n°8, Paris, Dec. 1983, p. 52-57.

BONAMI (Francesco), 'Dislocations: The Place of Installation', *Flash Art*, n°162, Milan, Jan.-Feb. 1992, p. 128.

BOS (Saskia), 'Nobody's Fools', *De Appel Bulletin*, n°1, Amsterdam, 1989, p. 7-17.

BOURDON (David), 'Bruce Nauman at Leo Castelli and Sperone Westwater', *Art in America*, 85, n°2, Feb. 1997, p. 95.

BOWMAN (Russell), 'Words and Images: A Persistent Paradox', *Art Journal*, 45, n°4, New York, winter 1985, p. 335-343.

BRADLEY (Kim), 'Bruce Nauman: The Private and the Public', *Artspace* 11, n°3, summer 1987, p. 62-64.

BRÜDERLIN (Markus), 'Vienna: Climbing in the Dark: Bruce Nauman', *Artscribe International*, n°89, London, Nov.-Dec. 1991, p. 94.

BRUGALLA (Laura) and MASSABE (Olga), 'Bruce Nauman: Cronología', *Creacion*, Madrid, 15 May 1992, p. 107-113.

BRUGGEN (Coosje van), 'Context: Light and Space as Art', *Journal: A Contemporary Art Magazine*, 4, n°2, Los Angeles, spring 1982, p. 57-61.

BRUGGEN (Coosje van), 'Bruce Nauman: Entrance, Entrapment, Exit', *Artforum*, 24, n°10, New York, summer 1986, p. 88-97.

BURTON (Scott), 'Time on Their Hands', *Art News*, 68, n°4, New York, summer 1969, p. 40-43.

BUTTERFIELD (Jan), 'Context: Light and Space', *Journal*, 4, n°2, Los Angeles, spring 1982, p. 57-61.

CALAS (Nicolas), 'Bodyworks and Porpoises', *Artforum*, 16, n°5, New York, Jan. 1978, p. 33-37.

CALDWELL (John), 'Creating Taste: The Carnegie International as a Case in Point', *Dialogue*, 9, n°2, Los Angeles, March-April 1986, p. 14-16.

CAMERINI (Silvia), 'Los Angeles: Bruce Nauman al MOCA', *Vogue*, n°455, Milan, Feb. 1988, p. 254.

CAMERON (Dan), 'A Whitney Wonderland', *Arts Magazine*, 59, n°10, New York, summer 1985, p. 66-69.

CAMERON (Dan), 'Opening Salvos, Part One', *Arts Magazine*, 62, n°4, New York, Dec. 1987, p. 89-93.

CAMERON (Dan), 'Anxieties of Influence: Regionalism, Arte Povera, and the Cold War', *Flash Art*, n°164, Milan, May-June 1992, p. 75-81.

CAMERON (Eric), 'On Painting and Video (Upside Down)', *Parachute*, n°11, Montreal, summer 1978, p. 14-17.

CARLUCCIO (Luigi), 'Nelle Scuderie a Varese: Un Tempo per l'Arte Americana d'Oggi', *BolaffiArte*, 3, n°17, Turin, Feb. 1972, p. 42-45.

CATOIR (Barbara), 'Über den Subjektivismus bei Bruce Nauman', *Das Kunstwerk*, 26, n°6, Stuttgart, Nov. 1973, p. 3-12.

CAVALIERE (Barbara), 'Bruce Nauman', *Arts Magazine*, 56, n°7, New York, March 1982, p. 26.

CELANT (Germano), 'Bruce Nauman', *Casabella*, 345, n°34, Milan, Feb. 1970, p. 38-41.

CHADWICK (Susan), 'Being There', *Houston Post*, Houston, 14.05.1989, p. 14.

CHADWICK (Susan), 'The Riddle of Our Existence and Animal Shapes', *Houston Post*, Houston, 25.05.1989, p. 4.

CHRISTOV-BAKARGIEV (Carolyn), 'Arte Povera 1967-1987', *Flash Art*, n°137, Milan, Nov.-Dec. 1987, p. 52-69.

CLOTHIER (Peter), 'Jay Chiat: Order and Mystery', *Art News*, 89, n°5, New York, May 1990, p. 113-116.

COHRS (Timothy), 'Bruce Nauman: Drawings', *Art News*, 86, n°9, New York, Nov. 1987, p. 200.

COOKE (Lynne), 'Minimalism Reviewed', *Burlington Magazine*, 131, n°1038, London, Sept. 1989, p. 641-645.

CORA (Bruno), 'Aquel vino tinto de Bruce Nauman como misterio contemporáneo', *Creacion*, Madrid, 5 May 1992, p. 102-106.

CORNWELL (Regina), 'A Question of Public Interest', *Contemporanea*, 3, n°2, New York, Feb. 1990, p. 38-45.

COTTER (Holland), 'Dislocating the Modern', *Art in America*, 80, n°1, New York, Jan. 1992, p. 100-107.

CRIQUI (Jean-Pierre), 'Pour un Nauman', *Les Cahiers du Musée national d'art moderne*, n°62, winter 1997, p. 5-25 and cover.

CRIQUI (Jean-Pierre), 'Bruce Nauman: Kunstmuseum Wolfsburg', *Artforum*, 36, n°3, Nov. 1997, p. 122-123.

CROWTHER (Hal), 'Nauman Juxtaposes Concepts, Media and Fuses New Meaning', *Buffalo Evening News*, Buffalo, 24.09.1975.

CUEFF (Alain), 'Le cirque expérimental de Bruce Nauman', *Beaux-Arts Magazine*, n°91, Paris, June 1991, p. 53-56.

DA VINCI (Mona), 'Bruce Nauman: Sperone Westwater Fischer; Castelli; Sonnabend', *Art News*, 76, n°3, New York, March 1977, p. 142-144.

DANIELI (Fidel A.), 'The Art of Bruce Nauman', *Artforum*, 6, n°4, New York, Dec. 1967, p. 15-19.

'Dans le courant de l'art conceptuel', *Art Actuel* in *Skira Annuel*, n°1, Lausanne, 1975, p. 38-59.

DANTO (C. Arthur), 'Bruce Nauman', *The Nation*, 8.05.1995.

DAURIAC (Jacques Paul), 'Paris, Musée d'Art Moderne de la Ville de Paris, Exposition : Electra', *Pantheon*, 42, n°2, Munich, April-June 1984, p. 188-189.

DAVIS (Bruce), 'Printed in Los Angeles', *Apollo*, n°124, London, Nov. 1986, p. 435.

DAVIS (Douglas), 'Veni, Vidi, Video', *Newsweek*, 75, n°15, New York, 13.04.1970, p. 98-99.

DAVIS (Douglas), 'Man of Parts', *Newsweek*, 77, n°9, New York, 1.03.1971, p. 70.

DECTER (Joshua), 'Bruce Nauman: Sperone Westwater', *Flash Art*, n°143, Milan, Nov.-Dec. 1988, p. 118.

DECTER (Joshua), 'Stupidity As Destiny', *Flash Art*, Milan, Oct. 1994, p. 72-76.

DEITCHTER (David), 'Art on the Installation Plan', *Artforum*, 30, n°5, New York, Jan. 1992, p. 78-84.

DELACOMA (Wynne), 'Nauman Wins with Neon: Artist Gets $50,000 in Exhibit', *Chicago Sun-Times*, Chicago, 6.06.1985, p. 70.

DESMOND (Michael), 'Lightworks', *Craft Australia*, n°3, London, spring 1986, p. 22-27.

DOMINGO (Willis), 'New York Galleries', *Arts Magazine*, 45, n°5, New York, March 1971, p. 55-57.

DOMINGO (Willis), 'New York Galleries', *Arts Magazine*, 45, n°6, New York, April 1971, p. 82-84.

DONOHUE (Marlena), 'The Galleries: Wilshire Center', *The Los Angeles Times*, Los Angeles, 19.04.1989, p. 18.

DORRA (BODO), 'Holografie—Ein neues Künstlerisches Medium?', *Das Kunstwerk*, n°1, Stuttgart, Feb. 1984, p. 5-27.

DREISHPOON (Douglas), 'Dislocations', *Arts Magazine*, 66, n°6, New York, Feb. 1992, p. 68.

DUFOUR (Gary), 'Bruce Nauman', *Vancouver Art Gallery*, Vancouver, 1993.

FARGIER (Jean-Paul), 'Bruce Nauman à l'ARC : No Man', *Cahiers du Cinéma*, n°389, Paris, Nov. 1986, p. 10.

FITZGIBBON (John), 'Sacramento !', *Art in America*, 59, n°6, New York, Nov.-Dec. 1971, p. 78-83.

FORSTBAUER (Nikolai), 'Bruce Nauman: Das Schreien der Stille', *ZYMA—ART TODAY*, n°3, Stuttgart, June-July 1991, p. 4-11.

FRACKMAN (Noel) and KAUFMANN (Ruth), 'Documenta 7: The Dialogue and a Few Asides', *Arts Magazine*, 57, n°2, New York, Oct. 1982, p. 91-97.

FRANKENSTEIN (Alfred), 'A Disciple of Paul Klee', *San Francisco Chronicle*, San Francisco, 14.10.1966, p. 52.

FRENCH (Christopher), 'The Slant Step Reappears', *Artweek*, 14, n°4, San Jose, 29.01.1983, p. 1, 16.

FRENCH (Christopher), 'Bruce Nauman: Humor versus Terror', *Journal* of Art, 1, n°5, New York, May 1989, p. 53-55.

FREY (Patrick), 'The Sense of the Whole', *Parkett*, n°10, Zurich, Sept. 1986, p. 34-41.

GALLOWAY (David), 'Report from Italy: Count Panza Divests', *Art in America*, 72, n°11, New York, Dec. 1984, p. 9-19.

GARDNER (Colin), 'The Esthetics of Torture', *Artweek*, 18, n°12, San Jose, 4.04.1987, p. 7.

GARDNER (Colin), 'The Body as Signifier', *Artweek*, 19, n°11, San Jose, 19.03.1988, p. 1.

GEER (Suvan), 'The Galleries: La Cienega Area', *The Los Angeles Times*, Los Angeles, 1.12.1989, p. 16.

GILARDI (Piero), 'Da New York', *Flash Art*, Milan, n°5, 1967, p. 1-2.

GILARDI (Piero), 'Micro-emotive Art', *Museumjournaal*, 13, n°4, Amsterdam, 1968, p. 198-203.

GILARDI (Piero), 'Primary Energy and the "Microemotive Artists"', *Arts Magazine*, 43, n°1, New York, Sept.-Oct. 1968, p. 48-51.

GILLICK (Liam), 'Bruce Nauman/Robert Mangold: Saatchi Collection', *Artscribe International*, n°78,
London, Nov.-Dec. 1989, p. 73-74.

GINTZ (Claude), 'Bruce Nauman aujourd'hui', *Art Studio*, n°3, Paris, winter 1986-1987, p. 128-137.

GLOWEN (Ron), 'Six Exemplars of Recent Sculpture', *Artweek*, 10, n°4, San Jose, 27.01.1979, p. 17.

GLOWEN (Ron), 'Scene and Unseen: Art in Los Angeles', *Vanguard*, 10, n°9, Vancouver, Nov. 1981, p. 30-35.

GLUECK (Grace), 'Bruce Nauman: No Body but His', *The New York Times*, New York, 1.04.1973, p. 24.

GLUECK (Grace), 'Kunst mit moralischem Imperativ [Bruce Nauman]', *Art*, Hamburg, 6-1992, p. 56-57.

GODFREY (Tony), 'Bruce Nauman: ICA Gallery', *Burlington Magazine*, 134, London, March 1992, p. 198-199.

GOLD (Barbara), 'Corcoran Biennial: New Sensibility in Washington', *Arts Magazine*, 43, n°6, New York, April 1969, p. 28-31.

GOLDBERG (Roselee), 'Space as Praxis', *Studio International*, 190, n°977, London, Sept.-Oct. 1975, p. 130-135.

GOLDRING (Nancy), 'Identity: Representations of the Self', *Arts Magazine*, 63, n°7, New York, March 1989, p. 85.

GOODMAN (Jonathan), 'From Hand to Mouth to Paper to Art: The Problems of Bruce Nauman's Drawings', *Arts Magazine*, 62, n°6,
New York, Feb. 1988, p. 44-46.

GOPNIK (Adam), 'The Art World. Bits and Pieces', *The New Yorker*, 66, n°13, New York, 14.05.1990, p. 88-92.

GOPNIK (Adam), 'Empty Frames', *The New Yorker*, 67, n°40, New York, 25.11.1991, p. 111-120.

GOPNIK (Adam), 'The Nauman Principle', *The New Yorker*, New York, 27.03.1995, p. 1-4.

GOTTLIEB (Carla), 'Addendum à l'Art de la Signature : La Signature au XXe Siècle', *Revue de l'Art*, n°34, Paris, 1976, p. 70-80.

GOTTLIEB (Carla), 'Self Portraiture in Postmodern Art', *Westdeutsches Jahrbuch für Kunstgeschichte*, n°42, R. F. A., 1981, p. 267-302.

GRAEVENITZ (Antje von), 'Amsterdam, Stedelijk Museum Ausstellung: Von Bildhauern Gemacht', *Pantheon*, 37, n°2,
Munich, April-June 1979, p. 119-120.

GRAEVENITZ (Antje von), 'San Giovanni Evangelista Ausstellung: Quartetto', *Pantheon*, 42, n°4,
Munich, Oct.-Dec. 1984, p. 384-386.

GRAEVENITZ (Antje von), 'Geloof en twijfel in het werk van Christo en Bruce Nauman: Rituele aspecten in het existentialistisch
perpectief', *Archis, Maanblad vor Architectuur, Stedebouw, Beeldende Kunst*, Utrecht, 6 June 1990, p. 28-33.

GRAW (Isabelle), 'Bruce Nauman: Being Is Nothing', *Flash Art*, n°169, Milan, March-April 1993, p. 71-73.

GRAW (Isabelle), 'Sein ist noch lange nichts (einige Themen bei Bruce Nauman)', *Texte zur Kunst*, 7-1992, p. 89-95.

GREENSPUN (Roger), 'Screen: Palette of Art', *The New York Times*, New York, 14.04.1972, p. 23.

GRUTERICH (Marlis), 'Krefeld, Museum Haus Lange Ausstellung: Wahrnehmungen-Aufzeichnungen-Mitteilungen.
Die Erweiterung des Wirlichkeitsbegriffs in der Kunst der 60er und 70er Jahre', *Pantheon*, n°3, Munich, July-Sept. 1979, p. 210.

HAGEN (Charles), 'At the Whitney Biennial: Good Morning America', *Artforum*, 23, n°10, New York, summer 1985, p. 56-57.

HALDER (Johannes), 'Bruce Nauman: Staatliche Kunsthalle, Baden-Baden', *Das Kunstwerk*, 34, n°5, Stuttgart, 1981, p. 90-91.

HANDY (Ellen),'Bruce Nauman/Judy Tomkins/Keith Haring', *Arts Magazine*, 60, n°5, New York, Jan. 1986, p. 134.

HARTEN (Jürgen), 'T for Technics, B for Body', *Art and Artists*, 8, n°8, London, Nov. 1973, p. 28-33.

HEARTNEY (Eleanor), 'Bruce Nauman: Sperone Westwater, Castelli, Thompson Street', *Art News*, 89, n°7,
New York, Sept. 1990, p. 153-154.

HEARTNEY (Eleanor), 'Dislocations: Museum of Modern Art', *Art News*, New York, 91, n°1, Jan. 1992, p. 117.

HEIN (B.), 'Film as Art: Part 1', *Heute Kunst*, n°13, R.F.A., Feb.-April 1976, p. 5-6.

HENTSCHEL (Martin), 'Bruce Nauman: Konrad Fischer, Düsseldorf', *Artforum*, 27, n°1, New York, Sept. 1988, p. 156-157.

HENTSCHEL (Martin), 'Bruce Nauman: Konrad Fischer, Düsseldorf', *Artforum*, 28, n°7, New York, March 1990, p. 175.

HIXSON (Kathryn), 'Good and Bad', *New Art Examiner*, Chicago, Dec. 1994.

HÖFLIGER (Yvonne), 'Ein Hauch von Hudson über dem Rheinfall', *Du*, n°8, 1984, Zurich, p. 58-63.

HONNEF (Klaus), 'Conceptual Art', *Louisiana Revy*, 12, n°1, Humlebaek, Sept. 1971, p. 32-34.

HUGHES (Robert), 'Being a Nuisance', *Time*, New York, 24.04.1995.

HUGO (Joan), 'Los Angeles Survey: Oversight and Overreach', *Artweek*, 12, n°31, San Jose, 26.09.1981, p. 1, 16.

JOCKS (Heinz Norbert), 'Bruce Nauman. 'Ein Auge zwischen Apathie und Hellsherei'', Galerie Konrad Fischer, *Kunstforum International*, 128, Cologne, Oct.-Dec. 1994, p. 391-392.

JOHNSON (Ellen H.) and SPEAR (Athena T.), 'Three Young Americans: Krueger, Nauman, Saret', *Bulletin of the Allen Memorial Art Museum* 25, n°3, Oberlin, spring 1968, p. 92-103.

JOHNSTONE (Christopher), 'Bruce Nauman: Opening the P.M.J. Self Gallery, London', *Studio International*, 189, n°973, London, Jan.-Feb. 1975, Oberlin, p. 8-9.

JONES (Ronald), 'Bruce Nauman', *Arts Magazine*, 59, n°6, New York, Feb. 1985, p. 4.

JONES (Ronald), 'Bruce Nauman', *Frieze*, London, May 1995, p. 58.

JOSELIT (David), 'Lessons in Public Sculpture', *Art in America*, 77, n°12, New York, Dec. 1989, p. 130-135.

KAGENECK (Christian von), 'Franz Gertsch und Bruce Nauman', *Das Kunstwerk*, 39, n°6, Stuttgart, Dec. 1986, p. 48.

KALIL (Susie), 'Houston: Metal Energy', *Art News*, 80, n°9, San Jose, Nov. 1981, p. 182, 184.

KALIL (Susie), 'Dimensional Dichotomies', *Artweek*, 12, n°41, San Jose, 5.12.1981, p. 6.

KALINA (Richard), 'Bruce Nauman: Leo Castelli Gallery; Sperone Westwater Gallery', *Arts Magazine*, 64, n°10, New York, summer 1990, p. 75.

KANDEL (Susan), 'Bruce Nauman', *Arts Magazine*, 65, n°8, New York, April 1991, p. 109.

KAZANJIAN (Dodie), 'New Image', *Vogue*, 180, n°5, New York, May 1990, p. 292-298, 320, 323.

KIMMELMAN (Michael), 'Two Who Define Today Amble in the Past', *The New York Times*, New York, 21.02.1997, p. C1 and C26.

KINGSLEY (April), 'New York Letter', *Art International*, 17, n°8, Lugano, Oct. 1973, p. 51-54.

KIRSCHNER (Judith Russi), '74th American Exhibition, Art Institute of Chicago', *Artforum*, 21, n°2, New York, Oct. 1982, p. 74-76.

KNIGHT (Christopher), 'A Three-Gallery Tribute to Nicholas Wilder', *The Los Angeles Times*, Los Angeles, 16.03.1990, p. 26.

KOEPPLIN (Dieter), 'Drei Zeichnungen von Bruce Nauman', *Das Kunstbulletin des Schweizerischen Kunstvereins*, n°7 and 8, Kriens, July 1986, p. 8-11.

KOETHER (Jutta), 'Keith Sonnier: Rolf Ricke, Cologne', *Flash Art*, n°138, Milan, Jan.-Feb. 1988, p. 130-130.

KOZLOFF (Max), '9 in a Warehouse', *Artforum*, 7, n°6, New York, Feb. 1969, p. 38-42.

KRAMER (Hilton), 'In Footsteps of Duchamp', *The New York Times*, New York, 30.03.1973, p. 28.

KRAMER (Hilton), 'Avant-Garde Academician', *The New York Times*, New York, 8.04.1973, p. 25.

KRAMER (Hilton), 'Idiotic Curators Present Wretched Nauman Show', *The New York Observer*, New York, 13.03.1995.

KRAYNAK (Janet), 'Bruce Nauman: Kunstmuseum Wolfsburg', *Frieze*, n°36, Sept.-Oct. 1997, p. 92.

KURTZ (Bruce), 'Interview with Giuseppe Panza di Biumo', *Arts Magazine*, 46, n°5, New York, March 1972, p. 40-43.

KURTZ (Bruce), 'Documenta 5: A Critical Review', *Arts Magazine*, 46, n°8, New York, summer 1972, p. 30-46.

KURTZ (Stephen A.), 'Reviews and Previews', *Art News*, 68, n°5, New York, Sept. 1969, p. 20.

KUSPIT (Donald B.), 'Bruce Nauman: Leo Castelli Gallery, Lorence-Monk', *Artforum*, 28, n°5, New York, Jan. 1990, p. 137.

KUTNER (Janet), 'The Visceral Aesthetic of a New Decade's Art', *Arts Magazine*, 51, n°4, New York, Dec. 1976, p. 100-103.

LAMBRECHT (Luk), 'Bruce Nauman: Museum für Gegenwartskunst Basel', *Forum International*, n°6, Antwerp, Jan.-Feb. 1991, p. 75.

LARSON (Kay), 'Privileged Access', *New York Magazine* 18, n°28, New York , 22.07.1985, p. 61-62.

LARSON (Philip), 'Words in Print', *Print Collector's Newsletter* 5, n°3, July-August 1974, p. 53-56.

LAUF (Cornelia), 'Neon Nights', *Artscribe International*, n°89, London, Nov.-Dec. 1991, p. 84-85.

LEIDER (Philip), ''The Properties of Materials': In the Shadow of Robert Morris', *The New York Times*, New York, 22.12.1968, p. 31.

LEIDER (Philip), 'New York', *Artforum*, 8, n°6, New York, Feb. 1970, p. 68-70.

LEVIN (Kim), 'New York, Bruce Nauman: Stretching the Truth', *Opus International*, n°46, Paris, Sept. 1973, p. 44-46.

LICHTENSTEIN (Therese), 'Bruce Nauman: Leo Castelli, Sperone Westwater', *Arts Magazine*, 59, n°5, New York, Jan. 1985, p. 36.

LINKER (Kate), 'Bruce Nauman: Leo Castelli Gallery, Sperone Westwater Gallery', *Artforum*, 23, n°5, New York, Jan. 1985, p. 86-87.

LIPPARD (Lucy), 'Eccentric Abstraction', *Art International*, 10, n°9, Lugano, Nov. 1966, p. 28, 34-40.

LÜTGENS (Annelie), 'Das Komplott des Künstlers: Bruce Nauman in Berlin und Retrospektiv in Zürich', *Neue bildende Kunst*, 4/5, 1995, p. 138.

LYON (Christopher), 'Bruce Nauman: Sperone Westwater', *Art News*, 87, n°10, New York, Dec. 1988, p. 145.

MacWILLIAM (David), 'Making Faces', *Vanguard*, 7, n°2, Vancouver, March 1978, p. 18.

MAHONEY (Robert), 'Bruce Nauman: Sperone Westwater', *Arts Magazine*, 63, n°4, New York, Dec. 1988, p. 107.

MARIONI (Tom), 'Out Front', *Vision*, n°1, Angers, Sept. 1975, p. 8-11.

MASON (Willis), ''Electric' Art Exhibit to Be Opened Sunday', *Durham Morning Herald*, London, 18.01.1975.

McCANN (Cecile N.), 'Bruce Nauman', *Artweek*, 4, n°1, San Jose, 6.01.1973, p. 1, 12.

McCORMICK (Carlo), 'Bruce Nauman: Sperone Westwater, Leo Castelli', *Flash Art*, n°120, Milan, Jan. 1985, p. 42.

McINTYRE (Arthur), 'L'Art corporel (Body Art)', *Art and Australia*, 14, n°1, Killara, July-Sept. 1976, p. 74-78.

McKENNA (Kristina), 'Bruce Nauman: Dan Weinberg Gallery', *The Los Angeles Times*, Los Angeles, 27.01.1991, p. 4, 84.

McKENNA (Kristina), 'Paroles d'artiste...', *Art Press*, n°184, Paris, October 1993, p. 21-23.

MOORE (Alan), 'Bruce Nauman: Leo Castelli Gallery', *Artforum*, 13, n°8, New York, April 1975, p. 79-80.

MORGAN (Robert C.), 'Eccentric Abstraction and Postminimalism: From Biomorphic Sensualism to Hard-Edge Concreteness', *Flash Art*, n°144, Milan, Jan.-Feb. 1989, p. 73-81.

MORGAN (Robert C.), 'Jasper Johns, David Salle, Bruce Nauman: Leo Castelli', *Flash Art*, n°44, Milan, Jan.-Feb. 1989, p. 123.

MORGAN (Stuart), 'Past Present Future: Count Giuseppe Panza di Biumo Interviewed by Stuart Morgan', *Artscribe International*, n°76, London, summer 1989, p. 53-56.

MOSER (Ulli), 'Bruce Nauman: "Okay, Okay, Okay, Okay, Okay..."', *Kunstforum International*, n°117, Cologne, 1992, p. 384-385.

MOURE (Gloria), '¿ Está el artista disponible ? A propósitio de Bruce Nauman', *Creacion*, Madrid, 5 May 1992, p. 98-102.

MUCHNIC (Suzanne), 'Nauman's Self-Involved, Clinical, Examining Eye', *The Los Angeles Times*, Los Angeles, 5.04.1988, p. 1-2.

MUCHNIC (Suzanne), "'Vices and Virtues': Word Association', *The Los Angeles Times*, Los Angeles, 9.04.1989, p. 87-88.

MÜLLER (Hans van), 'Bilder wie Unfälle', *Basler Magazin*, n°24, Basle, 19.06.1982, p. 6-7.

NADELMAN (Cynthia), 'A Star Struck Carnegie International', *Art News*, 85, n°3, New York, March 1986, p. 115-118.

'Nauman and Social Madness in Basel', *Art Newspaper* 1, n°3, Dec. 1990, p. 5.

NEMSER (Cindy), 'Subject-Object: Body Art', *Arts Magazine*, 46, n°1, New York, Sept.-Oct. 1971, p. 38-42.

NESBITT (Lois E.), 'Lie Down, Roll Over: Bruce Nauman's Body-Conscious Art Reawakens New York', *Artscribe International*, n°82, London, summer 1990, p. 48-51.

NESBITT (Lois E.), 'No Place: Dislocations', *Artscribe International*, n°90, London, Feb.-March 1992, p. 81-82.

NISSELSON (Jane E.), 'Contemporary Sculpture at MoMA', *Skyline*, 2, n°3, New York, summer 1979, p. 10.

NITTVE (Lars), 'Quartetto', *Artforum*, 23, n°1, New York, Sept. 1984, p. 107-108.

NOVAK (Linda), 'Bruce Nauman: Drawings, 1965-1986', *High Performance*, 11, n°1-2, Los Angeles, spring-summer 1988, p. 114-115.

NUSBAUM (Eliot), 'Pyramid: Ugly and Beautiful', *Des Moines Register*, Des Moines, 13.01.1991, p. 8.

O'BRIEN (John), 'The Epitome of Minimal Sculpture', *Artweek*, 20, n°37, San Jose, 9.11.1989, p. 15, 27.

OLLMAN (Leah), 'Bruce Nauman: Vices and Virtues', *High Performance*, 12, n°3, Los Angeles, autumn 1989, p. 42-43.

Painting, Object, Film, Concept: Works from the Herbig Collection, exhibition catalogue, Christie's, New York, 1998.

PARENT (Béatrice), 'Le Néon dans l'art contemporain', *Chroniques de l'Art Vivant*, n°20, Paris, May 1971, p. 4-6.

PERREAULT (John), 'The Act of Seeing', *Village Voice*, 13, n°17, New York, 8.02.1968, p. 19-21.

PERREAULT (John), 'Bruce Nauman', *Art News*, 67, n°1, New York, March 1968, p. 22.

PERREAULT (John), 'Downtown Is Uptown, Not 10th Street', *Village Voice*, 16, n°48, New York, Dec. 1971, p. 24.

PERRONE (Jeff), 'Bruce Nauman: Leo Castelli Gallery Downtown, Sonnabend, Sperone Westwater Fischer', *Artforum*, 15, n°5, New York, Jan. 1977, p. 58-60.

PERRONE (Jeff), "'Words': When Art Takes a Rest', *Artforum*, 15, n°10, New York, summer 1977, p. 34-37.

PERRONE (Jeff), 'The Salon of 1985', *Arts Magazine*, 59, n°10, New York, summer 1985, p. 70-73.

PERUCCHI-PETRI (Ursula), 'Hinweis auf einige Neuerwerbungen: Bruce Nauman und Robert Ryman', *Jahresbericht*, Zurich, 1985, p. 96-99.

PETERSON (William), 'Albuquerque: The Kitsch of Death', *Art News*, 87, n°8, New York, Oct. 1988, p. 188.

PETHERBRIDGE (Deanna), 'Liquorice Allsorts: Gravity and Grace: The Changing Condition of Sculpture', *Women's Art Magazine*, n°51, London, March-April 1993, p. 17-18.

PHILLIPS (Patricia C.), 'Bruce Nauman: Sperone Westwater Gallery', *Artforum*, 27, n°4, New York, Dec. 1988, p. 115.

PICAZO (Glòria), 'Time Span: Fundación Caixa de Pensions, Barcelona', *Contemporanea*, 3, n°5, New York, May 1990, p. 103.

PINCUS (Robert L.), 'The Good, Bad, Dramatic in Nauman's Neon Pieces', San Diego Union, San Diego, 15.10.1988.

PINCUS (Robert L.), "'Vices and Virtues': An Artistic Flashback', *San Diego Union*, San Diego, 6.11.1988.

PINCUS-WITTEN (Robert), 'Bruce Nauman: Leo Castelli Gallery', *Artforum*, 6, n°8, New York, April 1968, p. 63-65.

PINCUS-WITTEN (Robert), 'Bruce Nauman: Another Kind of Reasoning', *Artforum*, 10, n°6, New York, Feb. 1972, p.30-37.

PLAGENS (Peter), 'Roughly Ordered Thoughts on the Occasion of the Bruce Nauman Retrospective in Los Angeles', *Artforum*, 11, n°7, New York, March 1973, p. 57-59.

PLAGENS (Peter), 'Bruce Nauman: Nicholas Wilder Gallery', *Artforum*, 12, n°6, New York, March 1974, p. 85-86.

PLAGENS (Peter), 'Art in Los Angeles: Seventeen Artists in the Sixties', *Art Journal*, 41, n°4,
London, winter 1981, p. 375-379.

PLAGENS (Peter), 'Nine Biennial Notes', *Art in America*, 73, n°7, New York, July 1985, p. 114-119.

PLAGENS (Peter), 'I Just Dropped in to See What Condition My Condition Was In', *Artscribe International*, n°56,
London, Feb.-March 1986, p. 22-29.

PLAGENS (Peter), 'Under Western Eyes', *Art in America*, 77, n°1, New York, Jan. 1989, p. 32-41.

PLAGENS (Peter), 'A Matter of Horsepower', *Newsweek*, 121, n°8, New York, 22.02.1993, p. 62-63.

PLAGENS (Peter), 'Return of the Galisteo Kid', *Newsweek*, New York, 30.05.1994.

PLUCHART (François), 'L'Art corporel', *Artitudes International*, n°18-20, Paris, Jan.-March 1975, France, p. 49-96.

POHLEN (Annelie), 'Bruce Nauman: Galerie Fischer, Düsseldorf; Museum Haus Esters, Krefeld', *Artforum*, 22, n°9,
New York, May 1984, p. 95-96.

POINSOT (Jean-Marc), 'Bruce Nauman : La problématique du non-sens', *Art Press*, n°10, Paris, March-April 1974, p. 12-15.

PREVOST (Jean-Marc), 'Les vérités de Bruce Nauman', *Beaux-Arts Magazine*, Paris, Sept. 1995, p. 115.

PRICE (Jonathan), 'Video Art: A Medium Discovering Itself', *Art News*, 76, n°1, New York, Jan. 1977, p. 41-47.

PRINCETHAL (Nancy), 'Bruce Nauman: Sperone Westwater and Leo Castelli', *Art News*, 84, n°1, New York, Jan. 1985, p. 137.

RACZKA (Robert), 'From There to Here: Tracking Video's Pioneers', *High Performance*, 14, n°2,
Los Angeles, summer 1991, p. 70-72.

RATCLIFF (Carter), 'New York Letter (Spring Part I)', *Art International*, Lugano, 15, n°4, 20.04.1971, p. 25-28, 31, 69.

RATCLIFF (Carter), 'New York Letter (Spring Part II)', *Art International*, Lugano, 15, n°5, 20.05.1971, p. 32-39, 45.

RATCLIFF (Carter), 'New York Letter', *Art International*, 16, n°2, Lugano, 20.02.1972, p. 52-56.

RATCLIFF (Carter), 'Adversary Spaces', *Artforum*, 11, n°2, New York, Oct. 1972, p. 40-44.

RATCLIFF (Carter), 'Notes on Small Sculpture', *Artforum*, 14, n°8, New York, April 1976, p. 35-42.

RATCLIFF (Carter), 'Bruce Nauman at Castelli Greene Street and Sperone Westwater', *Art in America*, 73, n°3,
New York, March 1985, p. 151.

RAUH (Emily S.), 'Among Recent Acquisitions', *Bulletin of the Saint Louis Art Museum*, 7, n°6, St Louis, March-April 1972, p. 4-6.

'Recent Acquisitions', Albright-Knox Art Gallery Calendar, Feb. 1976.

REEDIJK (Hein), 'Bruce Nauman: Kunst voor navelstaarders (Art for Navel Contemplators)?', *Museumjournaal*, 18, n°4,
Amsterdam, Sept. 1973, p. 154-159.

REEVES (Jean), 'Simple Children's Show Moves, Floats, Blinks, Leads Viewer into the Complexity of Art', *Buffalo Evening News*,
Buffalo, 30.06.1971.

REIN (Ingrid), 'Amerikanische Zeichnungen der Siebziger Jahre', *Das Kunstwerk*, 35, n°3, Stuttgart, June 1982, p. 79-81.

RICHARDSON (Brenda), 'Bay Area Survey: The Myth of Neo-Dada', *Arts Magazine*, 44, n°8, New York, summer 1970, p. 46-49.

RICKEY (Carrie), 'Studs and Polish: L.A. in the Sixties', *Art in America*, 70, n°1, New York, Jan. 1982, p. 80-89.

ROBBINS (Robin), 'Picture Concepts', *Times Literary Supplement*, New York, 14.11.1980, p. 1290.

RORIMER (Anne), 'Blinky Palermo: Objects, "Stoffbilder", Wall Paintings', *Artforum*, 17, n°3, New York, Nov. 1978, p. 28-35.

RUSSELL (John), 'Bruce Nauman', *The New York Times*, New York, 12.11.76, p. 18.

RUSSELL (John), 'Art: "Contemporary Sculpture" at Modern', *The New York Times*, New York, 15.06.1979, p. 25.

RUSSELL (John), 'A Contemplative Chicago Show', *The New York Times*, New York, 29.07.1979, p. 31.

RUSSELL (John), 'Bruce Nauman: Sperone Westwater Gallery and Leo Castelli Gallery', *The New York Times*, New York,
12.10.1984, p. 24.

SALTZ (Jerry), 'Assault and Battery, Surveillance and Captivity: Brauce Nauman's Rats and Bats (Learned Helplessness in Rats) II',
Arts Magazine, 63, n°8, New York, April 1989, p. 13.

SCHAWELKA (Karl), 'Der Körper als Komplize und Widersacher. Bruce Naumans Videoinstallationen', *Im Blickfeld* I,
Jahrbuch der Hamburger Kunsthalle, Hamburg, 1994, p. 89-109.

SCHENKER (Christoph), 'Ende der InK: Bruce Nauman', *Kunstforum International*, n°2, 3, Cologne, May-August 1981, p. 346-348.

SCHENKER (Christoph), 'Museum für Gegenwartskunst and Kunsthalle, Basel', *Flash Art*, n°131, Milan, Dec.-Jan. 1987, p. 94-95.

SCHENKER (Christoph), 'Bruce Nauman: Tears of a Clown', *Flash Art*, n°158, Milan, May-June 1991, p. 126.

SCHILLING (Jürgen), 'Zur Entwicklungsgeschichte der Performance', *Heute Kunst*, n°25, R.F.A., March-April 1979, p. 22-23.

SCHIMMEL (Paul), '"Four Corner Piece": Bruce Nauman', Museum of Contemporary Art, *Calendar*,
Los Angeles, Feb.-March 1993, p. 4.

SCHJELDAHL (Peter), 'New York Letter', *Art International*, Lugano, 13, n°7, Sept. 1969, p. 70-73.

SCHJELDAHL (Peter), 'Only Connect', *Village Voice*, 27, n°4, New York, 20-26.01.1982, p. 72.

SCHJELDAHL (Peter), 'Profoundly Practical Jokes: The Art of Bruce Nauman', *Vanity Fair*, 46, n°3,
New York, May 1983, p. 88-93.

SCHJELDAHL (Peter), 'Daredevil', *7 Days*, New York, 28.03.1990, p. 52-53.

SCHJELDAHL (Peter), 'The Trouble with Nauman', *Art in America*, New York, April 1994, p. 82-91.

SCHNECKENBURGER (Manfred), 'Wahrnehmung, dingfest gemacht: ein Problemkreis um Chuck Close und Bruce Nauman
in der Ausstellung 'Project 74'', *Museen in Köln*, 13, n°8, Cologne, August 1974, p. 262-263.

SCHÖTTLE (Rüdiger), 'Ager Publicus', *Kunstforum International*, 81, n°4, Cologne, Oct.-Nov. 1985, p. 103-113, 300.

SELDIS (Henry J.), 'A Critical Guide to the Galleries: La Cienega Area', *The Los Angeles Times*, Los Angeles, 23.11.1973, p. 20.

SHARP (Willoughby), 'Body Works', *Avalanche*, n°1, New York, autumn 1970, p. 14-17.

SILVERTHORNE (Jeanne), 'To Live and to Die', *Parkett*, n°10, Zurich,, Sept. 1986, p. 18-33.

SIMAS (Joseph), 'Letter from Belgium and France', *Arts Magazine*, 64, n°3, New York, Nov. 1989, p. 113-116.

SIMON (Joan), 'Bruce Nauman: Work in Progress', *Beaux Arts*, Dec. 1997, p. 54-60.

SINGERMAN (Howard), ''Art in Los Angeles', Los Angeles County Museum of Art', *Artforum*, 20, n°7,
New York, March 1982, p. 75-77.

SMITH (Roberta), 'Endless Meaning at the Hirshhorn', *Artforum*, 23, n°8, New York, April 1985, p. 81-85.

SMITH (Roberta), 'Art: Bruce Nauman Retrospective', *The New York Times*, New York, 30.10.1987, p. 34.

SMITH (Roberta), 'An Array of Artists, Styles and Trends in Downtown Galleries', *The New York Times*, New York, 20.02.1988, p. 28.

SMITH (Roberta), 'Bruce Nauman: Prints 1970-1989', *The New York Times*, New York, 6.10.1989, p. 25.

SMITH (Roberta), 'Sculpture at the Whitney: The Radical Years', *The New York Times*, New York, 9.03.1990, p. 1, 28.

SMITH (Roberta), 'Extremes of Sculpture in 3 Bruce Nauman Shows', *The New York Times*, New York, 16.03.1990, p. 32.

SMITH (Roberta), 'Power and American Art: A View of the Fist That Grips the Brush', *The New York Times*,
New York, 24.10.1991, p. 1, 4.

SMITH (Roberta), 'Prospects of Bonding With a You, a Me and a Them', *The New York Times*, New York, 15.11.1996.

SOLOMON (Andrew), 'Complex Cow-boy', *The New York Times Magazine*, New York, 5.03.1995.

STAVITSKY (Gail), 'California in Print 1: A Series', *Artweek*, 10, n°16, San Jose, 21.04.1979, p.1, 20.

STAVITSKY (Gail), 'The 1985 Carnegie International', *Arts Magazine*, 60, n°7, New York, March 1986, p. 58-59.

STECKER (Raimund), 'Zerstückelt, geklont und aufgehängt: Bruce Naumans Ausstellung "Heads and Bodies" in Düsseldorf',
Frankfurter Allgemeine Zeitung, n°219, Frankfurt, 25.09.1989, p. 35.

STEIN (Donna M.), 'New Editions', *Art News*, 73, n°3, New York, March 1974, p. 48.

STEIR (Pat), 'The Word Unspoken', *Artforum*, 28, n°4, New York, Dec. 1989, p. 125-127.

STEVENS (Mark), 'An American Nightmare', *New York*, New York, 20.03.1995.

STILES (Knute), 'San Francisco: William Geis and Bruce Nauman', *Artforum*, 5, n°4, New York, Dec. 1966, p. 64-66.

STITELMAN (Paul), 'Bruce Nauman at the Whitney Museum', *Arts Magazine*, 47, n°7, New York, May-June 1973, p. 54-55.

STORR (Robert), 'Bruce Nauman, Le Fou-pas-si-saint', *Art Press*, n°89, Paris, Feb. 1985, p. 64-66.

STORR (Robert), 'Nowhere Man', *Parkett*, n°10, Zurich, Sept. 1986, p. 70-90.

STUTTAFORD (Geneviève), 'Nonfiction: Bruce Nauman by Coosje van Bruggen', *Publishers Weekly*, 235, n°4, 27.01.1989, p. 459.

SUDERBURG (Erika), 'Defining an Art Form', *Artweek*, 19, n°5, San Jose, 20.02.1988, p. 11.

TALLMAN (Susan), 'Clear Vision: The Prints of Bruce Nauman', *Arts Magazine*, 64, n°3, New York, Nov. 1989, p. 17-18.

TARSHIS (Jerome), 'San Francisco', *Artforum*, 9, n°6, New York, Feb. 1971, p. 85-87.

TARZAN (Deloris), 'No Pedestal Needed', *Seattle Times*, Seattle, 24.12.1978, p. 6.

TAUBIN (Amy), 'Clowning Around', *Village Voice*, 34, n°52, New York, 26.12.1989, p. 75-76.

TAZZI (Pier Luigi), 'Dear Harry...', *Artforum*, 27, n°1, New York, Sept. 1988, p. 131-134.

TEMIN (Christine), 'Conservative Art Is Hot in London', *Boston Globe*, New York, 17.08.1989, p. 91.

THURLEMANN (Felix), 'Dream Passage de Bruce Nauman : un espace d'énonciation paradoxale', *Part de l'oeil*, vol. 5,
Brussels, 1989, p. 188-193.

TREBAY (Guy), 'Bruce Nauman', *Village Voice*, 27, n°4, New York, 20-26.01.1982, p. 56.

TREIB (Marc), 'Architecture versus Architecture: Is (an) Image (a) Reality?', *Architectural Association Quarterly*, 9, n°4,
New York, 1977, p. 3-14.

TUCHMAN (Phyllis), 'American Art in Germany: The History of a Phenomenon', *Artforum*, 9, n°3, New York, Nov. 1970, p. 58-69.

TUCKER (Marcia), 'PheNAUMANology', *Artforum*, 9, n°4, New York, Dec. 1970, p. 38-44.

VACHTOVA (Ludmilla), 'Bruce Nauman: der Körper als Kunststück', *Kunstforum International*, 119, Cologne, spring 1992, p. 138-142.

WALLACE (Joan) and MILLER (John), 'Artists' Films: The Body as Site', *Flash Art*, n°161, Milan, Nov.-Dec. 1991, p. 96-99.

WALLACH (Amei), 'Artist of the Show Down', *New York Newsday*, New York, 8.01.1989, p. 4-5, 23.

WARREN (Lynne), 'Bruce Nauman: Marianne Deson Gallery', *New Art Examiner*, 6, n°8, Chicago, May 1979, p. 13.

WARREN (Ron), 'Bruce Nauman: Leo Castelli/Sperone Westwater', *Arts Magazine*, 59, n°4, New York, Dec. 1984, p. 39-40.

WATKINS (Jonathan), 'London: Promises Promises', *Art International*, n°8, Lugano, autumn 1989, p. 64-67.

WECHSLER (Max), 'Bruce Nauman: Museum für Gegenwartskunst', *Artforum*, 29, n°4, New York, Dec. 1990, p. 152.

WEINER (Daniel), 'Bruce Nauman: Castelli, Sperone Westwater, 65 Thompson', *Flash Art*, n°153, Milan, summer 1990, p. 145.

WELISH (Marjorie), 'Who's Afraid of Verbs, Nouns, and Adjectives?', *Arts Magazine*, 64, n°8, New York, April 1990, p. 79-84.

WIEGAND (Ingrid), 'Video Shock', *Print*, 30, n°4, New York, July-August 1976, p. 63-69.

WILLIG (Nancy Tobin), 'Show of Contemporary Art Set for Parents, Children', *Buffalo Courier-Express*, Buffalo, 25.07.1971.

WILSON (William), 'A Critical Guide to the Galleries', *The Los Angeles Times*, Los Angeles, 14.02.1969, p. 4.

WILSON (William), 'Bruce Nauman's Unsettling Art Given a Masterful Touch', *The Los Angeles Times*,
Los Angeles, 23.03.1970, p. 6.

WINER (Helene), 'How Los Angeles Looks Today', *Studio International*, 183, n°937, London, Oct. 1971, p. 127-131.

WOLFS (Rein), 'Bruce Nauman: Director of Violent Incidents', *Parkett*, n°10, Zurich, Sept. 1986, p. 42-49.

WORTZ (Melinda), 'Measurements of Time and Structures for Experience', *Artweek*, 11, n°36, San Jose, 1.11.1980, p. 5.

WORTZ (Melinda), 'Art in Los Angeles: Seventeen Artists, Sixteen Projects', *Art News*, 80, n°9,
New York, Nov. 1981, p. 161-165.

WORTZ (Melinda), 'Bruce Nauman', *Art News*, 81, n°4, New York, April 1982, p. 108.

YAU (John), 'Bruce Nauman: Leo Castelli', *Flash Art*, n°126, Milan, Feb.-March 1986, p. 48.

YAU (John), 'Bruce Nauman: Leo Castelli Gallery, Sperone Westwater Gallery, 65 Thompson Street', *Contemporanea*,
New York, n°20, Sept. 1990, p. 97.

YOUNG (Joseph E.), 'Los Angeles', *Art International*, 14, n°6, Lugano, summer 1970, p. 111-115.

ZANDEE (Trudy), 'Kunst Kritiek en de Reelzijdige Lijfelijkheid Van Body Art', *Museumjournaal*, 21, n°3,
Amsterdam, June 1976, p. 97-106.

ZORETICH (Frank), 'Tunnel Vision: Bruce Nauman's Walk-through Concrete Art Causes Critical Campus Controversy',
Albuquerque Journal Magazine, Albuquerque, 8.03.1988, p. 4-7.

ZUTTER (Jörg), 'Alienation of the Self, Command of the Other in the Work of Bruce Nauman', *Parkett*, n°27,
Zurich, March 1991, p. 155-158.

CATALOGUES OF SOLO EXHIBITIONS

Bruce Nauman,
Leo Castelli Gallery, New York, 1968.
Text by David Whitney.

Bruce Nauman: Work from 1965 to 1972,
Los Angeles County Museum of Art, Los Angeles, 1972.
Texts by Jane Livingstone and Marcia Tucker.

The Consummate Mask of Rock,
Albright-Knox Art Gallery, Buffalo, 1975.
Text by Linda L. Cathcart.

Dokumentation 1,
InK. Halle für Internationale neue Kunst, Zurich, 1978.
Text by Christel Sauer.

Dokumentation 8,
InK. Halle für Internationale neue Kunst, Zurich, 1980.
Text by Christel Sauer.

Bruce Nauman: 1/12-Scale Models for Underground Pieces,
Albuquerque Museum, Albuquerque, 1981.
Text by Jennie Lusk.

Bruce Nauman, 1972-1981,
Rijksmuseum Kröller-Müller, Otterlo, 1981.
Texts by Siegmar Holsten, Ellen Joosten, Rudolf Oxenaar
and Katharina Schmidt.

Bruce Nauman: Neons,
Baltimore Museum of Art, Baltimore,1982.
Text by Brenda Richardson. Catalogue raisonné.

*Bruce Nauman: Stadium Piece, Musical Chairs,
Dream Passage*,
Museum Haus Esters, Krefeld, 1983.
Text by Julian Heynen.

Bruce Nauman: Drawings 1965-1986,
Museum für Gegenwartskunst, Basle, 1986.
Texts by Coosje van Bruggen, Dieter Koepplin
and Franz Meyer. Catalogue raisonné.

Bruce Nauman,
Whitechapel Art Gallery, London, 1986.
Texts by Jean-Christophe Ammann, Nicholas Serota
and Joan Simon.
(French edition: *Bruce Nauman*, ARC, Musée d'Art Moderne
de la Ville de Paris, Paris, 1986.)

Bruce Nauman: Prints, 1970-89: A Catalogue Raisonné,
Castelli Graphics and Lorence-Monk Gallery, New York, 1989.
Texts by Christopher Cordes and John Yau.

Bruce Nauman: Skulpturen und Installationen, 1985-1990,
Museum für Gegenwartskunst, Basle, 1990.
Texts by Franz Meyer and Jörg Zutter.
(French edition: *Bruce Nauman: Sculptures and Installations*,
1985-1990, Musée Cantonal des Beaux-Arts, Lausanne, 1991)

Bruce Nauman,
Museo Nacional Centro de Arte Reina Sofía, Madrid;
Walker Art Center, Minneapolis; Museum of Contemporary
Art, Los Angeles; Hirshhorn Museum and Sculpture Garden,
Smithsonian Institution, Washington D.C.;
Museum of Modern Art, New York, 1994.
Catalogue raisonné
Texts by Neal Benezra, Kathy Halbreich, Paul Schimmel,
Joan Simon and Robert Storr.

Bruce Nauman: Image/Text, 1966-1996,
Mnam-Cci, Centre Georges Pompidou, Paris, 1997;
Kunstmuseum Wolfsburg, Wolfsburg, 1997;
Hayward Gallery, London, 1998;
Nykytaiteen museo/The Museum of Contemporary Art Kiasma,
Helsinki, 1998.
Texts by François Albera, Christine van Assche,
Vincent Labaume, Jean-Charles Masséra, Gijs van Tuyl.

SELECTED CATALOGUES OF GROUP EXHIBITIONS

Aanwinsten/Acquisitions, 1985-1993,
Stedelijk Museum, Amsterdam, 1993.

About Sculpture,
Anthony d'Offay Gallery, London, 1987.

A Century of Modern Drawing from the Museum of Modern Art, New York,
British Museum Publications Ltd., London, 1982.
Texts by John Elderfield and Bernice Rose.

Affiliations: Recent Sculpture and Its Antecedents,
Whitney Museum of American Art at Champion, Stamford, 1985.

Affinities and Intuitions: The Gerald S. Elliott Collection of Contemporary Art,
Art Institute of Chicago, Chicago, 1990.
Texts by Neal Benezra, Michael Auping, Lynne Cooke,
I. Michael Danoff, Douglas W. Druick, Judith Russi Kirshner,
Mary Murphy, Roald Nasgaard, Mark Rosenthal, Norman
Rosenthal and Charles F. Stuckey.

Against Order: Chance and Art,
Institute of Contemporary Art, University of Pennsylvania,
Philadelphia, 1970.
Text by Robert Pincus-Witten.

The Age of Modernism: Art in the 20th Century,
Martin-Gropius-Bau, Berlin, 1997.

Air,
National Gallery of Victoria, Melbourne, 1970.
Text by James Harithas.

Allegories of Modernism: Contemporary Drawing,
Museum of Modern Art, New York, 1992.
Text by Bernice Rose.

Altered States,
Kent Fine Art, New York, 1988.

American Art in Belgium,
Palais des Beaux-Arts, Brussels, 1977.
Texts by Georges Roque and Karel J. Geirlandt.

American Art 1930-1970,
Lingotto, Turin, 1992.

American Art Since 1960,
Art Museum, Princeton University, Princeton, 1970.
Texts by John Hand, Michael D. Levin and Peter P. Morrin.

American Art: Third Quarter Century,
Art Museum, Seattle,1973.
Text by Jan Van der Marck.

*The American Artist as Printmaker:
23rd National Print Exhibition*,
Brooklyn Museum, Brooklyn, New York, 1983.
Text by Barry Walker.

American Drawing In Black and White, 1970-1980,
Brooklyn Museum, Brooklyn, New York, 1981.
Text by Gene Baro.

American Drawings, 1963-1973,
Whitney Museum of American Art, New York, 1973.

American Masters of the 60's: Early and Late Works,
Tony Shafrazi Gallery, New York, 1990.

American Portraits of the Sixties and Seventies,
Center for the Visual Arts, Aspen, 1979.

American Sculpture of the Sixties,
Los Angeles County Museum of Art, Los Angeles, 1967.
Texts by Maurice Tuchman, Lawrence Alloway,
Wayne V. Andersen, Dore Ashton, John Coplans,
Clement Greenberg, Max Kozloff, Lucy R. Lippard,
James Monte, Barbara Rose and Irving Sandler.

*Amerikanische Kunst im 20. Jahrhundert:
Malerei und Plastik 1913-1993*,
Martin-Gropius-Bau, Berlin, 1993.

Amerikanische und englische Graphik der Gegenwart,
Staatsgalerie, Stuttgart, 1972.
Text by Gunther Thiem.

Amerikanische: Zeichnungen in den achtziger Jahren,
Museum Morsbroich, Leverkusen, 1990.
Text by Roberta Smith.

Amerikanische Zeichnungen in den achtziger Jahren,
Graphische Sammlung Albertina, Vienna, 1990.

Amerikanische Zeichnungen 1930-1980,
Städtische Galerie im Städelschen Kunstinstitut,
Frankfurt, 1985.
Texts by Walter Hopps and Dominique de Menil.

Amerikansk Kunst 1950-1970,
Louisiana Museum of Modern Art, Humlebaek, 1971.

An American Renaissance: Painting and Sculpture Since 1940,
Museum of Art, Fort Lauderdale, 1986.
Texts by Malcom R. Daniel, Harry F. Gaugh,
Sam Hunter, Karen Koehler, Kim Levin, Robert C. Morgan
and Richard Sarnoff.

Anti-Illusion: Procedures/Materials,
Whitney Museum of American Art, New York, 1969.
Texts by Marcia Tucker and James Monte.

*L'Architecte est absent: Works from the Collection
of Annick and Anton Herbert: Répertoire*,
Stedelijk Van Abbe Museum, Eindhoven, 1984.
Texts by Rudi H. Fuchs and Jan Debbaut.

Architectural Sculpture,
Los Angeles Institute of Contemporary Art, Los Angeles, 1980.
Texts by Debra Burchett, Susan C. Larsen, Lucy R. Lippard
and Melinda Wortz.

Art at Work,
Des Moines Art Center, Iowa, 1997-1998.

Art by Telephone,
Museum of Contemporary Art, Chicago, 1969.
Text by Jan Van der Marck.

L'Art au corps. Le corps exposé de Man Ray à nos jours,
Éditions de la Réunion des musées nationaux, M.A.C.,
Musées de Marseille, Marseilles, 1996.

L'Art conceptuel, une perspective,
A.R.C., Musée d'Art Moderne de la Ville de Paris, Paris, 1989.

*Art contemporain dans la collection FCM : Acquisitions
1977-1986/Zeitgenössiche Kunst aus der Sammlung MGB:
Erwerbungen 1977-1986/Contemporary Art from the FMC
Collection: Acquisitions 1977-1986*,
Kunsthaus Zürich, Zurich; Musée Rath Genève, Geneva, 1984.
Texts by Pierre Arnold, Arina Kowner and Christel Sauer.

L'Art corporel,
Galerie Stadler, Paris, 1975.
Text by François Pluchart.

L'Art des années soixante and soixante-dix : La collection Panza,
Musée d'Art Moderne, Lyons; Musée d'Art Contemporain,
Saint-Étienne, 1989.

Art in Los Angeles: Seventeen Artists in the Sixties,
Los Angeles County Museum of Art, Los Angeles, 1982.
Texts by Maurice Tuchman, Anne Bartlett Ayres,
Michele De Angelus, Christopher Knight and Susan C. Larsen.

Art in Process IV,
Finch College Museum of Art, New York, 1969.
Text by Elayne H. Varian.

Art in the Mind,
Allen Memorial Art Museum, Oberlin, 1970.
Text by Athena T. Spear.

Art Now 74: A Celebration of the American Arts,
John F. Kennedy Center for the Performing Arts,
Washington D.C., 1974.
Texts by Henry T. Hopkins, Maurice Tuchman, David Ross
and Richard Henshaw.

Art What Thou Eat: Images of Food in American Art,
Edith C. Blum Art Institute, Bard College,
Annandale-on-Hudson, 1991.
Texts by Donna Gustafson, Nan A. Rothschild, Kendall Taylor,
Gilbert T. Vincent and Linda Weintraub.

Arte minimal de la Colección Panza,
Museo Nacional Centro de Arte Reina Sofía, Madrid, 1988.

Arte Povera, Antiform,
Capc, Bordeaux, 1982.
Text by Germano Celant.

Artist and Camera,
Mappin Art Gallery, Sheffield, 1980.
Text by Miranda Strickland-Constable.

The Artist and the Photograph (II),
Israël Museum, Jerusalem, 1976.
Text by Yona Fischer.

Artists' Books USA,
Independent Curators Incorporated, New York, 1978.
Text by Peter Frank and Martha Wilson.

Artists Choose Artists III,
CDS Gallery, New York, 1984.
Text by Donald B. Kuspit.

*Artists of 20th-Century New Mexico: The Museum of Fine
Arts Collection*,
Museum of Fine Arts, Santa Fe, 1992.

SELECTED CATALOGUES OF GROUP EXHIBITIONS

At the Edge of Chaos: New Images of the World,
Louisiana Museum of Modern Art, Humlebaek, 1993.

Ausstellung im Bereich Dom-Römer: "zeitgenössische Kunst im Städtischen Raum",
Förderverein schöneres Frankfurt e.V., Frankfurt, 1990.

Avant-Garde in the Eighties,
Los Angeles County Museum of Art, Los Angeles, 1987.
Text by Howard N. Fox.

Un' avventura internazionale: Torino e le arti 1950-1970,
Castello di Rivoli, Museo d'Arte Contemporanea, Turin, 1993.
Texts by Ida Gianelli, Germano Celant, Paolo Fossati and Giorgio Verzotti.

A View from the Sixties: Selections from the Leo Castelli Collection and the Michael and Ileana Sonnabend Collection,
Guild Hall Museum, East Hampton, New York, 1991.
Texts by Sam Hunter and Robert C. Morgan.

A View of a Decade,
Museum of Contemporary Art, Chicago, 1977.
Texts by Martin Friedman, Robert Pincus-Witten and Peter Gay.

Beuys zu Ehren,
Städtische Galerie im Lenbachhaus, Munich, 1986.

Beyond the Frame: American Art 1960-1990,
Setagaya Art Museum, Tokyo, 1991.
Text by Lynn Gumpert and Brian Wallis.

La Biennale di Venezia 1978: Dalla natura all'arte, dall'arte alla natura,
Edizioni "La Biennale di Venezia", Venice, 1978.

La Biennale di Venezia: Section of Visual Arts,
Edizioni "La Biennale di Venezia", Venice, 1980.
Texts by Achille Bonito Oliva, Michael Compton, Martin Kunz and Harald Szeemann.

4e Biennale de Lyon d'art contemporain,
Halle Tony Garnier, Lyons, 1997.

Bilder, Objekte, Filme, Konzepte: Werke aus der Sammlung Herbig,
Städtische Galerie im Lenbachhaus, Munich, 1973.

Bilderstreit: Widerspruch, Einheit und Fragment in der Kunst seit 1960,
Museum Ludwig, Cologne, 1989.
Texts by Siegfried Gohr and Johannes Gachnang.

Black and White Since 1960,
City Gallery of Contemporary Art, Raleigh, 1989.
Text by Reba and Dave Williams.

Bodyworks,
Museum of Contemporary Art, Chicago, 1975.

Carl Andre, Günther Förg, Hubert Kiecol, Richard Long, Meuser, Reinhard Mucha, Bruce Nauman, Ulrich Rückriem,
Galerie Max Hetzler, Cologne, 1985.
Text by Ad Reinhardt.

Carnegie International,
Carnegie Museum of Art, Pittsburgh, 1988.
Texts by John Caldwell, Vicky A. Clark, Thomas McEvilley, Lynne Cooke, Milena Kalinovska and Nancy Princethal.

Carnegie International 1991,
Carnegie Museum of Art, Pittsburgh, 1991.
Texts by Lynne Cooke, Mark Francis, Fumio Nanjo and Zinovy Zinik.

Castelli and His Artists/Twenty-five Years,
Aspen Center for the Visual Arts, Aspen, 1982.
Text by Julie Augur.

Castelli at Dayton's,
Dayton's Gallery 12, Minneapolis, 1969.

Chambres d'Amis,
Museum van Hedendaagse Kunst, Ghent, 1986.
Text by Jan Hoet.

Collection Agnès and Frits Becht,
Musée d'Art Moderne de Villeneuve d'Ascq, Villeneuve d'Ascq, 1988.
Text by Frank Lubbers.

Collection Sonnabend : 25 années de choix et d'actualités d'Ileana et Michael Sonnabend,
Capc, Bordeaux, 1988.

Collector's Choice: Where I've Been—Where I'm Going,
Los Angeles Institute of Contemporary Art, Los Angeles, 1975.
Text by Marcia S. Weisman.

*Committed to Print: Social and Political Themes
in Recent American Printed Art*,
Museum of Modern Art, New York, 1988.
Text by Deborah Wye.

*Concept Art, Minimal Art, Arte Povera, Land Art,
Sammlung Marzona*,
Kunsthalle Bielefeld, Bielefeld, 1990.
Texts by Werner Lippert and Erich Franz.

Conceptual Art and Conceptual Aspects,
New York Cultural Center, New York, 1970.

Conceptual Art, Arte Povera, Land Art,
Galleria Civica d'Arte Moderna, Turin, 1970.
Texts by Germano Celant, Lucy R. Lippard and Aldo Passoni.

Concetto-Imago: Generationswechsel in Italien,
Bonner Kunstverein, Bonn, 1983.
Text by Zdeneck Felix.

Contemporanea: Incontri Internazionali d'Arte,
Parcheggio di Villa Borghese, Rome, 1973.

Contemporary Art in Southern California,
High Museum of Art, Atlanta, 1980.
Text by Clark V. Poling.

*Contemporary Sculpture: Selections from the Collection
of the Museum of Modern Art*,
Museum of Modern Art, New York, 1979.

Content: A Contemporary Focus, 1974-1984,
Hirshhorn Museum and Sculpture Garden,
Washington D.C., 1984.
Texts by Miranda McClintic, Howard Fox and Phyllis Rosenzweig.

The Dada/Surrealist Heritage,
Sterling and Francine Clark Art Institute, Williamstown, 1977.
Text by Sam Hunter.

*De Beuys à Trockel. Dessins contemporains du
Kunstmuseum de Basle*,
Mnam-Cci, Centre Georges Pompidou, Paris, 1996.

Deconstruct/Reconstruct,
John Gibson Gallery, New York, 1987.
Texts by Robert Nickas and William Childress.

Departures: Photography 1924-1989,
Hirschl and Adler Modern, New York, 1989.
Text by Simon Watney.

Devil on the Stairs: Looking Back on the Eighties,
Institute of Contemporary Art, University of Pennsylvania,
Philadelphia, 1991.
Text by Robert Storr.

Diagrams and Drawings,
Rijksmuseum Kröller-Müller, Otterlo, 1972.
Texts by Carter Ratcliff and Rudolf Oxenaar.

Diagrams and Drawings,
Kunstmuseum, Basle, 1973.
Texts by Franz Meyer and Rudolf Oxenaar.

Digital Visions: Computers and Art,
Everson Museum of Art, Syracuse, 1987.
Text by Cynthia Goodman.

DISLOCATIONS,
Museum of Modern Art, New York, 1991.
Text by Robert Storr.

Documenta 4, vol.1,
Museum Fridericianum, Kassel, 1968.
Texts by Arnold Bode, Max Imdahl, Jean Leering,
Jürgen Harten and Janni Müller-Hauck.

Documenta 5,
Museum Fridericianum, Kassel, 1972.
Texts by Harald Szeemann, Hans Heinz Holz
and Johannes Cladders.

*Documenta 6, Band 3: Handzeichnungen,
Utopisches Design, Bücher*,
Museum Fridericianum, Kassel, 1977.
Text by Wieland Schmied.

Documenta 7, vols. 1, 2,
Museum Fridericianum, Kassel, 1982.
Texts by Rudi H. Fuchs, Coosje van Bruggen,
Germano Celant, Johannes Gachnang and Gerhard Storck.

Documenta 9, vols. 1, 3,
Museum Fridericianum, Kassel, 1992.
Texts by Denys Zacharopoulos, Bart De Baere,
Pier Luigi Tazzi, Claudia Herstatt. Introduction by Jan Hoet.

Door beeldhouwers gemaakt/Made by Sculptors,
Stedelijk Museum, Amsterdam, 1978.
Texts by Rini Dippel and Geert van Beijeren.

*Drawings by Sculptors: Two Decades of Non-Objective Art
in the Seagram Collection,*
Joseph E. Seagram and Sons, Inc., New York, 1984.
Text by David Bellman.

Drawing Distinctions: American Drawings of the Seventies,
Louisiana Museum of Modern Art, Humlebaek, 1981.
Texts by Richard Armstrong, Alfred Kren, Carter Ratcliff
and Peter Schjeldahl.

Drawing for Outdoor Sculpture: 1946-1977,
John Weber Gallery, New York, 1977.

Drawing Now: 1955-1975,
Museum of Modern Art, New York, 1976.
Text by Bernice Rose.

*Drawings: An Exhibition of Contemporary American
Drawings Organized by the Fort Worth Art Center Museum,*
Fort Worth Art Center Museum, Fort Worth, 1969.
Texts by Henry T. Hopkins and Peter Plagens.

Drawings from the Collection of Dorothy and Herbert Vogel,
University of Arkansas at Little Rock, Little Rock, 1986.
Texts by Vivian Endicott Barnett, Floyd W. Martin,
Lloyd W. Benjamin III, Randy Ploog, Julie McGuire
and Steven Stinnett.

*Drawings since 1960: A Selection of the Collection
of Drawings of the Stedelijk Museum,*
Stedelijk Museum, Amsterdam, 1989.

*Dreissig Jahre durch die Kunst:
Museum Haus Lange 1955-1985,*
Museum Haus Lange and Museum Haus Esters, Krefeld, 1985.
Texts by Gerhard Storck, Britta Buhlmann, Christian Nagel,
Julian Heynen and Paul Wember.

Eccentric Abstraction,
Fischbach Gallery, New York, 1966.
Text by Lucy R. Lippard.

Eighteenth National Print Exhibition,
Brooklyn Museum, Brooklyn, New York, 1973.

Einleuchten, Will, Vorstel & Simul in HH,
Deichtorhallen Hamburg, Hamburg, 1989.

11 Los Angeles Artists,
Hayward Gallery, Arts Council of Great Britain, London, 1971.
Texts by Maurice Tuchman and Jane Livingston.

Emanuel Hoffmann-Stiftung Basel,
Museum für Gegenwartskunst, Basle, 1991.
Texts by Vera Oeri-Hoffmann, Christian Geelhaar
and Katharina Steib.

Energieen,
Stedelijk Museum, Amsterdam, 1990.

*Entre la Geometría y el Gesto: Escultura Norteamericana
1965-1975/Between Geometry and Gesture: American
Sculpture 1965-1975,*
Palacio de Velazquez, Madrid, 1986.
Texts by Richard Armstrong, Richard Marshall and Marga Paz.

Entre la géométrie et le geste : Œuvres sur papier 1965-1975,
Galerie Georges-Philippe Valois, Paris, 1990.
Text by Catherine Francblin.

*L'Epoque, la mode, la morale, la passion :
Aspects de l'art d'aujourd'hui, 1977-1987,*
Mnam-Cci, Centre Georges Pompidou, Paris, 1987.
Under the direction of Bernard Blistène, Catherine David
and Alfred Pacquement.

1. Klischee + Antiklischee: Bildformen der Gegenwart,
Neue Galerie, Aachen, 1970.
Text by Wolfgang Becker.

*Les Extrêmes se touchent : La collection d'art moderne
du Musée Boymans-van Beuningen Rotterdam,*
Institut Néerlandais, Paris, 1992.

*Fifty Years of Collecting: An Anniversary Selection–
Sculpture of the Modern Era,*
Solomon R. Guggenheim Museum, New York, 1987.
Text by Thomas Messer.

Films by American Artists: One Medium Among Many,
Arts Council of Great Britain, London, 1981.
Text by Regina Cornwell.

*First Exhibition-Dialogue on Contemporary Art in
Europe/Primeira Exposição-Diálogo sobre a Arte
Contemporâneo na Europa,*
Fundação Calouste Gulenkian, Centro de Arte Moderna,
Lisbon, 1985.
Texts by W.A.L. Beeren (among others).

*First Impressions: Early Prints
by Forty-six Contemporary Artists,*
Walker Art Center, Minneapolis, 1989.
Texts by Elizabeth Armstrong and Sheila McGuire.

SELECTED CATALOGUES OF GROUP EXHIBITIONS

*The First Show: Painting and Sculpture
from Eight Collections 1940-1980*,
Museum of Contemporary Art, Los Angeles, 1983.
Texts by Julia Brown, Pontus Hulten and Susan C. Larsen.

*Five Decades: Recent Works by Alumni
of the Department of Art*,
Museum of Art, University of Wisconsin, Madison, Elvehjem, 1980.
Texts by E. David Cronon, John Palmer and Victor Kord.

*420 West Broadway at Spoleto Festival: 33 Artists Shown
by Leo Castelli, André Emmerich, Sonnabend, John Weber*,
Festival dei due Mondi, Spoleto, 1972.
Text by Barbara Rose.

*From Reinhardt to Christo: Works Acquired through
the Benefaction of the Late Ruth C. Roush*,
Allen Memorial Art Museum, Oberlin, 1980.

Fünf Sammler–Kunst unserer Zeit,
Von der Heydt-Museum, Wuppertal, 1971.
Text by G. Aust.

Funkties van Tekenen/Functions of Drawing,
Rijksmuseum Kröller-Müller, Otterlo, 1975.
Texts by R.H. Fuchs and Rudolf Oxenaar.

*The Future of the Object! A Selection of American Art:
Minimalism and After*,
Galerie Ronny van de Velde, Antwerp, 1990.
Text by Kenneth Baker.

*Den Gedanken auf der Spur bleiben: Zeichnungen 1960 bis
1990 aus der Sammlung des Kaiser Wilhelm Museums*,
Museum Haus Lange and Museum Haus Esters, Krefeld, 1991.

Gemini G.E.L.: Art and Collaboration,
National Gallery of Art, Washington D.C., 1984.
Text by Ruth E. Fine.

German and American Art from Beuys and Warhol,
Tate Gallery Publishing, London, 1996.

*Gravity & Grace: The Changing Condition
of Sculpture 1965-1975*,
Hayward Gallery, Arts Council of Great Britain, London, 1993.
Texts by Jon Thompson, William Tucker and Yehuda Safran.

Here & Now: An Exhibition of Thirteen Artists,
Washington University Gallery of Art, St Louis, 1969.

The Hirshhorn Collects: Recent Acquisitions 1992-1996,
Hirshhorn Museum and Sculpture Garden,
Washington D.C., 1997.

Holografi: det 3-dimensionella mediet,
På Kulturhuset, Stockholm, 1976.

Hommage à Toiny Castelli,
Galerie des Ponchettes, Musées de Nice, Nice, 1988.

Idea and Image in Recent Art,
Art Institute of Chicago, Chicago, 1974.
Text by Anne Rorimer.

Ideas in Sculpture 1965-1977,
Renaissance Society at the University of Chicago,
Chicago, 1977.

Ideas on Paper 1970-1976,
Renaissance Society at the University of Chicago,
Chicago, 1976.
Text by Dennis Adrian.

Illumination: The Quality of Light,
Three Rivers Arts Festival and Pittsburg Center for the Arts,
Pittsburgh, 1985.
Text by Elaine King.

Image World: Art and Media Culture,
Whitney Museum of American Art, New York, 1989.
Texts by Marvin Heiferman, Lisa Phillips and John G. Hanhardt.

Images du Futur 88,
La Cité des Arts et des Nouvelles Technologies de Montréal,
Montreal, 1988.

Images of the Self,
Hampshire College Gallery, Amherst, 1979.
Text by Irving Sandler.

Immaterial Objects,
Whitney Museum of American Art, Downtown at Federal
Reserve Plaza, New York, 1991.

*Indiana Influence: The Golden Age of Indiana Landscape
Painting: Indiana's Modern Legacy*,
Fort Wayne Museum of Art, Fort Wayne, 1984.

*Individuals: A Selected History
of Contemporary Art 1945-1986,*
Museum of Contemporary Art, Los Angeles, 1987.
Texts by Kate Linker, Donald Kuspit, Hal Foster,
Ronald J. Onorato, John C. Welchman and Thomas Lawson.

Information,
Museum of Modern Art, New York, 1970.
Text by Kynaston L. McShine.

The Interrupted Life,
New Museum of Contemporary Art, New York, 1991.
Text by France Morin.

Instruction Drawings: The Gilbert and Lila Silverman Collection,
Cranbrook Academy of Art Museum, Bloomfield Hills, 1981.
Texts by Roy Slade and Michael Hall.

I Triennal de Dibuix Joan Miró,
Fundación Joan Miró, Barcelona, 1989.
Texts by Margit Rowell, Miquel Molins i Nubiola
and Rosa Queralt.

*Jardin Secret : ou la collection privée de quatre marchands
de tableaux : Bruno Bischofberger, Konrad Fischer,
Pierre et Marianne Nahon, Ileana Sonnabend,*
ARCA, Centre d'art contemporain, Marseilles, 1986.

*Johns, Kelly, Lichtenstein, Motherwell, Nauman,
Rauschenberg, Serra, Stella: Prints from Gemini G.E.L.,*
Walker Art Center, Minneapolis, 1974.
Text by Philip Larson.

¿Kid Stuff?,
Albright-Knox Art Gallery, Buffalo, 1971.
Text by William Burback.

Kompass: West Coast USA,
Museum am Ostwall, Dortmund, 1970.

Kompas 4: West Coast USA,
Stedelijk Van Abbe Museum, Eindhoven, 1969.
Text by Jean Leering.

*Konzeption—Conception: Dokumentation einer heutigen
Kunstrichtung: Documentation of a To-day's Art Tendency,*
Schloss Morsbroich, Städtisches Museum Leverkusen,
Leverkusen, 1969.
Texts by Rolf Wedewer, Konrad Fischer and Sol LeWitt.

Kounellis, Merz, Nauman, Serra: Arbeiten um 1968,
Museum Haus Lange, Krefeld, 1981.
Texts by Gerhard Storck and Marianne Stockebrand.

*Kunst aus Fotografie: Was machen Künstler heute
mit Fotografie?: Montagen—Übermalungen—Gemälde—
Dokumente—Fotobilder,*
Kunstverein Hannover, Hanover, 1973.
Text by Helmut R. Leppien.

*Kunst bleibt Kunst: Aspekte internationaler Kunst am Anfang
der 70er Jahre: Projekt '74,*
Kunsthalle Köln and Kölnischer Kunstverein, Cologne, 1974.

Kunst mit Photographie: Die Sammlung Dr. Rolf H. Krauss,
Neue Nationalgalerie, Berlin, 1983.
Texts by Rolf H. Krauss, Manfred Schmalriede
and Michael Schwarz.

Kunst nu/Kunst unserer Zeit,
Groninger Museum, Groningen, 1982.
Text by Antje von Graevenitz.

*Kunst werkt: International moderne kunst in de industriële
werkongeving, een meer dan 30-jaar durend experiment/
Art Works: International Modern Art in the Industrial Working
Environment, an Experiment over More Than Thirty Years,*
Stedelijk Museum, Amsterdam, 1992.

97 Kwangju Biennale: Unmapping the Earth,
Kwangju, Korea, 1997.

*Language and Structure in North America: The First Large
Definitive Survey of North American Language Art,*
Kensington Arts Association, Toronto, 1975.

Large Drawings,
Independent Curators Incorporated, New York, 1984.
Text by Elke Solomon.

Lead,
New York, Hirschl and Adler Modern, 1987.
Text by Klaus Kertess.

Leo Castelli: A Tribute Exhibition,
Butler Institution of American Art, Youngstown, 1987.
Text by Louis Zona.

Leo Castelli Post Pop Artists,
Nadia Bassanese Studio d'Arte, Trieste, 1990.

Leo Castelli y sus Artistas,
XXX Años de Promocion del Arte Contemporaneo,
Centro Cultural Arte Contemporaneo, Mexico City, 1987.

Life-Size: A Sense of the Real in Recent Art,
Israel Museum, Jerusalem, 1990.
Texts by Suzanne Landau, Douglas Crimp,
Carolyn Christov-Bakargiev, Germano Celant, Robert Storr
and Christian Leigh.

Light/Sculpture,
William Hayes Ackland Memorial Art Center,
University of North Carolina at Chapel Hill, Chapel Hill, 1975.

*Little Arena: Drawings and Sculptures from the Collection
of Adri, Martin and Geertjan Visser,*
Rijksmuseum Kröller-Müller, Otterlo, 1984.
Text by Rudolf Oxenaar.

*Live in Your Head: When Attitudes Become Form:
Works—Concepts—Processes—Situations—Information,*
Kunsthalle, Berne, 1969.
Texts by Harald Szeemann, Scott Burton,
Grégoire Muller and Tommaso Trini.

Looking West,
Joslyn Art Museum, Omaha, 1970.
Text by LeRoy Butler.

LA Hot and Cool,
MIT List Visual Arts Center, Cambridge, 1987.
Texts by Dana Friis-Hansen, Dennis Cooper, Rita Valencia,
Christopher Knight, Howard Singerman and Benjamin Weissman.

Los Angeles Prints: 1883-1980,
Los Angeles County Museum of Art, Los Angeles, 1981.
Texts by Ebira Feinblatt and Bruce Davis.

Los 80 en la Colección de la Fundación "la Caixa",
Estacion Plaza de Armas, Seville, 1992.

Lumières : Perception-Projection,
Centre International d'Art Contemporain de Montréal,
Montreal, 1986.
Texts by Danielle Roy, Luc Courchesne and Robert White.

Maelstrom: Contemporary Images of Violence,
Emily Lowe Gallery, Hofstra University, Hempstead, 1986.
Text by Pamela Gettinger.

Marking the Decades: Prints 1960-1990,
Baltimore Museum of Art, Baltimore, 1992.
Text by Jan Howard.

The Maximal Implications of the Minimal Line,
Edith C. Blum Art Institute, Bard College,
Annandale-on-Hudson, 1985.
Texts by Linda Weintraub, Donald Kuspit and Phyllis Tuchman.

Mechanika,
Contemporary Arts Center, Cincinnati, 1991.
Text by Jan Riley.

Menace,
Museum of Contemporary Art, Chicago, 1975.

Metropolis-International Art Exhibition Berlin 1991,
Martin-Gropius-Bau, Berlin, 1991.

Minimal + Conceptual Art aus der Sammlung Panza,
Museum für Gegenwartskunst, Basle, 1980.
Text by Franz Meyer.

Minimalism,
Nicola Jacobs Gallery, London, 1990.

*Minimalism to Expressionism, Painting and Sculpture
since 1965 from the Permanent Collection,*
Whitney Museum of American Art, New York, 1983.

*Modern Painting, Drawing and Sculpture Collected by
Louise and Joseph Pulitzer Jr,*
Fogg Art Museum, Cambridge,1971.

Modes of Address: Language in Art Since 1960,
Whitney Museum of American Art, Downtown at Federal
Reserve Plaza, New York, 1988.
Text by Tom Hardy.

Monumental Drawing: Works by 22 Contemporary Americans,
Brooklyn Museum, Brooklyn, 1986.
Text by Charlotta Kotik.

*Motion and Document—Sequence and Time: Eadweard
Muybridge and Contemporary American Photography,*
Addison Gallery of American Art, Phillips Academy,
Andover, 1991.
Texts by James L. Sheldon and Jock Reynolds.

Moving Image: Images in Movement: Electronic Art, Karlsruhe,
Zentrum für Kunst und Medientechnologie Karlsruhe,
Fundación Joan Miró, Barcelona, 1992.
Text by Heinrich Klotz.

Multiples,
Hirschl and Adler Modern, New York, 1990.
Text by Dan Cameron.

Multiples: The First Decade,
Philadelphia Museum of Art, Philadelphia, 1971.
Text by John L. Tancock.

Museum für Moderne Kunst und Sammlung Ströher,
Museum für Moderne Kunst, Frankfurt, 1991.
Texts by Jean-Christophe Ammann and Christmut Präger.

Nachtregels/Night Lines: Words Without Thoughts
Never To Heaven Go,
Centraal Museum Utrecht, Utrecht, 1991.
Texts by Atte Jongstra, Sjarel Ex, Leo Delfgaauw,
Franck Hoenjet, Bert Jansen, Ellen de Bruijne,
Patricia Deiters, Frank-Alexander Hettig, Marja Bosma,
Let Geerling, Hans Schopping, Eveline Vermeulen,
Sonja Herst, Wim van Sinderen and Leontine Coelewij.

The Nathan Manilow Sculpture Park,
Governors State University Foundation, University Park, 1987.
Text by Peter Schjeldahl.

N Dimensional Space,
Finch College Museum of Art, New York, 1970.
Text by Elayne H. Varian.

Neue Zeichnungen aus dem Kunstmuseum Basel,
Kunstmuseum Basel, Basle, 1982.
Text by Dieter Koepplin.

Neon-Kunst: Bruce Nauman, Richard Serra, Keith Sonnier,
Städtisches Museum Abteiberg, Mönchengladbach, 1987.
Texts by Dierk Stemmler and Marcia Tucker.

NEONstücke (NEONpieces),
Sprengel Museum, Hanover, 1990.
Text by Dietmar Elger.

New Dimensions in Drawing 1950-1980,
Aldrich Museum of Contemporary Art, Ridgefield, 1981.

New Directions: The Tenth SECA Show, San Francisco
Museum of Modern Art, San Francisco, 1966.

The New Sculpture 1965-75:
Between Geometry and Gesture,
Whitney Museum of American Art, New York, 1990.
Texts by Richard Armstrong, John G. Hanhardt
and Robert Pincus-Witten.

New Spaces: The Holographer's Vision,
Franklin Institute, Philadelphia, 1980.
Text by Karen Spitulnik Peiffer.

New York on Paper 3,
Museum of Modern Art, New York, 1985.
Text by Bernice Rose.

9 Young Artists: Theodoron Awards,
Solomon R. Guggenheim Museum, New York, 1969.
Texts by Edward F. Fry, Thomas M. Messer
and Diane Waldman.

The 1980s: Prints from the Collection of Joshua P. Smith,
National Gallery of Art, Washington D.C., 1989.
Text by Charles M. Ritchie.

1988: The World of Art Today,
Milwaukee Art Museum, Milwaukee, 1988.

1985 Biennial Exhibition,
Whitney Museum of American Art, New York, 1985.

1985 Carnegie International,
Carnegie Museum of Art, Pittsburgh, 1985.
Texts by John R. Lane, John Caldwell, Rudi H. Fuchs,
Jannis Kounellis, Germano Celant, Per Kirkeby,
Johannes Gachnang, Bazon Brock, Achille Bonito Oliva,
Nicholas Serota, Benjamin H.D. Buchloch, Hal Foster,
Donald B. Kuspit, Mark Rosenthal, Peter Schjeldahl,
Thomas McEvilley and Hilton Kramer.

1987 Biennial Exhibition,
Whitney Museum of American Art, New York, 1987.
Texts by Richard Armstrong, John G. Hanhardt,
Richard Marshall and Lisa Phillips.

1991 Biennial Exhibition,
Whitney Museum of American Art, New York, 1991.
Texts by Richard Armstrong, John G. Hanhardt,
Richard Marshall and Lisa Phillips.

1970 Annual Exhibition of Contemporary
American Sculpture,
Whitney Museum of American Art, New York, 1970.

1977 Biennial Exhibition,
Whitney Museum of American Art, New York, 1977.
Texts by Barbara Haskell, Marcia Tucker, Patterson Sims,
John G. Hanhardt and Mark Segal.

1967: At the Crossroads,
Institute of Contemporary Art, University of Pennsylvania,
Philadelphia, 1987.
Texts by Hal Foster and Irving Sandler.

Objects, Structures, Artifice: American Sculpture 1970-1983,
SVC Fine Arts Gallery, University of South Florida, Tampa, 1983.
Text by Michael Klein.

Op Losse Schroeven: Situaties en Cryptostructuren,
Stedelijk Museum, Amsterdam, 1969.
Texts by Wim Beeren and Piero Gilardi.

*Open Mind (Gesloten Circuits/Circuiti Chiusi):
Hommage Aan Vincent*,
Museum van Hedendaagse Kunst, Ghent, 1989.
Texts by Constant Ansoms, Michel Outtier,
Annemie Van Kerckhoven, Bruno Corá, Pier Luigi Tazzi,
Frank Vande Veire and Daniele Pieroni.

Ouverture: Arte Contemporanea,
Castello di Rivoli-Comitato per l'arte in Piemonte, Turin, 1985.
Text by Rudi Fuchs.

Oversize Prints,
Whitney Museum of American Art, New York, 1971.
Text by Elke Solomon.

Painting and Sculpture in California: The Modern Era,
San Francisco Museum of Modern Art, San Francisco, 1977.
Text by Henry T. Hopkins.

Painting and Sculpture Today 1974,
Indianapolis Museum of Art, Indianapolis, 1974.

*Painting, Drawing and Sculpture of the '60s and the '70s
from the Dorothy and Herbert Vogel Collection*,
Institute of Contemporary Art, University of Pennsylvania,
Philadelphia, 1975.
Text by Suzanne Delehanty.

Personal Environments,
Museum of Fine Arts, Santa Fe, 1986.
Text by David Turner.

*Peter Stuyvesant Collectie: Een keuze uit een keuze/
Peter Stuyvesant Collection: A Choice within a Choice/
Collection Peter Stuyvesant : Un choix parmi un choix*,
Provinciaal Museum Hasselt, Hasselt, 1981.

Pier+Ocean: Construction in the Art of the Seventies,
Hayward Gallery, Arts Council of Great Britain, London, 1980.
Text by Gerhard von Graevenitz.

Photographic Portraits,
Moore College of Art, Philadelphia, 1972.

Photography and Art: Interactions Since 1946,
Los Angeles County Museum of Art, Los Angeles, 1987.
Texts by Andy Grundberg and Kathleen McCarthy Gauss.

Planes of Memory,
Long Beach Museum of Art, Long Beach, 1988.
Texts by Jacqueline Kain and Anne-Marie Duguet.

The Pleasure Machine: Recent American Video,
Milwaukee Art Museum, Milwaukee, 1991.

Points of Departure: Origins in Video,
Independent Curators Incorporated, New York, 1990.
Texts by Jacqueline Kain and William D. Judson.

Points of Departure: Origins in Video,
Carnegie Museum of Art, Pittsburgh;
Independent Curators Incorporated, New York, 1990.
Texts by Jacqueline Kain and William D. Judson.

PostMINIMALism,
Aldrich Museum of Contemporary Art, Ridgefield, 1982.

Power: Its Myths and Mores in American Art, 1961-1991,
Indianapolis Museum of Art, Indianapolis, 1991.
Texts by Holliday T. Day, Brian Wallis, Anna C. Chave
and George E. Marcus.

Praxis Collection,
Vancouver Art Gallery, Vancouver, 1984.
Texts by Scott Watson, Ann Morrison, Peter Blackman
and Marnie Fleming.

Print Acquisitions,
Whitney Museum of American Art, New York, 1984.

Project: World's Fairs, Waterfronts, Parks and Plazas,
Rhona Hoffman Gallery, Chicago, 1984.

Projects: Architectural Sculpture,
Los Angeles Institute of Contemporary Art, Los Angeles, 1980.
Texts by Debra Burchett, Craig Hodgetts, Louise Lewis,
Mac McCloud, Merle Schipper, Michael Smith, Richard Turner
and Melinda Wortz.

Projects: Architectural Sculpture,
Baxter Art Gallery, California Institute of Technology,
Pasadena, 1980.

*Prospect 68: Internationale Vorschau auf die Kunst
in den Galerien der Avantgarde,*
Städtische Kunsthalle, Düsseldorf, 1968.
Texts by Konrad Fischer and Hans Strelow.

Prospect 71−Projection,
Städtische Kunsthalle, Düsseldorf, 1971.
Texts by Konrad Fischer, Jürgen Harten and Hans Strelow.

*Quartetto: Joseph Beuys, Enzo Cucchi,
Luciano Fabro, Bruce Nauman,*
L'Accademia Foundation, Venice, 1984.
Texts by Kaspar König, Achille Bonito Oliva and Julian Heynen.

4e Semaine Internationale de Video,
Saint-Gervais, Geneva, 1989.
Texts by Alain Vaissade, André Iten, Lysianne Léchot,
Peggy Gale, David A. Ross, Catherine David,
Rosanna Albertini, Chris Dercon, Jean-Paul Fargier,
Anne-Marie Duguet, Christine van Assche,
Erwan Huon Depenanster and Yves Kropf.

*Raüme heutiger Zeichnung: Werke aus dem Basler
Kupferstichkabinett,*
Staatliche Kunsthalle, Baden-Baden, 1985.
Texts by Siegmar Holsten, Dieter Koepplin,
Marie Therese Hurni and Paul Tanner.

*Raüme heutiger Zeichnung: Werke aus dem Basler
Kupferstichkabinett,*
Kunstmuseum Basel, Basle, 1985.

*The Readymade Boomerang: Certain Relations in 20th
Century Art: The Eighth Biennale of Sydney,*
Art Gallery of New South Wales, Sydney, 1990.
Texts by René Block, Lynne Cooke, Bernice Murphy,
Anne Marie Freybourg and Dick Higgins.

The Real Big Picture,
Queens Museum, Flushing, New York, 1986.
Text by Marvin Heiferman.

Recent American Etching,
Davison Art Center, Wesleyan University, Middletown, 1975.
Text by Richard S. Field.

Recent American Etching,
National Collection of Fine Arts, Smithsonian Institution,
Washington D.C., 1975.
Text by Richard S. Field.

Recent Works on Paper by American Artists,
University of Wisconsin, Madison, 1977.

Recorded Activities,
Moore College of Art, Philadelphia, 1970.
Text by Lucy Lippard.

Repetition,
Hirschl and Adler Modern, New York, 1989.
Text by John Yau.

Rooms, P.S. 1,
P.S. 1, Institute for Art and Urban Resources Inc.,
New York, 1977.
Texts by Alanna Heiss and Linda Blumberg.

*Sammlung Helga und Walther Lauffs
im Kaiser Wilhelm Museum Krefeld,*
Kaiser Wilhelm Museum, Krefeld, 1984.

Scene of the Crime,
UCLA at the Armand Hammer Museum of Art
and Cultural Center, Los Angeles, 1997.

Schlaf der Vernunft,
Museum Fridericianum, Kassel, 1988.
Text by Hubertus Gassner, Markus Brüderlin,
Veit Loers and Lucius Burckhardt.

Schwarz auf Weiss: von Manet bis Kiefer,
Galerie Beyeler, Basle, 1984.
Text by Reinhold Hohl.

*Schwerpunkt Skulptur: Hundertvierzig Werke
von achtzig Künstler, 1950-1990,*
Kaiser Wilhelm Museum, Krefeld, 1992.
Texts by Gerhard Storck and Julian Heynen.

*Schwerpunkt Skulptur: Wie Vorstellungen Form
angenommen haben: Ausstellungsbilder seit 1969,*
Kaiser Wilhelm Museum, Krefeld, 1992.
Texts by Gerhard Storck and Eva Meyer-Hermann.

The Sculptor as Draftsman: Selections from the Permanent Collection,
Whitney Museum of American Art, New York, 1983.
Text by Paul Cummings.

Sculptors at UC Davis: Past and Present,
Richard L. Nelson Gallery, University of California, Davis, 1982.

Sculptors' Drawings 1910-1980: Selections from the Permanent Collection,
Whitney Museum of American Art, New York, 1984.

Sculptors on Paper: New York,
Madison Art Center, Madison, 1987.
Text by René Paul Barilleaux

De Sculptura,
Wiener Festwochen im Messepalast, Vienna, 1986.

Sculpture: American Directions 1945-1975,
National Collection of Art, Washington D.C., 1975.

La Sculpture contemporaine après 1970,
Fondation Daniel Templon, Musée temporaire, Fréjus, 1991.

La Sculpture et son dessein,
JGM Galerie, Paris, 1991.

Sculpture in California 1975-80,
San Diego Museum of Art, San Diego, 1980.
Text by Richard Armstrong.

"Sélection" : Œuvres de la collection,
FAE Musée d'Art Contemporain, Pully-Lausanne, 1991.

Selections from the Collection: A Focus on California,
Los Angeles County Museum of Art, Los Angeles, 1984.

Selections from the William J. Hokin Collection,
Museum of Contemporary Art, Chicago, 1985.
Text by Terry A.R. Neff.

The Sense of Self: From Self-Portrait to Autobiography,
Independent Curators Incorporated, New York, 1978.
Texts by Ira Licht, Nina Sundell and Richard King.

7e Biennale de Paris, Parc Floral de Vincennes, Paris, 1971.

74th American Exhibition,
Art Institute of Chicago, Chicago, 1982.
Text by Anne Rorimer.

7 Objects/69/90,
University of Massachusetts, Amherst, 1990.
Texts by Phyllis Blau and Eric Vieland.

Seventy-second American Exhibition,
Art Institute of Chicago, Chicago, 1976.
Text by Anne Rorimer.

73rd American Exhibition,
Art Institute of Chicago, Chicago, 1979.
Texts by A. James Speyer and Anne Rorimer.

Singular Visions: Contemporary sculpture in New Mexico,
Museum of Fine Arts, Santa Fe, 1991.
Text by Sandy Ballatore.

6th Guggenheim International Exhibition 1971,
Solomon R. Guggenheim Museum, New York, 1971.
Texts by Diane Waldman and Edward F. Fry.

'60 '80: Attitudes/Concepts/Images,
Stedelijk Museum, Amsterdam, 1982.
Texts by Ad Petersen, Edy de Wilde, Gijs van Tuyl, Wim Beeren, Antje von Graevenitz and Cor Blok.

Skulptur-Ausstellung in Münster,
Westfälisches Landesmuseum für Kunst und Kulturgeschichte, Munster, 1977.
Text by Lazlo Glozer.

Skulptur im 20. Jahrhundert,
Wenkenpark, Riehen, Basle, 1980.
Text by Reinhold Hohl.

Skulptur im 20. Jahrhundert,
Skulpturenausstellung Merian-Park, Basle, 1984.
Text by Antje von Graevenitz.

Skulptur Projekte in Münster 1987,
Westfällisches Landesmuseum für Kunst und Kulturgeschichte, Munster, 1987.
Texts by Klaus Bussmann and Kaspar König.

The Slant Step Revisited,
Richard L. Nelson Gallery, University of California, Davis, 1983.
Texts by Cynthia Charters and L. Price Amerson.

Sonsbeek '71,
Sonsbeek Foundation, Arnhem, 1970.

Sonsbeek '86: Internationale Beelden
Tentoonstelling/International Sculpture Exhibition,
Sonsbeek Foundation, Arnhem, 1986.
Texts by Saskia Bos, Antje von Graevenitz
and Marianne Brouwer.

Soundings, Neuberger Museum,
State University of New York at Purchase, Purchase, 1981.
Texts by Suzanna Delehanty, Dore Ashton, Germano Celant
and Lucy Fischer.

Space, Time, Sound: Conceptual Art
in the San Francisco Bay Area: The 1970s,
San Francisco Museum of Modern Art, San Francisco, 1981.
Texts by Suzanna Foley and Constance Lewallen.

Die Spirale im menschlichen Leben und in der Natur:
eine interdisziplinäre Schau,
Museum für Gestaltung, Gewerbemuseum Basel, Basle, 1985.
Text by Jean-Christophe Ammann.

Spirals and Progressions: Robert Filliou, Paul Klee,
Richard Long, Mario Merz, Bruce Nauman, Robert Smithson,
Kunstmuseum, Lucerne, 1975.
Texts by Pierre Gaudibert, Christian Geelhaar, Max Wechsler
and Jean Christophe Ammann.

The Spiritual in Art: Abstract Painting, 1890-1985,
Los Angeles County Museum of Art, Los Angeles, 1986.
Texts by Maurice Tuchman (among others).

Stations,
Centre International d'Art Contemporain de Montréal,
Montreal, 1987.

De Statua,
Stedelijk Van Abbe Museum, Eindhoven, 1983.
Text by R. H. Fuchs.

Stedelijk '60-70: Verzameling 1960-1970,
Palais des Beaux-Arts, Brussels, 1971.

Strike Restrike: The Revitalized Print,
Gallery II, Western Michigan University, Kalamazoo, 1984.
Texts by Curtis Rhodes and John Link.

String and Rope,
Sidney Janis Gallery, New York, 1970.

Sunshine & Noir: Art in L.A., 1960-1997,
Louisiana Museum of Modern Art, Humlebaek;
Kunstmuseum Wolfsburg, 1997-1998.

Szenenwechsel,
Museum für Moderne Kunst, Frankfurt, 1992.
Text by Jean-Christophe Ammann.

Territorium Artis,
Kunst- und Ausstellungshalle der Bundesrepublik
Deutschland, Bonn, 1992.
Text by Pontus Hulten.

30 Years of TB-9: A Tribute to Robert Arneson,
John Natsoulas Gallery, Davis, 1991

31st Biennial of American Painting,
Corcoran Gallery of Art, Washington D.C., 1969.
Text by James Harithas.

Three Decades of Exploration: Hommage to Leo Castelli,
Museum of Art, Fort Lauderdale, 1987.

Three Decades: The Oliver-Hoffmann Collection,
Museum of Contemporary Art, Chicago, 1988.

3-∞: New Multiple Art,
Whitechapel Art Gallery, London, 1970.

3D into 2D: Drawings for Sculpture,
New York Cultural Center, New York, 1973.
Text by Susan Ginsburg.

Three L.A. Sculptors: Lloyd Harol, George Herms,
Bruce Nauman,
Los Angeles Institute of Contemporary Art, Los Angeles, 1975.
Text by Peter Lodato.

Three Young Americans: Krueger, Nauman, Saret,
Allen Memorial Art Museum, Oberlin, 1968.
Text by Ellen H. Johnson and Athena T. Spear.

Time Photography,
School of Visual Arts, New York, 1969.
Text by Robert Fiore.

Time Span: Jenny Holzer, On Kawara, Bruce Nauman,
Lawrence Weiner,
Fundación Caixa de Pensions, Barcelona, 1990.
Text by Manel Clot.

Tokyo Biennale '70: Between Man and Matter,
Tokyo Metropolitan Art Gallery, Tokyo, 1970.

The Trans Parent Thread: Asian Philosophy
in Recent American Art,
Hofstra Museum, Hofstra University, Annandale-on-Hudson;
Edith C. Blum Art Institute, Bard College, Hempstead, 1990.
Texts by Gail Gelburd and Geri De Paoli.

Transform: BildObjektSkulptur im 20. Jahrhundert,
Kunstmuseum and Kunsthalle, Basle, 1992.

Transformations in Sculpture: Four Decades of American
and European Art,
Solomon R. Guggenheim Museum, New York, 1985.
Text by Diane Waldman.

3ᵉ Salon international de Galeries pilotes :
Artistes et découvreurs de notre temps,
Musée cantonal des beaux-arts, Palais de Rumine, Lausanne;
ARC, Musée d'Art Moderne de la Ville de Paris, Paris, 1970.

Tropismes: Colección d'Art Contemporani
Fundación "la Caixa",
Centre Cultural Tecla Sala, L'Hospitalet de Llobregat, 1992.

20th Century American Drawings, Five Years of Acquisitions,
Whitney Museum of American Art, New York, 1978.
Text by Paul Cummings.

20 American Artists: Sculpture 1982,
San Francisco Museum of Modern Art, San Francisco, 1982.
Text by George W. Neubert.

200 Years of American Sculpture,
Whitney Museum of American Art, New York, 1976.
Texts by Tom Armstrong, Wayne Craven, Norman Feder,
Barbara Haskell, Rosalind E. Krauss, Daniel Robbins
and Marcia Tucker.

Übrigens sterben immer die anderen:
Marcel Duchamp und die Avantgarde seit 1950,
Museum Ludwig, Cologne, 1988.

Un choix d'art minimal dans la Collection Panza,
ARC, Musée d'Art Moderne de la Ville de Paris, Paris, 1990.

U.S.A. West Coast,
Kunstverein, Hamburg, 1972.
Texts by Helmut Heissenbuttel and Helene Winer.

Variants: Drawings by Contemporary Sculptors,
Sewall Art Gallery, Rice University, Houston, 1981.
Texts by Esther de Vécsey and Laura W. Russell.

Verbiage: An Exhibition of Words,
Kettle's Yard, Cambridge University, Cambridge, 1979.

Video Art,
Institute of Contemporary Art, University of Pennsylvania,
Philadelphia, 1975.

Video as Attitude,
Museum of Fine Arts, Museum of New Mexico, Santa Fe, 1983.
Text by Patrick Clancy.

Video-Skulptur: retrospektiv und aktuell 1963-1989,
Kölnischer Kunstverein, Cologne, 1989.
Texts by John G. Hanhardt, Friedemann Malsch,
Vittorio Fagone, Wulf Herzogenrath and Edith Decker.

Views from Abroad: European Perspectives on American
Art 3. American Realities,
Whitney Museum of American Art, New York, 1997.

Vom Zeichnen: Aspekte der Zeichnung 1960-1985,
Frankfurter Kunstverein, Frankfurt, 1985.
Text by Peter Weiermair

Die Wahlverwandtschaften-Zitate,
Stadtmuseum Graz, Graz, 1986.

Wahrnehmungen, Aufzeichnungen, Mitteilungen:
Die Erweiterung des Wirklichkeitsbegriffs in der Kunst
der 60er und der 70er Jahre,
Museum Haus Lange, Krefeld, 1979.
Texts by Gerhard Storck and Marianne Stockebrand.

Was die Schönheit sei, das weiss ich nicht
(II Biennale Nürnberg), Kunsthalle, Nuremberg, 1971.

Watercolors and Related Media by Contemporary Californians,
Baxter Art Gallery, California Institute of Technology,
Pasadena, 1977.
Text by Michael Smith.

Werke aus der Sammlung Crex,
Kunsthalle, Basle, 1982.
Text by Jean-Christophe Ammann.

Werke aus der Sammlung Crex, Zürich,
InK. Halle für Internationale neue Kunst, Zurich, 1978.
Texts by Urs Raussmüller and Christel Sauer.

West Coast 1945-1969,
Pasadena Art Museum, Pasadena, 1969.
Text by John Coplans.

The West Coast Now,
Portland Art Museum, Portland, 1968.
Texts by Rachel Griffin and Henry T. Hopkins.

Westkunst: Zeitgenössische Kunst seit 1939,
Kunsthalle Köln and Kölnischer Kunstverein, Cologne, 1981.
Texts by Marcel Baumgartner, Kaspar König and Laszlo Glozer.

What Is Political, Anyway?,
Borås Konstmuseum, Borås, 1992.
Text by Peter Schjeldahl.

Wiener Diwan: Sigmund Freud heute,
Museum des 20. Jahrhunderts, Vienna, 1989.

William Geis and Bruce Nauman,
San Francisco Art Institute, San Francisco, 1966.

Word as Image: American Art, 1960-1990,
Milwaukee Art Museum, Milwaukee, 1990.
Texts by Russell Bowman and Dean Sobel.

De Woorden en de Beelden: Tekst en beeld in de kunst van de twintigste eeuw/The Words and the Images: Text and Image in the Art of the Twentieth Century,
Centraal Museum Utrecht, Utrecht, 1991.
Texts by Kees Broos, Erick Slagter, Michael Gibbs, Bert Jansen and Antje von Graevenitz.

Words,
Seoul, Kukje Gallery, 1992.

Words: A Look at the Use of Language in Art, 1967-1977,
Whitney Museum of American Art, Downtown at Federal Reserve Plaza, New York, 1977.
Texts by Isabella Puliafito and Martha Winans.

Words at Liberty,
Museum of Contemporary Art, Chicago, 1977.

Works Concepts Processes Situations Information,
Galerie Hans Mayer, Düsseldorf, 1989.

Zeichnen/Bezeichnen: Zeichnungen aus der Sammlung Mia und Martin Visser, Bergeyk, mit Beiträgen aus der Sammlung Geert Jan Visser, Antwerpen,
Kunstmuseum, Basle, 1976.
Texts by Franz Meyer, R. H. Fuchs and Zdenek Felix.

Zeichnungen amerikanischer Künstler,
Galerie Ricke, Cologne, 1970.

Zeichnungen: Aus dem Kupferstichkabinett Basel,
Kunsthalle, Nuremberg, 1990.
Text by Dieter Koepplin.

Zeichnungen der 50er bis 70er Jahre aus dem Kaiser Wilhelm Museum Krefeld, Graphische Sammlung und Sammlung Helga und Walther Lauffs,
Kaiser Wilhelm Museum, Krefeld, 1980.
Text by Gerhard Storck.

Zeitlos,
Hamburger Bahnhof, Berlin, 1988.